BLACK GENESIS

A Resource Book for African-American Genealogy

BLACK GENESIS

GENESIS

A Resource Book for
African-American Genealogy

2nd Edition

James M. Rose, Ph.D.
&
Alice Eichholz, Ph.D., C.G.

Contents

Foreword vii
Preface ix
How to Use This Book xiii
Acknowledgments xv

PART I An Overview 1
Chapter 1 The Beginning 3
Chapter 2 Important Dates in U.S. African-American History 13
Chapter 3 Oral History 17
Chapter 4 National Archives and Federal Records 21
Chapter 5 Military Records 27
Chapter 6 Migratory Patterns 31
Chapter 7 Slavery 35

PART II Survey of the States 45

Alabama 53	Kansas 155
Alaska 61	Kentucky 161
Arizona 63	Louisiana 167
Arkansas 67	Maine 175
California 73	Maryland 179
Colorado 79	Massachusetts 193
Connecticut 85	Michigan 199
Delaware 95	Minnesota 205
District of Columbia ...99	Mississippi 209
Florida 105	Missouri 217
Georgia 111	Montana 227
Hawaii 125	Nebraska 229
Idaho 129	Nevada 235
Illinois 133	New Hampshire 239
Indiana 145	New Jersey 243
Iowa 151	New Mexico 249

New York 253
North Carolina 263
North Dakota 273
Ohio 277
Oklahoma 285
Oregon 289
Pennsylvania 293
Rhode Island 299
South Carolina 307
South Dakota 317
Tennessee 321

Texas 327
Utah 333
Vermont 337
Virginia 341
Washington 349
West Virginia 355
Wisconsin 359
Wyoming 365

Canada 369
West Indies 373

APPENDIX A General References 381
APPENDIX B African-American Family History Research
Bibliography 385
APPENDIX C National Archives and Records Administration
Facilities 391
APPENDIX D Library Symbols 397

Index 407

Foreword

Black Genesis is back in print!

Originally published in 1978, *Black Genesis* was the first book to provide researchers with access to family history information and materials for African Americans. The continued interest in the now out-of-date first edition of the book persuaded the authors that there was a need for an updated and expanded version of their original work.

Although there are now a number of books on African-American research available on the market, *Black Genesis* remains the standard-bearer. Its new format—organized by state and, within each state, by category—makes locating resources pertaining to slaves and free blacks in the United States easier than ever.

Thanks to the editors—James M. Rose and Alice Eichholz—for presenting more assistance to researchers to uncover African-American contributions to the cultural and historical formation of the United States.

Barbara Dodson Walker
President of The Afro-American
Historical and Genealogical Society

Preface

The formal study of African-American genealogy probably began with the historian Carter G. Woodson, who authored many books, including *Free Negro Heads of Families in the United States Census of 1830,* published in 1925 by the Association for the Study of Negro Life and History (reprinted by Carter G. Woodson in his book *Major Works by Carter G. Woodson,* Associated Publishers Incorporated: Washington, D.C., n.d.).

While the social, historical, and economic study of African-American families continued to develop, a study of the ancestral roots of individuals remained extremely limited. Then, Alex Haley began the Kinte Library Project as an outgrowth of his own research on his African and Irish roots. In 1973 Dr. James M. Rose, co-editor of this book, was privileged to work with Haley and became inspired by Haley's efforts to make records for the study of African-American ancestry more accessible. Dr. Rose began to work with students at Queens College, City University of New York, to collect and organize a massive amount of material for a resource book that would help African Americans research their ancestry.

At Queens College he was introduced to Dr. Alice Eichholz, who had been working with minority students at the college and had considerable experience researching and teaching genealogy. Together they started the Ethnic Genealogy Research Center at the college and began looking for a publisher interested in their project. With the assistance of Roger Scanlan at the Family History Library in Salt Lake City, Utah, and J. Carlyle Parker at Gale Research Publishing Company, *Black Genesis* was published in 1978. The previous year Haley's award-winning television mini-series, *Roots,* became a catalyst for a new era in ancestral research in the United States for all Americans.

That was more than twenty years ago. Today, the explosion of family history research has produced a growing body of African-American genealogy, supported by a considerable number of resources on the Internet. This new edition of *Black Genesis* provides guidance not only to the same basic resources presented in the original hardcover edition but also to a substantial amount of new material. The original goal remains the same—to introduce the novice and professional researcher to African-American genealogical research methods and resources.

The format of *Black Genesis* has changed slightly. In this new edition, the material is presented state-by-state instead of by region. The format is the same for each state, with information on resources available specifically for African-American genealogical research, organized in a manner consistent with the general research principles and methodology. Resources described include research and resource guides, published genealogies, community studies on African-American families and, most important, original research materials that can be found in national, state, county, and city archives, and in historical societies and libraries.

The number of "how-to books" and Internet resources for African-American genealogy, and the number of individuals doing genealogical research on African-American families, are proof that our first publication's original goal has been achieved. Although several books mentioned in the original publication are now out-of-print, they remain in this edition, since their historical and genealogical value is extremely important. Not all states have the same kinds of information or same depth of material. For example, manumission records depend on a state's legal history, and if they were kept, their existence depends on someone having preserved them. In some states the records are separated and labeled "colored" or "African American" and "white." In others, no ethnic or racial descriptions are included. As with other ethnic research, it is imperative that a researcher with African-American roots uses *all* the sources in that state in searching for clues to his or her family's past.

Massive amounts of source materials are becoming available through the Internet on listserves, surname bulletin boards, and free and subscription databases. Books like *Black Genesis*, however, are still invaluable for providing the fundamentals of research; others, like *Black Roots in Southeastern Connecticut, 1650–1900,* by James M. Rose and Barbara W. Brown (Reprint, New London Historical Society: New London, Conn., 2001), and *Free African- Americans of North Carolina, Virginia and South Carolina* by Paul Heinegg (4th ed., Baltimore: Genealogical Publishing Co., 2001) stand as models for comprehensive genealogical studies of African-American families. Community and plantation studies, and other similar studies, will make it easier for thousands of African Americans to trace their roots in North America.

Finally, researchers focusing on African-American roots should consider the following facts during their research process:

- The African-American family was not genealogically destroyed during slavery.

- Oral history can provide valuable clues, even if its accuracy is in doubt.

- Until the turn of the twentieth century, African Americans tended not to migrate far after slavery.

- Low-frequency African-American surnames like Broadnax, Cohen, and Avera are rarely made up and generally stem from a close proximity with the white family of that surname; there might even be a biological connection.

- Thousands of European-Americans may have some roots in African-American ancestry. African Americans may also have Native-American and European ancestry.

- Some African Americans have limited slave ancestry because ancestors attained freedom early after importation.

- Many African-American families enumerated in the 1870 census are third-, fourth-, and even fifth-generation Americans.

- Political, geographic, economic, sociological, physical, and psychological aspects of family life need to be included in research.

- African-American families who received or acquired property after slavery are easier to trace.

- Plantation records may not determine which slave listed is the right ancestor, but a great deal can still be learned about life on that plantation.

- More published primary sources and compilations are specifying "African American" in their indexes, making research in all records easier.

James M. Rose, Ph.D., Chesapeake, Virginia
Alice Eichholz, Ph.D., C.G., Montpelier, Vermont

How to Use This Book

When using this book, you will frequently notice abbreviations attached to specific sources in the individual state chapters. These abbreviations identify the libraries or repositories in which those particular sources can be located. A description of the abbreviations used appears in the back of the book, in Appendix D. Sometimes the actual manuscript number for a specific source at a repository is also given. Please keep in mind that resources listed for your area of interest are only samples of records that may be available. Every day new sources are either discovered or made available through the repositories, and many of these may become available online in the future. Look at other states in your research area to get an idea of other kinds of sources that might be available and become your own detective to scout them out.

Note: The authors have used the terms African Americans, Africans, Blacks, People of Color, and Negroes interchangeably in this book in the interest of keeping the source accurate and reflecting the time period of the record source.

Acknowledgments

Books as complex as this one require the efforts and dedication of many people. We are grateful to the hundreds of people all over the United States who responded to us when we requested information and assistance. The following people and organizations helped immeasurably to make this book become a reality:

South Carolina Department of Archives and History; Elizabeth I. Yeahquo, Washington State Library; Karl J. Niederer, Director, Department of State Division of Archives and Records Management, State of New Jersey; Curtis Greubel, Wyoming State Archives; Jesse White, Illinois State Archives; Ann Billesbach, Nebraska State Historical Society; Steve Nielsen, Minnesota Historical Society; Kathryn Otto, Montana Historical Society; Ohio Historical Society; Delaware Public Archives; Iris Agard Hawkins, President, Black Genealogy Search Group of Denver; Genevieve Troka, California State Archives; Texas State Archives; Archives and History Library: The Cultural Center Charleston, West Virginia; South Dakota State Historical Society; Ruth E. Hodge, Pennsylvania State Archives; State Historical Society of North Dakota; Dolores Vyzralek, Betty M. Epstein and Rebecca Preece, New Jersey State Library; Melissa T. Salazar, State Records Center and Archives of New Mexico; John Fowler, Louisiana State Archives; and the Florida Department of State.

Others went beyond the call of duty to provide information and expert assistance in the production and editing of the material collected and reviewed. To them we are particularly grateful. They include the following:

Jacqueline E.A. Lawson, former President of Black Heritage Society of Washington State and an accomplished genealogist, provided essential help in editing Part I.

Thelma Strong Eldridge, President of the Chicago chapter of the Afro-American Genealogical and Historical Society, updated the Illinois chapter.

Franzine Taylor reviewed the Alabama chapter, added information, and helped to edit part of the original material.

Annette W. Curtis, Mid-Continent Public Library, Independence, Missouri, supplied valuable information from her own book, noted in the Missouri chapter.

Jean Driggers and Alan Driggers helped by reviewing spelling, grammatical errors, bibliography entries, and even retyping sections of the book. Accepting nothing more than a thank-you, they kept offering their services. Alan spent his entire summer school break double-checking sources and the bibliography.

Julius O. Pearce and Joysetta Pearce, genealogist at the African-American Museum of Nassau County, scanned the original book into a word processing program. They operate a very successful genealogical organization in Freeport, Long Island.

Katy Hare and her mother, Mary Hare, researched the "Important Dates" section of each chapter, following up on valuable encyclopedic information that gave us hundreds of dates. The Hares spent hour after hour transcribing and verifying those dates.

Marian Hoffman at Genealogical Publishing Company provided the ablest of eyes and hands in editing the final manuscript.

Marcella Houle Pasay, author of *Full Circle: A Directory of Native and African-Americans in Windham County, CT, 1650–1900*, reviewed the final copy as a peer reader.

PART I
AN OVERVIEW

Chapter 1:
The Beginning

Prior to the publication of the first edition of *Black Genesis* and *Roots*, there was little attempt to spur the interest of African Americans in researching their ancestry. Many thought that the primary resources available for European-American family research were not available for researching African-American family ancestry. Nothing could be further from the truth. This updated volume sheds light on the available resources and hopefully continues to galvanize the interest in African-American genealogy into the twenty-first century.

Our purposes are to (1) help the novice in African-American family history search for roots in Western soil; (2) encourage the development of African-American genealogical research by suggesting and illustrating areas where records need to be diligently uncovered and published; (3) suggest ways that genealogical materials can be used to reexamine history; (4) consider new technological aspects of genealogy research for African Americans; and (5) continue to develop an African-American genealogical methodology that includes use of sources specific to that heritage.

Helping the Novice

The basic principles for genealogical research are to start with the present and work backward one generation at a time; find and use original sources whenever possible; focus not only on your direct ancestors but also on your extended family or collateral relatives; and always consider the time and place surrounding your ancestors' lives.

With African-American ancestry in mind, here are some basic steps to take in beginning genealogical research:

1. Read a general "how-to" genealogical research book. There are many such books in local and Internet bookstores. A listing of some can be found in Appendix A. Then, consider the major "how-to" books dealing specifically with African-American families, notably the following:

Ball, Edward. *Slaves in the Family.* New York: Ballantine Books, 1999.

Burroughs, Tony. *African American Roots: A Beginner's Guide to Tracing the African American Family Tree.* Chicago: Fireside Publications, 2000.

Parmer, Dee Woodtor. *A Place Called Down Home—An African American Guide to Genealogy and Historical Identity.* New York: Random House, 1999.

Rose, James M., and Alice Eichholz. *Black Genesis.* Detroit: Gale Research, 1978. (Gale Genealogy and Local History Series; vol. 1).

> The original still exists in many state archives and libraries and includes many resources and bibliographical citations not included in the updated version. More publications dealing specifically with methodology and sources for African-American ancestry can be found in Appendix B, "African-American Family History Research Bibliography."

2. Conduct interviews with older members of your family: The purpose is to gather as much family data as possible, including dates and places of births, deaths, and marriages. Carefully document your sources of information. Oral history gathered in interviews is a very important aspect of African-American family research. Chapter 3, "Oral History," describes how to do this part of the research.

Note: Other sources can fill in the gaps in data when necessary. Vital records are listed under each state's listing. Addresses of the state archives are also listed.

3. Find your ancestors in the federal census records. There are federal census records available from 1790 to 1930; however, only those African Americans who obtained their freedom prior to 1865 will be listed in the 1850 and 1860 censuses, and only heads of households of free African-American families are listed in census records before 1850. Slave schedules are available for 1850 and 1860, listing slave owners and enumerating their slaves by age and gender only, not by name.

See Chapter 4, "National Archives and Federal Records," for a complete explanation of censuses. (See also Szucs and Luebking's *The Source* and Val D. Greenwood's *The Researcher's Guide to American Genealogy*, listed in Appendix A, for complete explanations of federal census records and their indexes. Or visit the National Archives web site: **www.nara.gov/genealogy**.)

The 1880 census has a soundex indexing system for all those households in which there was at least one child under ten years of age. Each person in the household is listed by name, sex, age, place of birth, and birthplace of parents. The 1900 and 1920 censuses have a soundex for all heads of households, as well as for children and people in a household who are not directly related. In some states, the 1910 census has a similar Miracode index for households and people. The 1930 census has soundexes available for some states and some counties within other states.

Soundex and census records can be obtained in a number of ways. They can be found on microfilm at state libraries and state archives or borrowed through a local library with interlibrary loan. The National Archives in Washington, D.C. and its regional branches have microfilm copies of all federal census records (see Appendix C). For a comprehensive description of where to locate and obtain census records, see Eichholz's *Ancestry's Red Book: American State, County, and Town Sources* and Greenwood's *The Researcher's Guide to American Genealogy*, listed in Appendix A.

Subscription database services on the Internet (**www.ancestry.com** or **www.genealogy.com**, for example) make digitalized views of census records—as well as most published census indexes—available online. The Family History Library, Salt Lake City, Utah, has produced an every-name index to the 1880 census that is available either for purchase or for use at local Family History Centers (see **www.familysearch.com**). U.S. federal census records from 1790–1930 are also available in microfilm and digital microfilm formats from Heritage Quest (**http://www.heritagequest.com**).

State censuses are as important a genealogical resource as federal censuses, but they do not exist for all states. State censuses and tax records can substitute for some of the missing or destroyed federal censuses and are valuable population enumerations in their own right. Many state censuses, for example, asked different questions than the federal census, so they record information that cannot be found elsewhere in federal schedules. (See Szucs and Luebking's *The Source* and Greenwood's *The Researcher's Guide to American Genealogy,* listed in Appendix A, for a rundown of available state censuses.)

4. Secure vital documents such as birth, marriage, and death records to verify oral history and provide leads to additional sources.

5. Research county records (i.e., wills, deeds, court proceedings, etc.), military records, church records, and miscellaneous records for family information. It is in this area that *Black Genesis* can be particularly helpful. Chapter 5 of *Black Genesis* covers military records available for African Americans. Chapter 6 briefly outlines the migrating patterns of African Americans—patterns that were similar in some ways to those of European-Americans, yet different in others. Chapter 7 follows with a discussion of records involving slavery and how they can be used to document and trace African-American family ancestry. Then, Part II provides a state-by-state listing of sources that particularly apply to African-American families.

Unearthing the Records

Many African Americans may be unfamiliar with the enormous scope of extant records documenting African-American life—both slave and free—in the United States in the last 350 years. As discussed in the first edition of *Black Genesis*, those records, though massive, were relatively unused because there had been no concerted effort to identify and publish them. In the years since the publication of *Black Genesis*, however, numerous efforts have been made to uncover and publish those resources by research publishing teams in African-American genealogical societies and independent researchers. The survey of state and county records in Part II illustrates the types of records and scope of information now available, but there are many more records that still need to be discovered and published.

Genealogical resource books generally include sections on African-American genealogy. Publications such as gravestone indexes, tax records, deed abstracts, or census extracts are more likely today to contain references to African Americans. As with all good genealogical research, the published record is not alone an adequate source. The original record, if it still exists, needs to be used not only for documentation and accuracy purposes but to view the original in its context. The context may provide other clues.

The following is our new, updated list of long- and short-term projects suggested for the twenty-first century. It is followed by our original list from the first edition of *Black Genesis*.

New List of Suggested Projects

• DNA testing should be conducted on a volunteer basis by African Americans in the United States and compared with various ethnic groups in Africa, i.e., Mandingoes or Ashanti. This would provide evidence not only of ethnic heritage but also of patterns of migration after importation. Oxford Ancestors (**www.oxfordancestors.com**) in England has been using this approach to map genetic origins for Europeans. Brigham Young University in Provo, Utah, is conducting a similar volunteer project for American migrations.

• Family reunions with both slave and slaveholder descendants are becoming more common. Documentation and publication of these events and their findings should be collected and published.

• Oral histories still need to be collected from African-American senior citizens.

• African-American genealogy web sites should continue to be created to provide sources for others.

• A compilation of all African-American genealogical records for a specific area, much like Brown and Rose's *African-American Roots in Southeastern Connecticut* and Marcella Pasay's *Full Circle: A Directory of Native and African-Americans in Windham County, CT, 1650–1900* (see Connecticut), needs to be published.

Suggested Projects from First Edition of Black Genesis

Since *Black Genesis* was originally published, many of the projects listed below have been started:

• While some census information regarding many free African Americans is now available in print, on the Internet, or published in CD-ROM form for the 1790 through 1830 censuses, similar projects should be undertaken for all census returns. There are CDs available of African Americans in the 1870 census. These cover Georgia; North Carolina; Pennsylvania; Virginia; West Virginia; Cook County, Illinois; Baltimore, Maryland; St. Louis, Missouri; and five New York City boroughs only.

• Revolutionary War records for African Americans are now available in print (See Chapter 5, "Military Records"). Other National Archives pension and war records involving African Americans need to be published.

• Vital records of African Americans found in family Bibles and diaries need to be located and indexed. Most family Bible records previously printed in genealogical magazines have omitted slave entries. Many Bible records gathered by the Daughters of the American Revolution are added to annually and are widely available on microfilm; however, these are indexed by state and by year of publication, making the search tedious. Some Bible records have been included in commercial Internet searchable databases and newsletters, but this is only a very small percentage of what must be available, and there is no state or national index of them.

• All individuals listed in the Freedman's Bank CD-ROM should be traced to an individual or family alive today, if possible.

• Records of slave traders should be found, indexed, and published.

• A search for slave-aid-society records needs to be undertaken.

• Archives of African-American religious organizations should be surveyed for genealogical material to be published.

• The obituaries and other vital events in African-American newspapers and magazines, especially those published by African-American churches, should be extracted and indexed.

• A nationwide alphabetical computerized index of all slave owners in the 1850 and 1860 U.S. Slave Schedules should be published. (Since the original *Black Genesis* an index has been published in book form.)

• The 1890 special census of Civil War veterans should be published, indicating all African Americans.

• The manumission records available for all counties in all states should be published. Many such records are available on microfilm through the Family History Library. But others are hidden in deeds and miscellaneous papers in town halls and courthouses.

• Marriage records of African Americans should be published for all states that kept segregated records, as well as for those where licenses identify African Americans.

• All court records involving African Americans should be found and published, especially for those states keeping segregated records.

• A bibliography of "Who's Who" books pertaining to African Americans should be published.

• Records of African-American cemeteries, including inscriptions of gravestones should be located and published.

• Extant records of African-American funeral homes could be published with the help of The National Funeral Directors and Morticians Association [NFDMA], located in Atlanta, Georgia.

• Yearbooks of African-American colleges and universities should be catalogued.

• Plantation records and diaries available on microfilm, microfiche, and in manuscript form need to be located, indexed, and published.

• Mortality schedules for the 1850, 1860, 1870, 1880 federal census schedules not already indexed and published should include all slaves and free African Americans.

The above suggested projects constitute only a small portion of the vast amount of work that is still left to be done in every state. But there are more than just names, dates, and places to be found. The character and quality of African-American life still need to be understood as part of the African-American experience in the United States.

Reexamining History

It is sometimes difficult to understand what family trees have to do with history. For many years genealogy was conducted mostly by those privileged with time and money. For a similar number of years, history has been thought of as dates, places, and wars.

Genealogy and history, in fact, go hand in hand. Together they can help us understand our past and our relationships to each other. Genealogy is primarily a quest for identity, not in terms of names or status (although it has been used that way sometimes), but as a basis for understanding the psychological, social, political, and economic forces that influenced us through our parents, grandparents, great-grandparents, and family life in general.

To understand what was happening in and to your family during a specific time, in a specific place, is to breathe life into history. Watch the excitement in a young person when he or she realizes that everything did not begin and end at 145th and Lenox (now Malcolm X Blvd.), that older people are a rich source of family information, that what happened in previous generations profoundly affects him or her. Then you will understand the joy of making history come alive. There are several ways genealogical tools and techniques can be used to uncover that history, providing different lenses on the past. The following examples of Joshua Hempstead and Richard Linville are two illustrations.

Joshua Hempstead's Diary

Joshua Hempstead was a prominent resident in New London, Connecticut, in the early 1700s. A widower, he lived in a moderately sized frame house that still stands on the corner of Truman and Hempstead Avenues. He kept an extensive diary between 1711 and 1758, which conveyed the names, places, dates, activities, economics, weather, and politics of that time. Although an index of all surnames was developed when *The Diary of Joshua Hempstead of New London, Connecticut* (New London, Conn.: New London County Historical Society, 1901) was published, it did not include an index of African Americans who were mentioned only by first name. The 1999 reprint has corrected this oversight. Information about the CD-ROM version is available at **http://www.newlondongazette.com/DiaryCD1.html**.

Retrieving all information from the diary about Adam, a slave, and the people he interacted with, and comparing that information with court and church records of the New London area, a remarkable tapestry of the interconnected life of African Americans, Native Americans, and European Americans emerges. (See James M. Rose and Barbara Brown's books, *Tapestry: A Living History of the Black Family in Southeastern Connecticut,* and *Black Roots in Southeastern Connecticut, 1650–1900*, which tell this story.)

Such community-based research serves as a methodological model for genealogical research in general and African-American genealogical research in particular, making it possible to piece together the ancestry of many African-American families. Other excellent community/plantation studies with examples of how to develop this methodology for African-American families include the following:

Ball, Edward. *Slaves in the Family.* New York: Ballantine Books, 1999.

Heinegg, Paul. *Free African Americans of Maryland and Delaware from the Colonial Period to 1810.* Baltimore: Genealogical Publishing Co., 2000.

Heinegg, Paul. *Free African Americans of North Carolina, Virginia and South Carolina from the Colonial Period to 1810.* 4th ed. Baltimore: Genealogical Publishing Co., 2001.

Richard Linville's Slaves in Oregon

Wills are a rich source for discovering African-American ancestors. But each will must be viewed in the perspective of the cultural, economic, and social occurrences surrounding the time that the will was written. One will written by Richard Linville in Polk County, Oregon, on February 25, 1847, states: "As it is my intention to live with my son Harrison Linville and he will probably be burdened with my property and myself in my declining years, I hereby will and bequeath to him and his heirs or legal representatives at my demise all rights I may have to my two slaves called Maria and Johnson *now in Oregon.*" (Emphasis added from original Oregon State Archives, Polk County, OR Estates, 1857, #0377.)

While there is a wealth of literature surrounding the 1846 migration to Oregon, there has been little mention of African Americans or slaves being part of that journey. Richard Linville, his wife, three of their children, and many grandchildren were the first settlers to take the Applegate Trail to Oregon in the late summer and fall of 1846. It is obvious from Richard's will, written shortly after their settlement in Oregon during the winter of 1846–47, that both Maria and Johnson had been on the journey. That fact is brought to light only by understanding the circumstances of the time and the words "now in Oregon"—implying their recent emigration with the family. Since slavery was illegal in Oregon at the time and no slave census was taken there in 1850, the knowledge of these two people would have been lost had not a family member recognized the importance of this historical discrepancy. How many other African Americans have been disregarded in the recounting of history, but can be found through concerted genealogical research?

Emergence of Research on the Internet

In the last two decades, the Internet has radically changed the nature of genealogy and the accessibility of records. This is particularly true for research materials on African-American genealogy. As with all published materials, it is important to see the original record, if it still exists, and to make sure that anything you find is thoroughly documented. The Internet has both original sources (as with digitized views of actual census pages) and secondary sources (as with transcriptions of records, in some cases, copied transcriptions of otherwise published material). Appendix A—General References has a section on resource guides for the Internet. Throughout this revised edition of *Black Genesis* there are web site addresses given for those places on the Internet that are not likely to change addresses quickly.

11

Conclusion

It is wonderful watching how research teams and individuals have unearthed and published so many materials in the past two decades. These publications give us a better understanding of the African-American past and American history. The novice is also helped by the publications and the source materials on the Internet. Our hope is that this publication will take the next step toward unlocking more doors to future research and discoveries.

Chapter 2:
Important Dates in
U.S. African-American
History

1619 Twenty Africans arrive from Curaçao to Jamestown, Virginia.

1664 Africans own considerable property in New Amsterdam (New York).

1775 General George Washington, revising an earlier decision, ordered recruiting officers to accept free "Negroes" in the American Army. More than 5,000 "Negroes," mostly Northern "blacks," fought against the British.

1776 The Declaration of Independence was approved in Philadelphia.

1777 Vermont took the lead in abolishing slavery. By 1804 all the states north of Delaware had taken action leading to the gradual abolition of slavery. (Some slaves were seen in New Jersey as late as 1860, however.) Pennsylvania passed a law for gradual abolition in 1780. New Hampshire's law was passed in 1783. In 1784 Connecticut and Rhode Island took similar action. Manumission acts were passed in New York in 1785, and in New Jersey in 1786, though effective legislation stipulating gradual abolition was not achieved in the states until 1799 and 1804.

1787	The Continental Congress prohibited slavery in the Northwest Territory under the famous Ordinance of 1787.
1808	A federal law prohibiting the importation of African slaves into United States went into effect.
1812–1814	War was waged between United States and Great Britain.
1820	The famous Missouri Compromise was approved by Congress. Slavery was prohibited north and west of the 36-30 parallel line within the Louisiana Territory. Missouri itself entered the Union as a slave state, while Maine entered as a free state.
1821	The African Republic of Liberia was founded under the auspices of the Colonization Society. African Americans were encouraged to emigrate to Liberia, and about 20,000 did so.
1857	The *Dred Scott* decision declared that African Americans were not citizens of the United States and denied to Congress the power to prohibit slavery in any federal territory.
1862	President Lincoln proposed to Congress a plan for gradual, compensated emancipation of slaves. Lincoln urged the Congressional delegations from Delaware, Kentucky, Maryland, Missouri, and West Virginia to support his proposal. They opposed it, as did Northern abolitionists, who felt that slaveholders should not be paid for property that they could not rightfully own. Congress, however, passed a joint resolution on April 10, 1862, endorsing the concept of gradual, compensated emancipation.
1862	The United States Senate passed a bill abolishing slavery in the District of Columbia. Slave owners were to be compensated at the rate of $300 per slave. One hundred thousand dollars were also allocated for the voluntary emigration of these freedmen to Haiti or Liberia.

1862   President Lincoln signed a bill abolishing slavery in the federal territories.

1862   Congress authorized President Lincoln to accept African Americans for service in the Union Army. Eventually, more than 186,000 African Americans served in the Union Army.

1862   President Lincoln issued a preliminary Emancipation Proclamation, giving rebellious states and territories until January 1, 1863 to abandon their hostilities or lose their slaves.

1863   President Lincoln signed the Emancipation Proclamation, which declared slaves free in some states, selected counties, and territories then in rebellion against the United States.

1865   Congress established, within the War Department, a Bureau of Refugees, Freedmen, and Abandoned Lands, known as the Freedmen's Bureau. In its five years of existence, the Bureau set up 4,330 schools, enrolling 247,000 students, and aided in the establishment of such African-American colleges as Atlanta University, Fisk University, Hampton Institute, and Howard University. The United States government also chartered the Freedman's Bank in Washington, D.C. to encourage financial responsibility among the former slaves. On April 4, 1865, the headquarters of the Freedman's Bank opened in New York. Shortly thereafter, branches were established in Louisville, Nashville, New Orleans, Vicksburg, and Washington. By 1872 there was a total of thirty-four branches, all located in the South, with the exception of the New York and Philadelphia offices. The Freedman's Bank closed its doors on June 28, 1874.

1865   The Thirteenth Amendment prohibiting involuntary servitude, except as punishment for a crime, was adopted.

1865	The Reconstruction Period began.
1870	Most African Americans, both former slaves and those newly freed, appeared by name in the federal census.
1898	Several thousand African Americans served in the Spanish-American War, serving in Cuba with distinction.
1917	The United States entered World War I. Approximately 300,000 African Americans served during this conflict.
1941	The bombing of Pearl Harbor brought on World War II. Thousands of African Americans served in the European and Pacific theater.

Note: More information on the above dates can be found in the *Encyclopedia of African American Culture and History,* edited by Jack Salzman, David Lionel Smith, and Cornel West. 5 vols. New York: Simon and Schuster, 1996.

Chapter 3:
Oral History

The process of collecting data concerning genealogy and history through informal but informative conversation with people is known as oral history. "Informal but informative" means that the conversation is kept flowing while predetermined questions are asked. You will want to have these conversations with the older members of your family.

The first step is to look over the information you already know, and then determine what you need to find out and which people in your family are likely to know the answers. Write the questions down for easy recall during your conversation. In addition to the names, dates, and places of births, marriages, and deaths, you will want to understand something of the social, economic, and psychological circumstances surrounding each generation. An older person may not initially remember the vital statistics but will probably recall them easily when discussing various experiences. Do not pass up the opportunity to ask about religious, educational, and political practices in the family, as well as local customs. An important part of oral history is understanding how attitudes and experiences have changed or have been carried on through the generations.

You should also have a basic geographic understanding of the area you are researching, and should be sure to get the names of counties or cities, not just states. For this, it is a good idea to carry a county or township map with you for easy reference. If you are not able to talk with a particular person, most of these suggestions can be adapted to letter writing. For those whose elders have died, there are other possible resources for reconstructing the lives of ancestors. For example, a minister or others who may have had a relationship with the family member can be a source of information.

Since many of the people you will want to interview will be elderly, you should be respectful and considerate. If you hold the interview in a place where they feel comfortable and dress in a way that they would consider appropriate, you are more likely to conduct a successful interview. Their age and health should always be considered—under most circumstances, sixty to ninety minutes should be the limit for each interview.

The list of questions should be asked in a respectful manner. After asking a question, listen to the response and take notes on points for follow-up. Allow time for a response. While your family member is answering, you will be able to restructure one of your questions or ask a probing one suggested below. It should be remembered that with oral history, conversation means that you will do most of the listening, not talking.

When rapport has been established, your family member will probably want to share photographs, letters, and family papers with you. You, in turn, will want to share what progress you have made in putting the family tree together. For various reasons, a family member will often not want to let you know some of the family's past. If this is the case, patience and acceptance of the right to privacy will go a long way. Your interviewee will usually be helpful once he or she knows that you will not use the information in any harmful way. Asking family members to get involved in the research problems with you will help increase their confidence in the project and make them feel more comfortable about sharing information.

Here are a few specific guidelines to follow during the interview:

• Keep notes while interviewing, even if you use a recorder. The purpose is to keep track of the chronology of events and record information in order to re-word questions.

• Try not to ask a double question, or one that you answer yourself. The way you ask questions can influence the answer you receive. Short, clear questions prevent confusion and are easy to answer.

• Guard against your own feelings by avoiding negative physical mannerisms, and do not interrupt your interviewee's response (except to focus a response).

• Show concern and interest. Try to conceal boredom. Keeping eye contact with the person will help.

Finally, the following questions or responses will help probe the psychological and social factors surrounding particular experiences. They can easily be introduced into the conversation once it is flowing: "Tell me more." "I'm not sure I understand." "What led up to that?" "What happened next?" "How did it turn out?"

There are several Internet sites that are dedicated to how to conduct an oral interview. The sites also include forms that you can use in gathering your information. Try **http://www.rootsweb.com/~genepool/ oralhist.htm** or type "oral history" into the search box on your Internet browser or a search engine to see other possibilities. You may want to purchase a genealogy software package for organizing your research.

The following sources will help you develop your oral history:

Clark-Lewis, Elizabeth. "Oral History: Its Utilization in the Genealogical Research Process." *National Genealogical Society Quarterly.* 67 (March 1979): 25–33.

Blassingame, John W. *Slave Testimony: Two Centuries of Letters, Speeches, Interviews and Autobiographies.* Baton Rouge, La.: Louisiana State University Press, 1977.

Brecher, Jeremy. *History from Below: How to Uncover and Tell the Story of Your Community, Association or Union.* New Haven, Conn: Advocate Press, 1986.

Burroughs, Tony. "Slave Oral History." *African American Genealogical Sourcebook.* Edited by Paula K. Byers. Detroit: Gale Research, 1995.

Erickson, Stacy. *A Field Notebook for Oral History,* 2d ed. Diane Publishing Company, 1996. Presents in simple outline form, basic information about the oral history process, primarily directed toward those who have no experience with oral history.

Gwaltney, John Langston, ed. *Drylongs: A Self-Portrait of Black America.* New York: Random House, 1980.

Havlice, Patricia P. *Oral History: A Reference Guide and Annotated Bibliography.* Jefferson, N.C.: McFarland & Company, Inc., 1985.

Ritchie, Donald A. *Doing Oral History.* New York: Twayne Publishers, 1995.

Wright, Giles R. "Oral History and the Writing of Afro-American History: The Great Migration Experience 1915–1930." *Journal of the Afro-American Historical and Genealogical Society.* 10:1 (January 1989).

Chapter 4:
National Archives and
Federal Records

Once you have completed a preliminary chart of a few generations of your family, the next step is to locate each generation in the federal population census. The federal government maintains extensive groups of primary materials useful for genealogical research, including those specifically related to African Americans. If you have the resources to travel, the National Archives or one of its regional branches (see Appendix C) is the place to start. A fine explanation of the sources and publications available there can be located on the Internet at **http://www.nara.gov/genealogy**. Fortunately, many records within the National Archives have been inventoried and materials relevant to African Americans have been identified and extracted. The following guides will be helpful:

Black Studies: Select Catalog of National Archives Microfilm Publications. United States National Archives and Records Service. Washington, D.C.: National Archives Trust Fund Board, 1984.

Guide to Genealogical Research in the National Archives. 4th ed. Washington, D.C.: National Archives and Records Administration, 2001.

National Archives Microfilm Resources for Research: A Comprehensive Catalog. Washington, D.C.: National Archives and Records Administration, 1991.

Newman, Debra L. *Black History: A Guide to Civilian Records in the National Archives.* Washington, D.C.: National Archives and Records Administration, 1984, 1996.

Walker, James D. "The National Archives and Records Service." *Ethnic Genealogy.* Edited by Jessie Carney Smith. Westport, Conn.: Greenwood Press, 1983.

The major records discussed here are the federal census schedules, including their indexes and mortality schedules. The National Archives also have the original files of the Freedmen's Bureau and Freedman's Bank records discussed in the next section of this chapter. Those records concerning military service, which are also located at the National Archives, are discussed in the next chapter, "War Records."

Federal Census Records

Beginning in 1790, and every ten years afterwards, a federal census has been taken. Over the years, the records for each census have varied. Even though census taking continues today, the records are not available to the general public for seventy-two years. This means that, currently, the 1790–1930 census records are open for public use. What follows is a description of the valuable information related to African Americans that can be obtained from these records.

1790—First Census of the United States
Arranged by state and then by county. Lists free African Americans who were heads of households by name; other members are numbered, not named; slaves are listed by number within the slave owner's household. Other free African Americans living with white families are not named, only numbered. See Debra Newman Ham's *List of Free Black Heads of Families in the First Census of the United States, 1790.* Washington, D.C.: National Archives and Records Service, 1973.

1800—Second Census of the United States
Same as 1790 census.

1810—Third Census of the United States
Same as 1790 census.

1820—Fourth Census of the United States
Arranged by state and then by county. Lists free African Americans who were heads of households by name. Other African Americans in the household, slaves living with owners, and free African Americans living in white households are not named but are numbered within age groupings (under 14, 14–26, 26–45, and 45 and over). The number of persons engaged in agriculture, commerce, and manufacturing is recorded.

1830—Fifth Census of the United States
Same as 1820 census except that the age groupings are under 10, 10–25, 25–36, 36–55, 55–100, and 100 and over. The number of persons engaged in agriculture, commerce, or manufacturing is not included.

1840—Sixth Census of the United States
Same as 1830 census.

1850—Seventh Census of the United States
Arranged by state and then divided into free schedules and slave schedules, both organized by county. Free schedules list names of all members of a household and indicate age; sex; color (black, mulatto, or white— in some cases "Indian"); place of birth; and profession, trade, or occupation for males over fifteen. Other information includes whether married within the year, attending school, or unable to read or write, and if pauper or convict. Slave schedules list number of slaves by age and sex under each owner's name. There is also a slave schedule for the 1860 census.

1860—Eighth Census of the United States
Same as 1850 census except that females over fifteen have their profession, trade, or occupation listed.

1870—Ninth Census of the United States
Arranged by state and then by county. This is the first federal census that includes names of all people counted.

1880—Tenth Census of the United States
Arranged by state and then by county. Includes the same information as the 1870 census with the addition of the relationship to head of household (especially important regarding African Americans because of extended family relationships), and birthplace for each person as well as that of their mother and father. The 1880 census has a Soundex for all households with children under ten years of age. This system of indexing by sounds of the last name means that, if someone lived in a household with children under ten, you only need to know the person's name and state of residence in order to locate them on the census for this year.

1890—Eleventh Census of the United States
As much as 99 percent of the 1890 census was destroyed by water and smoke from a fire in the Commerce Building in 1921. However, a special census for 1890 remains. See "Special Census Schedules" below for further information.

1900—Twelfth Census of the United States
Same information as the 1880 census, with the addition of a number of socioeconomic facts on each family, including number of children born to women and number still living, and year of immigration to U.S. There

is a Soundex for all states in the 1900 census that includes all people, not just those who lived in a household with children under ten.

1910—Thirteenth Census of the United States
Soundex or Miracode for 21 states. Information provided is similar to the 1900 census, with the addition of whether the person is a survivor of the Union or Confederate Army or Navy.

1920—Fourteenth Census of the United States
Similar information as in 1900 and 1910. Soundex available for all states.

1930—Fifteenth Census of the United States
Includes answers to thirty-two questions, with similar categories as in the 1900–1920 censuses.

For a complete listing of information on each census, go to **http://www.census.gov:80/prod/2/gen/cff/cff-9702.pdf**. You will need to download Adobe Acrobat Reader to view the complete file.

Mortality Records

Another group of census records taken by the federal government is the mortality records for 1850, 1860, 1870, 1880, and for five states, in 1885. Information in these records includes name, age, sex, color, birthplace, occupation, and marital status. There is an indication as to whether an African-American person was a slave or free, the month of death and cause, and, by 1880, the birthplace of mother and father and name of attending physician. This group of records is, consequently, a nationwide list of African Americans who died from June 1849 to May 1850; June 1859 to May 1860; June 1869 to May 1870; June 1879 to May 1880; and for Colorado, Florida, Nebraska, New Mexico, and the Dakotas, June 1884 to May 1885.

The records may not be complete regarding the deaths of slaves. Although indexes to the mortality records have been published, they generally omit African Americans. Consequently, the originals must be consulted until a complete index is available. The location of the mortality records for the various states is noted in the survey of states that follows.

Special Census Schedules

In 1890 a special census was prepared to record persons who served in the Army, Navy and Marine Corps of the United States during the War of the Rebellion (who are survivors) and widows of such persons. The information captured on these records includes the name of the veteran, post office address, rank, company, regiment or vessel, dates of enlistment and discharge, disability, length of service and, if applicable, the widow's name. These records are housed at the National Archives.

Agricultural information was recorded briefly in 1820, but a more complete list that includes free African-American farmers is included in Schedule 2, the Agricultural Schedules. These schedules were prepared in 1850–1880 for several states, as well as in 1885 for Colorado, Florida, Nebraska, New Mexico, and the Dakotas. The information recorded includes the farmer's name and a description of the land, animals, and equipment.

Freedmen's Records

The records of the Bureau of Refugees, Freedmen, and Abandoned Lands, popularly referred to as the Freedmen's Bureau, are quite valuable. The Bureau existed during Reconstruction and kept such important records as marriages, contracts, abandoned and confiscated lands, and school reports. In addition to consulting the *Black Studies* guide cited at the beginning of this chapter, see **http://www.freedmensbureau.com/** for more information.

The Freedman's Savings and Trust Company, incorporated March 3, 1865 in Washington, D.C. for the benefit of freedmen, was not a part of the Freedmen's Bureau, though they both were chartered at the same time. The bank kept registers of those who deposited money in branches throughout the South and New York City. These records can be found on CDs, which can be purchased from The Church of Jesus Christ of Latter-day Saints, Family History Library, Salt Lake City, Utah.

Chapter 5:
Military Records

Service records for African Americans in the various wars of the United States are available and, in some cases, well indexed for general use. The National Archives, state archives and many libraries have begun the process of documenting military record sources. The Internet sites for many repositories have added these listings. In addition, several books have been written recently on military records. Some of the new and old sources for the records of the French and Indian War, American Revolution, War of 1812, Civil War, and other military pursuits are described below.

Black Studies: A Select Catalog of National Archives Microfilm Publications. Washington, D.C.: U.S. General Services Administration, 1984. For a full view of military records at the National Archives and their branches, see **http://www.nara.gov/ genealogy**.

Moebs, Thomas Truxtun. *Black Soldiers—Black Sailors—Black Ink: Research Guide on African-Americans in U.S. Military History, 1526–1900.* Chesapeake Bay, Va.: Moebs Publishing. Co., 1994.

French and Indian War

Black Soldiers in the Colonial Militia: Documents from 1639–1780. N.P.: Tabor-Lucas Publications, c1994.

Bowman, Larry G. "Virginia's Use of Blacks in the French and Indian War." *Western Pennsylvania History Magazine.* 53 (Jan 1970), 57–63.

Revolutionary War, 1776

The number of African Americans and their contributions to the Revolution were quite significant. For background reading in trying to trace African American ancestors who fought in this war, the following books and articles are suggested:

Greene, Robert Ewell. *Black Courage 1775–1783: Documentation of Black Participation in the American Revolution.* Washington, D.C.: National Society of the Daughters of the American Revolution, 1984.

Ham, Debra Newman. *List of Black Servicemen Compiled from the War Department Collection of Revolutionary War Records.* Washington, D.C.: National Archives and Records Service, 1974 (microfiche, 1996).

War of 1812

Early in the war the United States Navy petitioned for the right to recruit black sailors. In March of 1813 blacks began to enter the war and participated in many of the battles. Over 200 black marines also participated in battles. One unit was the 26th U.S. Infantry Regiment, which consisted of 247 African Americans from Philadelphia, Pennsylvania. See the web site **http://www.liunet.edu/cwis/cwp/library/aaffsfl.htm** for a list of some of the soldiers who fought in the war. Other good sites for information include **http://www.galafilm.com/1812/e/background/amer_afric_par.html** and **http://www.coax.net/people/lwf/war_1812.htm**, which has many interest links listed. The National Archives web page (**http://www.nara.gov/genealogy**) can be searched for *Genealogical Records of the War of 1812*, by Stuart L. Butler, or *Documenting African Americans in the Records of Military Agencies*, by Lisha Penn.

Also see Gerald T. Altoff's book *Amongst My Best Men: African Americans and the War of 1812.*

Civil War

Thousands of African Americans fought in the Civil War on both the Union and Confederate sides. Most of the records of their services are located at the National Archives, but others can be found at state libraries. Record Group 94, "Records of the Adjutant General's Office, 1780's–

1917," at the National Archives contains an index to Compiled Service Records of Volunteer Union Soldiers who served with U.S. Colored Troops. It is an alphabetical card index giving the name of a soldier, his rank, and service unit. The card file will then refer you to the complete service record of the soldier. A second part of this record group is the Compiled Records Showing Service of Military Units in Volunteer Union Organizations. Once the unit has been determined from the card index, this part of the records relates the activities and commander of each unit. The following books are suggested for background reading:

Barrow, Charles Kelly, J.H. Segars, and R.B. Rosenburg. *The Forgotten Confederates: An Anthology about Black Southerners.* Atlanta, Ga.: Southern Historical Press, 1995.
This book examines the role of African Americans who served within Southern armies.

Cornish, Dudley Taylor. *The Sable Arm: Black Troops in the Union Army, 1861–1865.* Lawrence, Kans.: University Press of Kansas, 1956.

Cox, Clinton. *Undying Glory: The Story of the Massachusetts 54th Regiment.* New York: Scholastic Inc., 1991.

Emiho, Luis F. *A Brave Black Regiment: History of the Fifty-Fourth Regiment of Massachusetts Volunteer Infantry, 1863–1865,* 3rd edition, with introductions by James M. McPherson and Edwin Gittleman. Salem, N.H.: Ayer Co. Publishers, 1990.

Foner, Eric. *Reconstruction: America's Unfinished Revolution, 1863–1877.* New York: Harper & Row, 1988.
An excellent bibliography of primary and secondary resources to help in locating African-American ancestors in the Civil War.

Hargrove, Herndon B. *Black Union Soldiers in the Civil War.* Jefferson, N.C.: McFarland & Company, 1988.

Helsley, Alexia Jones. *South Carolina's African-American Confederate Pensioners, 1923–1925.* Columbia, S.C.: South Carolina Department of Archives and History, 1998.

Jordan, Ervin L. *Black Confederates and Afro-Yankees in Civil War Virginia.* Charlottesville, Va.: University Press of Virginia, 1995.

Monaghan, Jay. *Civil War on the Western Border, 1854–1865.* Lincoln, Nebr.: University of Nebraska Press, 1955.

Rollins, Richard, ed. *Black Southerners in Gray: Essays on Afro-Americans in Confederate Armies.* Murfreesboro, Tenn.: Southern Heritage Press, 1994.

Secret-Braxton. Jeanette. *Guide to Tracing Your African American Civil War Ancestor*. San Pablo, CA: Craderson Pub. 1996.

This helpful guide describes how to use the following federal and state records: Military Records and Pension Records; U.S. Colored Troops' Records; Union Navy Seamen's Records; General Index to Pension Files, 1861–1865; Miscellaneous Records Relating to Veteran's Claims; General Correspondence of the Records and Pension Office, 1889–1920; and other national and state archives sources.

Other Military Resources

There were several units of African Americans who served in the infantry and cavalry on military posts in the West, in the Indian wars, in the Southwest, and in Cuba during the Spanish-American War and twentieth-century wars. Records of these units are available at the National Archives and described at their web page, **http://www.nara.gov/**. Also, see the individual state listings in Part II.

Chapter 6:
Migratory Patterns

Until the late eighteenth century, the African-American population remained relatively stable, not moving out of the geographic area in which they found themselves upon arrival in the colonies. At the start of the nineteenth century, and especially by 1830, thousands of African Americans began moving toward the cities or the western frontier. They, like the thousands of whites with whom they migrated, moved to other areas for a myriad of military, economic, and social reasons growing out of industrialization and western expansion.

In addition to the general migratory patterns in which all Americans moved, there were three important migratory patterns in which African Americans alone were involved: 1) the domestic slave trade; 2) the escape of slaves with and without the Underground Railroad; 3) the agricultural revolution of the early twentieth century.

The domestic slave trade resulted in the displacement of many African Americans. Consequently, it is significant to understand the areas and routes of trade in order to successfully explore African-American genealogical roots. The areas for slave sales and distribution, such as Charleston and Columbia, South Carolina, were busy and prosperous places. In fact, more than 40,000 slaves were imported from Africa to Charleston in anticipation of prohibition of foreign slave trade, which began in 1808. By the end of the 1850s, Columbia and Charleston were larger markets in the domestic slave trade than Richmond, Virginia. The southern counties in Virginia and Maryland supplied the largest number of slaves to the Deep South. Baltimore was the center for slave sales, and Alexandria the port of debarkation for slaves and free African Americans to be transported by boat to New Orleans.

Two methods frequently used for transporting slaves to distant markets were by ship—either along the Atlantic coast or down the Ohio and

Mississippi rivers and their tributaries—or overland by forced march and, later, railroad. The largest coast cargoes of slaves were shipped from Alexandria, Norfolk, and Richmond, Virginia; Baltimore, Maryland; or Charleston, South Carolina, to the ports of Natchez and Mobile, Alabama and New Orleans, Louisiana, where they were sold inland. The Mississippi River was a great inland channel of slave trade, with numerous African Americans being sold along the way. The relationship between migratory patterns and the domestic slave trade will continue to be a major focus of African-American genealogy in the future.

Some of the sources described in the various state chapters, along with the resources listed below, can be used as the basis for such research. In addition, there are massive numbers of slave sale advertisements found in early newspapers and early residential directories, which can be a rich source of slave traders. For example, the largest slave traders in Memphis, Tennessee were Bolton and Dickens. The New-York Historical Society and The New Hampshire Historical Society have Bolton and Dickens's list of more than 1,500 slaves and their purchasers. Alphabetizing and tracing the names in this list would be an excellent contribution to African-American family ancestry. Hundreds of other lists could be reclaimed and published for similar purposes. The following are examples:

Bancroft, Frederick. *Slave Trading in the Old South.* Baltimore: J.H. Furst Co., 1931.

Drago, Edmund L., ed. *Broke by the War: Letters of a Slave Trader.* Columbia, S.C.: University of South Carolina Press, 1991.

Tadman, Michael. *Speculators and Slaves: Masters, Traders, and Slaves in the Old South.* Madison, Wis.: University of Wisconsin Press, 1989.

The second African-American genealogical migration pattern was established by the escape of slaves and the Underground Railroad. Slaves escaped from nearly every geographical area and then traveled north and west. Slaves were known to have traveled from as far as Greenwich, Connecticut, to northern Ohio by freight car and to have stowed away on barges up the Ohio River from Virginia and Kentucky. African Americans also traveled by the Underground Railroad from Columbia, South Carolina and Wilmington, Delaware to New Haven, Connecticut; New Bedford and Boston, Massachusetts; Portland, Maine; and Canada. Another route on the Railroad existed from North Carolina through Tennessee, Kentucky, and Indiana, to Michigan. See **http:// www.undergroundrailroad.com**.

The following provides background for understanding the scope of migratory patterns created by escaped slaves and the Underground Railroad:

Blockson, Charles L. *The Underground Railroad: Dramatic First-hand Accounts of Daring Escapes to Freedom.* New York: Prentice Hall, 1987.

National Park Service. *The Underground Railroad, Official Map and Guide.* Washington, D.C.: U.S. Dept. of the Interior, 1997.

Siebert, Wilbur. *The Underground Railroad: From Slavery to Freedom.* New York: Arno Press, 1968.

Still, William. *The Underground Railroad.* Chicago: Johnson Publishing Co., 1970.

Switala, William J. *Underground Railroad in Pennsylvania.* Mechanicsburg, Pa.: Stackpole Books, 2001.

Trusty, Emma Marie. *The Underground Railroad: Ties That Bound Unveiled.* Privately printed, July 1999.

The agricultural revolution in the first half of the twentieth century had a profound effect on the lives of African Americans in the South. The unprecedented rate at which modern machinery replaced farm labor created a major geographic shift in the labor force. Farm laborers in the South headed to northern cities to find new kinds of work. The web site **http://www.northbysouth.org** examines the impact of the migration north with prose and pictures. For more information about the migration of African Americans during this time period, consult the following:

Grossman, James R. *Land of Hope: Chicago, Black Southerners, and the Great Migration.* Chicago: University of Chicago Press, 1989.

Henri, Florette. *Black Migration, 1900–1920.* New York: Doubleday Anchor Press, 1975.

Lemann, Nicholas. *The Promised Land: The Great Black Migration and How It Changed America.* New York: A.A. Knopf, 1991.

Marks, Carole. *Farewell, We're Good and Gone: The Great Black Migration.* Bloomington, Ind.: Indiana University Press, 1989.

Stewart, Roma Jones. The Migration of a Free People: Cass County's Black-Settlers from North Carolina. *Michigan History* 71 (January–February 1987).

Chapter 7: Slavery

Once you have traced your ancestors through oral history, census, and vital statistics records back to slavery, you will need to be familiar with the techniques of establishing family relationships through slave records. It is sometimes tedious work and will probably take you longer than you would like. If slave records were published and as easily accessible as other genealogical information, the task would be much easier.

Throughout the Western world and Africa there are thousands of records dealing with slavery. In many cases they were dutifully kept because of their importance to the growth of capitalism. When Africans were seized from their homeland and brought to the Americas, the slave ship captain recorded them in his manifest. Many such records still exist in vast quantities in the United States and several European and Caribbean countries. These were only the beginning of slave records. Once off the ship, if able to survive the journey, the slaves' lives were recorded in many ways—sometimes in separate records, but more often as part of the normal course of events in the slave owner's business affairs. One of the most effective approaches to researching enslaved ancestors is to identify the plantation on which the ancestor worked and the holder of the enslaved family. Research then focuses on the slave owner's family and the records it produced as slave owners, as well as on the enslaved family itself. There are many techniques that we have used throughout the years to find slave ancestry. Here is one approach:

1. Locate the records of your family members in the 1870 federal census or any special census conducted by the state in which they lived.

2. Construct the make-up of your family as it would have been in 1850–1860.

3. Check the 1850 or 1860 Slave Schedules for slaveholders' names in that same county, township or post office. Sometimes the surnames of ex-slaves recorded in the censuses are the surnames of former slaveholders.

4. Compare your family make-up with your findings in the Slave Schedules.

5. Once you have established the potential owner(s) of an enslaved ancestor, construct or find the slave-owning family genealogy. See Edward Ball's *Slaves in the Family* (New York: Ballantine Books, 1999); Mary L. Jackson Fears' *Slave Ancestral Research: It's Something Else* (Bowie, Md.: Heritage Books, Inc., 1995); and David H. Streets' *Slave Genealogy: A Research Guide with Case Studies* (Bowie, Md.: Heritage Books, Inc., 1986) for excellent examples of slave research.

6. If the slaveholder died before 1865, look at the clusters of first names found in the owners/holders estate records. First names can often be linked together from the population censuses after 1870.

7. If the slaveholder is still living after the Civil War (1865), begin to look at the owner's annual returns, account books, business receipts, medical notes, birth registers, diaries, letters, and bills of sale. Many of those ex-enslaved became tenant farmers or sharecroppers after the Civil War. If the family owned land, deed records are helpful in tracing the original owner. Any legal transactions concerning the land would be recorded.

8. Research the slave-owning family's genealogy by looking at all probate records, slave records, and county, state, and federal records. Make a chart with the family names and put underneath every name what slaves they owned and when. Very often you can trace the African-American family through this process, because slaves were more likely to be willed and sold within European family groupings.

9. If at all possible form a research team and compile all information on the slaves in the town or county. By doing this you will be able to track your family history and leave a valuable resource for others.

10. Read secondary sources on the area. You might get lucky and find information linking your family to a slave owner.

11. Don't assume your family was in slavery immediately before 1870. In many cases African Americans continued to live and work with the white family with whom they had lived during slavery at an earlier time. Some others were never slaves or had been free for many years.

If you have a low-frequency surname, it is more likely that you are related to the slave owner or were always free. Use circumstantial information and oral history to prove connections. If you have proof that your ancestors were on a specific plantation, "adopt" all related names as your extended family.

Lastly, try using Internet search engines for slave records. New records come to light yearly. Also see each state's web site for materials specific to that state. Use **http://www.USGENWEB.com** to check state and county web links for current information on what is available. There are plenty of sites not connected to this web site, so you will want to extend your search beyond it. The following sections provide a description, with some illustrations, of various types of records that are known to be available for some states.

Slave Trading Records

Valuable information on migration trails can be found in these records. See Chapter 6, "Migratory Patterns," for more information about this resource. In addition, naval shipping lists (which include slave arrivals) for east Florida, Georgia, Maryland, Massachusetts, New Hampshire, New Jersey, New York, South Carolina, and Virginia are on microfilm (1) at Columbia University in New York City, (2) at the National Archives, and (3) through the Family History Library in Salt Lake City and its local Family History Centers.

Bills of Slave Sales

In most cases these records, as well as those for indentured servants, are found as part of land deeds, since slaves were considered property. The name of the slave, the value, and some description of age plus the buyer's name, the seller's name, their counties of residence, and the date of the sale are usually included. Occasionally, such deeds are separate from land deeds or are in miscellaneous records at historical societies, libraries, and state, county, and city archives. They can be used in conjunction with other records to construct a genealogy.

Slave Advertisements

Local papers carried advertisements in local papers naming runaways and slaves for sale or hire. It is now possible to locate these advertisements by searching the *Index to Personal Names in the National Union Catalog of Manuscript Collections 1959–1984.* (Alexandria, Va.: Chadwyk-Healey, 1988). Once you have focused on a particular slaveholding family, consult this index to see if there are any listings for that family in the National Union Catalog of Manuscript Collections (NUCMC). This will provide the location of personal and business papers of members of that family. The NUCMC search process begins at **http://lcweb.loc.gov/coll/nucmc/nucmc.html**.

It's possible that records of interest have been microfilmed as part of the extensive microfilm series *Records of Ante-Bellum Southern Plantations From the Revolution Through the Civil War* (Frederick, Md.: University Publications of America, 1985), edited by the noted historian Kenneth Stampp. This ongoing series is available at many research libraries and is accompanied by very thorough descriptions and reel guides for the component collections. The following books are suggested additional reading:

Headley, Robert K., Jr. *Genealogical Abstracts From the 18th-Century Virginia Newspapers.* Baltimore: Genealogical Publishing Co., 1987.
Contains runaway advertisements from the eighteenth century.

Smith, Billy G., and Richard Wojtowicz. *Blacks Who Stole Themselves: Advertisements for Runaways in the Pennsylvania Gazette 1728–1790.* Philadelphia: University of Pennsylvania, 1989.

Tregillis, Helen Cox. *River Roads to Freedom: Fugitive Slave Notices and Sheriff Notices Found in Illinois Sources.* Bowie, Md.: Heritage Books, Inc. 1988.

Windley, Lathan A. *Runaway Slave Advertisements: A Documentary History From the 1730s to 1790,* 4 vols. Westport, Conn.: Greenwood, 1983.
Covers the states of Virginia, North Carolina, Maryland, South Carolina.

Birth, Baptism, Marriage, and Death Records

Vast numbers of vital records for slaves exist in historical societies; state, county, and city archives; and state libraries; and in the possession of private individuals. During the colonial period such records were often part of European-American church records, family papers, and wills. This was true for the North as well as the South. Local customs determine whether the records were kept separately or not.

Census and Tax Records

In addition to the federal census schedules already discussed, tax and census records were kept for business and governmental purposes, since slaves were considered property. There are census records for slaves as early as 1619, when twenty blacks arrived in Jamestown, Virginia. By 1623 another census was taken, which included the names of many of the blacks. But most often tax and census records contained numbers only and did not include names. Slaves were assessed periodically, and valuations were placed on them when estates were broken up. Often it is possible to approximate the ages and relationships of slaves by their value and order on such lists.

Court Records

Local customs and laws will determine how accessible the records of slaves in court records are. They are, however, among the most voluminous of existing records dealing with slavery. In Georgia, for example, separate tribunals were set up to try slaves, although little has been done to index the wealth of information in these records, which can be found at the Georgia State Archives. In addition, slave owners bringing slaves into Georgia had to register the names of their slaves in court. Other states handled court records and slavery in different ways. See the following references:

Finkelman, Paul. *Slavery in the Courtroom: An Annotated Bibliography of American Cases.* Washington: Library of Congress, 1985.

Catterall, Helen Tunnicliff, ed. *Judicial Cases Concerning American Slavery and the Negro.* 5 vols. New York: Negro Universities Press [1968]. Reprint. Originally published: Carnegie Institution of Washington, 1926. Includes indexes. Contents: v. 1. Cases from the courts of England, Virginia, West Virginia, and Kentucky. v. 2. Cases from the courts of North Carolina, South Carolina, and Tennessee. v. 3. Cases from the courts of Georgia, Florida, Alabama, Mississippi, and Louisiana. v. 4. Cases from the courts of New England, the middle states, and the District of Columbia. v. 5. Cases from the courts of states north of the Ohio and west of the Mississippi rivers; Canada and Jamaica.

Medical Records

Most slaves received some kind of care from doctors and hospitals. Miscellaneous medical records, which may be part of plantation records, and doctors' journals found at various state libraries and archives could be appropriate sources. All owners or employers were required to make health reports to the federal government during the pre-Civil War period in order to keep track of various epidemics. Among these records are the Mortality Schedules for 1850, 1860, discussed in Chapter 4.

Wills, Intestate Records, and Inventories

Essential to all genealogical documentation is the information obtained from wills, intestate records, and inventories. Their importance cannot be overstated. Whether a deceased left a will or not, if he owned property courts were required to appoint administration to divide the property and care for the dependents. When a will was left, the administrator was the executor appointed by the deceased. If there was no will (an intestate estate), administrators were appointed from the community. The job of the administrator or executor was to itemize and value all the property, which included slaves, and distribute it among the heirs.

The following probate record helps illustrate how a will can be used to construct genealogies:

Will of Elliott Futrell written September 20, 1836, in Northampton County, North Carolina. (*Journal of Negro History* 16 [July, 1931]: 332–3)

> In the name of God Amen. I Elliott Futrell of Northampton County, State of North Carolina being sick but of sound mind and memory do make and ordain this my last will and testament in manner as follows. Item lst. I give and bequeath unto my nephew Sander D. Futrell my plantation whereon I now live, also Negro woman Bridget and Negro girl named Elizabeth to him and his heirs forever. Secondly, I give and bequeath unto my niece Penelope Futrell daughter of Noah Futrell Negro girl named Notice to her and her heirs forever. 3rd. I give and bequeath unto my niece Mary Futrell Negro woman Nancy and her child to her and her heirs forever. 4th. I give and bequeath unto my niece Irene Futrell and daughter of Noah Futrell Negro woman Lavinia and her child Isabel to her and her heirs forever. 5th. I give and bequeath unto my nephew Noah Futrell son of Noah Futrell Negro boy named Moses to him and his heirs forever. 6th. I give and bequeath unto my niece Matilda Futrell daughter of Noah Futrell Negro girl Nancey to her and her heirs forever. 7th. I give and bequeath unto my brother Littleburg Futrell my track adjoining Willie Fennell and others, to him and his heirs. Item 8th. I give and bequeath unto my niece Mitchel Futrell daughter of Noah Futrell Negro girl named Amy to her and her heirs forever. Item 9. I give and bequeath unto my brother Hosea Futrell

Negro woman America and her three children named Henry, William, Daisy to him and his heirs forever. It is my will and desire that all of my property not herein given away be disposed of by my executor and so much thereof as may be necessary for the payment of my just debts to be equally divided between my brother Hosea Futrell and Sander D. Futrell, my nephew. I nominate and appoint my friend Bryan Randolph my lawful executor in witness thereof.

I have hereunto set my hand and seal this 20th day of September in the year of our Lord 1836 in the presence of Jordan Bell and Jacob Outland.
(signed) Elliott Futrell

From Elliott Futrell's will, it can be determined that he had three brothers and no surviving children. The children of his brothers, and the slaves who were distributed by the will, are shown in the following chart. Abbreviations used are (g) girl, (w) woman, and (b) boy.

BROTHER	CHILDREN	BEQUEST
Noah Futrell	i Penelope	Notice (g)
	ii Irene	Lavinia (w)
		i. Isabel (g)
		(daughter of Lavinia)
	iii Noah	Moses (b)
	iv Matilda	Nancey (g)
	v Mitchel (niece)	Amy (g)
	(?) vi Mary	Nancy (w)
		i. child (unnamed)
Hosea Futrell		America (w)
		i. Henry (b)
		ii. William (b)
		iii. Daisy (g)
	i. Sander D.	Bridget (w); Elizabeth (g)

In order to further follow the lives of these slaves, one would have to check the marriage and death records of any Futrells and research wills, bills of sale, and land and court records of all descendants and their spouses and children.

Manumissions

Before the Emancipation Proclamation some slaves did gain their freedom for various reasons. This process was called manumitting, and a freedom certificate was granted to the slave upon manumission. Freed slaves were required to carry their certificates of freedom at all times. In states where manumissions are found they are usually in separate court records. In the North, however, you will sometimes find manumissions filed with land records or recorded in the will of the slave owners. Manumission records are being recorded on the Internet. Access the National Union Catalog of Manuscript Collections [NUCMC] and search for manumissions. Below is an example of a Wayne County, North Carolina manumission entered on the Internet located at **http://www.co.wayne.in.us/recorder/manumission.html**.

Nov
13th
1835

To All People to whom these presents may come Know ye [*sic*] that I, David White at present in Wayne County State of Indiana do hereby by these presents release and set free from Slavery a certain Negro man named Willis, commonally [*sic*] called Willis Perry of very dark complexion of middle sise [*sic*], and about thirty five years of age, He being the same that I purchased of James Perry Esq. of Pasquetank [*sic*] County North Carolina the 27th day of the 7th month last -In witness whereof I the said David White hath to these presents set my hand and seal this the 11th day of the 9th month 1835-Sealed and delivered }

    In presence of
    Levi Coffin
    John Fellow

                    [signed] David White
                    ((Seal))

    State of Indiana
    Wayne County

Before me the undersigned an acting Justice of the peace in and for the county aforesaid this day personally came David White the within grantor and acknowledged the within deed of manumission to be his voluntary act and deed for the purposes therein specified-In testimony whereof I have hereunto set my hand and seal, September 11th 1835.

                    [signed] Joseph Morrow J.P.
                    ((Seal))

Where manumission records have been located and/or published in individual states, they are included in Part II under that state's sources.

Secondary Sources

Once you have located an ancestor living in a particular area or with a particular slave owner, you will want to research every aspect of that area or family. No guidebook or bibliography can tell you everything you need to know, but the records listed in the survey of states that follows are only those that specifically identify African Americans and not the immense volume of genealogically valuable material—available in every state archive, historical society, and library—that may apply to associates or relatives of your particular family. For a comprehensive reference to this large group of material, see Eichholz's *Ancestry's Red Book: American State, County, and Town Sources* and Szucs and Luebking's *The Source*, both cited in Appendix A. In addition, there are thousands of primary and secondary sources which exist but have not yet been identified, microfilmed, published, or recorded. Many are being added to web sites on the Internet (See Internet Resources, in Appendix A).

PART II
SURVEY OF THE
STATES

Survey of the States

Now that we've discussed general record categories available on a national level, we turn to the records of the individual states. The survey of the states in the original *Black Genesis* was organized by regions and included the West Indies and Canada. At that time very little was known about the extent of sources available for African-American genealogical research. Today, those sources are not only better known but also more available. Here, the presentation of states is organized alphabetically, with the West Indies and Canada following the fifty states. Particular emphasis is placed on states that had large African-American populations before 1900—they are considered "nucleus" states for the development of the African-American family in the United States.

Each state's resources specific to African-American research are organized by the following categories: Important Dates, State Archives, Census Records, State and County Records, Cemetery and Church Records, Military Records, Newspapers, Manuscript Sources, Internet Resources, Research Contacts, and Bibliography. Each is described below.

Information is not always available for each category under every state listing; however, in cases where a category is not included, the researcher is referred to genealogical resources available for all residents of that state. Research in African-American genealogy requires the use not only of the specific records described below but also of general resources not covered here. For information on the extensive general genealogical resources available, consult *Ancestry's Red Book: American State, County, and Town Sources*, by Alice Eichholz (rev. ed. Salt Lake City: Ancestry, Inc., 1992); *The Source* (rev. ed. Salt Lake City: Ancestry, Inc., 1996), by Loretto Szucs and Sandra Luebking; and *The Researcher's Guide to American Genealogy*, by Val Greenwood (3rd ed., Baltimore: Genealogical Publishing Company, 2000).

Important Dates

Dates significant to each state's African-American history and relative to genealogical research are presented first, in order to help you understand the context in which your ancestors lived and records about their lives emerged. Most dates are drawn from the *Encyclopedia of African-American Culture and History* (5 vols. New York: Simon and Schuster, 1996), edited by Jack Salzman, David Lionel Smith, and Cornel West.

State Archives

Listed under each state are the street, postal, and web addresses of the state archives, an important source for guides and research specific to that state. Also listed are many county, local, and historical society libraries that can be extremely helpful in your research. For a comprehensive listing of libraries, including their web addresses, refer to Elizabeth Petty Bentley's *The Genealogist's Address Book* (4th ed. Baltimore: Genealogical Publishing Company, 1999). Alternatively, go to **http://www.USGenWeb.com** and select a state to research, or use an Internet search engine and enter a state's or county's name and "library" or "historical society." Both approaches will lead you to the location of repositories within a state.

Census Records

For each state, available federal census schedules, mortality schedules, slave schedules, and state or special censuses are listed. In cases where states have materials that substitute for missing census records, those materials are included. State census records are widely available for research, not only within the state but also in other locations throughout the United States. They can be consulted at the National Archives and Records Administration in Washington, D.C. and its regional branches (see Appendix C), and through the Family History Library of the LDS Church and its regional Family History Centers (See **http://www.familysearch.com**). At least two Internet sites offer actual census views online for a research membership fee (see **http://www.ancestry.com** or **http://www.genealogy.com**).

State and County Records

In this section you'll find information about where to obtain birth-marriage-divorce-death records, including current postal and web addresses for each state's Vital Records Office. You can obtain more detailed information and order copies of current records directly through **http://www.vitalcheck.com**, which has individual links to each state agency. Thomas Kemp's *International Vital Records Handbook* (4th ed. Baltimore: Genealogical Publishing Company, 2001) provides vital records application forms and ordering information for each of the fifty states, the U.S. Trust Territories, and international countries. In addition, comprehensive and easy-to-read vital records information for each state can be found at **http://www.vitalrec.com/**.

Other state and county records, such as lists of "free persons of color," slave lists, voter registrations, slave trials, and manumission records, are found under this section if they are part of the known governmental records in that state.

Cemetery and Church Records

The location and availability of African-American cemetery and church records are indicated for each state. Considerably more attention must be given to uncovering these two important research sources before they'll be widely available. What is presently known is included here with the hope that new sources will continue to emerge. To keep current with new sources available on the Internet, see "African American Cemeteries Online" at **http://www.prairiebluff.com/aacemetery/**.

Military Records

In addition to the national military records available for all Americans (see Part I), some states have specific military sources for African-Americans. If available, these sources are reported in this section.

A national web site devoted to the Civil War has material on Colored Troops: **http://www.civilwararchive.com/unioncol.htm**.

Newspapers

Examples of African-American newspapers available for each state are listed in this section. Obituaries, death notices, and social and community events—as well as the African-American perspective of life in that location, as reported in the newspapers—all provide important contributions to the research process.

Manuscript Sources: Personal Papers, Slave Records, and Diaries

Known manuscript sources for personal papers, slave records, and diaries, including plantation records, are listed in this section. Some states have extensive collections that have been found and cataloged; others have few. While the listing for each state is not comprehensive, what is presented here are examples with their location indicated by library code (see Appendix D for library abbreviation codes). You may also want to consult the National Union Catalog (see Part I) and its Internet search site.

Internet Resources

Each state's presentation includes a brief sample of the kinds of sites or records found today on the Internet. The multitude of sources on the Internet are not all included, as they are growing exponentially every day, making any listing out-of-date before publication. Additional samples can be located through the state archives, state historical society, or library web sites, as well as online at **http://www.USGenWeb.com**, **http://www.Rootsweb.com**, and **http://www.cyndislist.com**.

Princeton University Library provides an excellent general site of African-American genealogical resources on the Internet at **http://www.princeton.lib.nj.us/robeson/genealogylinks.html**.

Research Contacts

Listed here are state libraries and organizations or individuals who have specific interests or collections in African-American genealogical research. In addition, the listing under District of Columbia includes some libraries of national significance for research.

Bibliography

Provided here are some books and articles that will give you a social, political, and historical context for your family history or provide additional examples of resources for African-American genealogical research. All books and articles listed can be found by accessing an online library catalog, such as the Library of Congress. See **http://www.loc.gov/ library/** or online search subscriptions such as FIRST SEARCH, available at most university and large libraries.

A Final Reminder

It's important not to overlook the large number of federal records located at the National Archives and its regional branches (see Part I). African-American genealogical research cannot be done in a vacuum; African-American lives are thoroughly integrated into the lives, records and sources pertaining to all Americans. While *Black Genesis* focuses on the records *specific* to African-Americans, be sure to consider *all* records and sources available to genealogical researchers.

Alabama

Important Dates

1702 – The Port of Mobile was founded as part of France's Louisiana Colony, and in 1719 the first enslaved blacks were brought in to work as laborers and domestics.

1783 – The area claimed by England and occupied by the English-allied Creek Indians became part of the territory of the United States.

1800 – The census of the American part of Alabama (established as Washington County in the Mississippi territory) listed only 494 blacks.

1820 – The year after Alabama achieved statehood the census counted 41,879 blacks. By 1860 the slave population reached 435,080— nearly half the state's population.

1859 – A group of Guinean Africans was brought illegally to Mobile on the slave ship *Clothilde,* one of the last recorded slave ship voyages to the United States. Unable to be sold, the slaves were freed; they formed a separate community called Africa Town in Mobile's northern suburb of Plateau, Alabama.

1862 – Over 10,000 Alabama freedmen served as soldiers in the Union Army.

1865 – Thirty-five black schools were set up by the Freedmen's Bureau and the American Missionary Association.

State Archives

Alabama Department of Archives & History
624 Washington Avenue
Montgomery, AL 36130
http://www.archives.state.al.us/

Since the publication of the first edition of *Black Genesis*, Alabama Department of Archives & History has made great strides in locating and organizing its records related to African-American genealogical research.

Census Records

Federal Census Records

1820–1880; 1890 (part of Perry County only); 1900–1930 (DNA, A–Ar, and Mobile and Birmingham public libraries)

Mortality Records

1850–80 (A–Ar)

Slave Schedules

1850, 1860 (A–Ar)

State Census Records

Of four state censuses for Alabama, the most helpful are 1855 census (for 14 counties: Autauga, Baldwin, Blount, Coffee, Franklin, Henry, Lowndes, Macon, Mobile, Montgomery, Pickens, Sumter, Tallapoosa, Tuscaloosa), which gives the name of the head of household and the number of slaves and free persons of color in age categories, and the 1866 (statewide) census, which provides the name of head of household for African Americans and whites, and the number of females and males in age categories. Both censuses are located at the Alabama Department of Archives & History. The 1866 returns for "Colored Population" can be found online at **http://members.aol.com/blountal/Gen.html**.

State and County Records

Birth-Marriage-Divorce-Death Records

Center for Health Statistics
201 Monroe St., Suite 1140   *Mailing Address:* P.O. Box 5625
Montgomery, AL 36104   Montgomery, AL 36103
http://www.alapubhealth.org/vital/vitalrcd.htm

Alabama did not require the recording of birth or death certificates until 1908. The statewide recording of marriage certificates began in 1936 and divorce certificates in 1950. All Alabama vital records are available from the state office and through a statewide computer system operational in all sixty-seven counties.

In many instances county records are separated by "colored" or "white" designations. Most birth records list sex, race, place, and date of birth of individual but no name. The names of parents and physician/midwife attending are also sometimes listed. Most death records list name of individual, and place of death, age at death and attending physician. Some include place of burial and cause of death. Most marriage records include names of husband and wife, presiding official at marriage, and signatures of two people who posted marriage bond. Most divorce records list only date of divorce and names of the parties and officials. One example of county records before mandatory recording are those for Baldwin County: Birth and Death Records, 1886–1919; Marriage Records (Colored), 1896–1935; see **http://www.archives.state.al.us/referenc/vital.html**.

Property Records

The state archives holds certain county land records indexed by county, name, and date of land purchase. Published land records can be found in the state archives and local public libraries. Some online sources are available through **http://www.rootsweb.com/~algenweb/index.html**.

Cemetery and Church Records

See the Alabama Department of Archives & History web site (**http://www.archives.state.al.us/**).

Military Records

Alabama service records for those who served in the Revolutionary War, Creek Indian Wars of 1813–1814 and 1836–1837, Civil War, Spanish American War, and WWI can be found at the Alabama Department of Archives & History. When researching slave owner(s), consider reviewing the Confederate Service Cards, 1861–1865, Alabama Confederate Pension Files, and Compiled Service Records of Volunteers. There also is a listing of African Americans in the Confederate Army, 1861–1865.

Newspapers

Newspapers published from 1800 to the present are indexed on microfilm at Alabama Department of Archives & History. The following is one example:

Huntsville Gazette. November 22, 1879, to October 29, 1894. Weekly. Holdings: 1881–94 (incomplete)

Manuscript Sources: Personal Papers, Slave Records, and Diaries

Alabama Department of Archives & History holds considerable manuscript material pertinent to African-American genealogy, including the following slave records:

Abraham, Jacob. Contract, 1860
Alabama Bills of Sale Collection, 1832–1863
Alabama Pamphlets Collection, 1821–1961
Allen, Wade Hampton, 1794–1851
Andrews, Eliza Frances, B. 1840. Papers, 1848–1908
Bass Family. Papers, 1839–1901
Bellinger, Carnot 1806–1876. Papers, 1864–1887
Bennett, Reuben, 1789–1868. Business Records, 1816–1863
Bill of Sale Collection, 1851
Bill of Sale, 1852
Blackspear, Alexander. Slave Deed of Gift, 1836
Blount, Richard A. (Richard Augustus), 1774–1849. Papers, 1792–1861
Branscomb Family. Letters, 1851–1865
Brown, Thomas. Will [Undated]
Chapron, Jean Marie. Letterbook, 1838–1841
Clements Family. Papers, 1855–1862
Cocke Family. Papers, 1820–1966
Coffee, John, 1772–1833. Papers, 1796–1887
Crenshaw, Edward, 1842–1911. Diary, 1861–1865
Crowell, John, 1785–1846. Journal, 1822–1830
Floyd, Charles. Account Book, 1833–1865
Hall, William B. Papers, 1858–1866
Hall, William, Bonnell. Papers, 1835–1910

Hall Family. Photographs

Harrison Family. Reminiscences, [186-]–[187-.]

Hill and Howth Plantation Records
>   "Rules and Regulations for the Management of Slaves" by William P. Gould.

Jones, B. R. (Benjamin Rush), 1813–1887. Receipts, 1836–1863

King, William R., 1786–1853. Family Papers, 1714–1964

Lowery, William. Diaries, 1862–1863

Mango County Probate Office
>   Reports of Slave Sales at Auction, Appraisement and Division of Slaves, 1820–1845.
>   Sale of Slaves, 1820–1845. Four file drawers of records are available.

Maxwell Family. Papers, 1859–1959

Mckee, Robert, 1830–1909. Papers, 1861–1899

Moseley, Lewis B. Account Book, 1833–1837

Oliver, William K. Papers, 1824–1859

Pamphlets Vertical File—subjects 1836

Perry, Sally, Randle. Diary, 1867–1868

Pickens, Isreal. Family Papers, 1805–1884
>   Includes information on the family slaves. Ms 60–1166

Ramsey, Richard C. Papers, 1834–ca.1874

Ray, W. B. Letter and Certificate, 1859

Slave Receipt, 1855

Slavery Pamphlet Collection, [1804–1909]

Stephens, Alexander H. (Alexander Hamilton), 1812–1883. Papers, 1863–1866

Torbet, James, and Tait, Charles. Family Papers, 1768–1874
>   Includes information on the family slaves. Ms 60–1444

Traylor, John G. B., 1809. Diary, 1834–1847

Vass, Elise Virginia Jones, 1852–1935. Reminiscences, Undated

Walker Family. Papers, 1798–1833

Williamson Family. Papers, 1862–1865

Yancey, William, Lowndes, 1814–1863. Papers, 1834–1941

Internet Resources

Alabama Department of Archives & History web site (**http:// www.archives.state.al.us/**), Alabama GenWeb (**http://www. rootsweb.com/~algenweb/index.html**), and Alabama GenWeb: African Americans (**http://members.aol.com/blountal/Gen.html**) each have a wealth of information and web links to assist in Alabama research. County resources listed include the following:

Butler County: 1860 Slave Schedules
Checklist of Records Available for Research on African-American History at the National Archives-Southeast Region.
Huntsville, Alabama Branch: Registers of Signatures of Depositors in Branches of the Freedmen's Saving and Trust Company 1865–1874
Index to Baptism of Blacks 1851–1855
United States Colored Troops: database of over 230,000 names of the men who served in the Civil War.

The Southern Historical Collection (**http://www.lib.unc.edu/mss/ shcabout.html#shc**) at the Wilson Library of University of North Carolina-Chapel Hill has a large manuscript collection containing vast amounts of information on slavery in Alabama. Other examples from the Southern Historical Collection are noted under other state chapters with the notation of (NcU). See North Carolina or access the collection's catalog on the Internet (**http://www.lib.unc.edu/search/mss.html**). Examples of materials found here include the following:

Thompson Family Papers, #1460, 1809–1924. Chiefly family letters and financial and legal materials of the Thompson family of Alabama, Louisiana, and Mississippi, and the related Malone family of Alabama. An account book belonging to Goodloe W. Malone contains a slave list of about seventy names and ages.

George Washington Allen Papers, #2711, 1832–1932. Predominantly correspondence between George Washington Allen, planter of Opelika and Lafayette, Alabama, and Alexander A. Allen, planter and lawyer of Bainbridge and Lexington, Georgia. Topics include the management of slaves (1832–1865); the murder of an Alexander relative in Ala. by a slave (1849); and former slaves renting houses in Tuskegee in order to qualify for the vote (1868).

Several web sites provide the opportunity to read a sample of slave narratives (see Part I) and view photographs of the former slaves. The following excerpt from George P. Rawick, ed., *The American Slave: A Composite Autobiography* (Westport, Conn.: Greenwood Press, 1972–79; Supplement Series 1, Vol. 1: 13–16) is found on the Internet at **http://afgen.com/slave_narrative.html**:

"Charity Anderson, 101 years old, lived near Mobile, Alabama at the time she was interviewed. She was born at Belle's Landing, in Monroe

County, Alabama. Her master operated a wood yard that supplied fuel to river boats. Anderson was a house slave. She recalls that her master treated all his slaves well, but she also remembered seeing slaves torn up by dogs and whipped unmercifully."

Research Contacts

Black Heritage Council of the Alabama Historical Commission
468 South Perry Street
Montgomery, AL 36130-0900
http://www.preserveala.org/intro1.htm
This fifteen-member council helps locate those who are working to preserve African-American places and makes sure they know about the resources available to help them.

Bibliography

Bailey, Richard. *They Too Call Alabama Home: African-American Profiles, 1800–1999.* Montgomery, Ala.: Pyramid Publishing, 1999.

Barefield, Marilyn D. *Researching in Alabama: A Genealogical Guide.* Tuscaloosa: University of Alabama Press, 1999.

Brewer, Willis. *Alabama: Her History, Resources, War Record & Public Men from 1540 to 1872.* Baltimore: Clearfield Company, 2000.

Davis, Charles S. *The Cotton Kingdom in Alabama, Perspectives in American History,* No. 3. (1939. Reprint.) Philadelphia: Porcupine Press, 1974.

Feldman, Lynne B. *A Sense of Place: Birmingham's Black Middle-Class Community, 1890–1930.* Tuscaloosa: University of Alabama Press, 1999.

Hester, Gwendolyn L. *Freedmen and Colored Marriage Records, 1865–1890, Sumter County, Alabama.* Bowie, Md.: Heritage Books, Incorporated, 1996.
The main body of this book is an index, organized by surnames of both brides and grooms, which gives the full names of both brides and grooms, license and marriage dates, and book and page numbers of the original records.

Johnson, Charles. *Shadow of the Plantation.* Chicago: University of Chicago Press, 1934. Reprint, Piscataway, N.J.: Transaction Publishers, 1996.

Jordan, Weymouth T. *Antebellum Alabama: Town & Country*. Tusca-loosa: University of Alabama Press, 1986.

Pinkard, Olivia T., and Barbara C. Clark. *The Descendants of Shandy Wesley Jones and Evalina Love Jones: The Story of an African-American Family of Tuscaloosa, Alabama*. Baltimore: Gateway Press, 1993.

Sellers, James Benson. *Slavery In Alabama*. Tuscaloosa: University of Alabama Press, 1994.
A fine description of the laws, customs, and effects of slavery in Alabama.

Wiggins, Sarah W., comp. *From Civil War to Civil Rights, Alabama, 1860–1960: An Anthology from the Alabama Review*. Tusca-loosa: University of Alabama Press, 1987.

Alaska

Important Dates

1861 – Gold was discovered on Stikine River near Telegraph Creek.

1867 – U.S. purchased Alaska from Russia. African Americans settle in the Alaskan frontier.

1890s – African Americans were among the large groups of prospectors who sought riches in the Klondike Gold Rush.

1943 – The all African-American Ninety-Seventh Division of the Corps of Engineers built the Alaskan section of the Alcan Highway.

1960 – Blanche Smith became the first African-American state legislator.

State Archives

Alaska State Archives
141 Willoughby Avenue
Juneau, AK 99801-1720
http://www.archives.state.ak.us/

Census Records

Federal Census Records

1900–1930 (DNA, A-Sr)

State and County Records

Birth-Marriage-Divorce-Death Records

Alaska State Vital Records Office
Department of Health and Social Services

Bureau of Vital Statistics
350 Main Street, Room 114
P. O. Box 110675
Juneau, AK 99811-0675

Internet Resources

Alaska State Archives web page (**http://www.archives.state.ak.us/**) and Alaska's Rootsweb page (**http://www.akgenweb.org/**) both provide a wealth of information for Alaska researchers.

Research Contacts

Alaska Historical Society
395 Whittier Street   *Mailing Address:* P.O. Box 100299
Juneau, AK 99801-1718   Anchorage, AK 99510-0299

A number of African Americans went to Alaska during the Gold Rush and ended up settling there permanently. A research project for the centennial of the Gold Rush, the Blacks in Alaska History Project, Inc. (**http://www.yukonalaska.com/akblkhist/**) has identified over forty African Americans in Alaska and Yukon Territory from the 1900 census, post returns, and newspapers.

Bibliography

Overstreet, Everett Louis. *Black on a Background of White: A Chronicle of Afro-Americans' Involvement in America's Last Frontier, Alaska.* Fairbanks: Alaska Black Caucus, 1988.

Spurr, Josiah Edward, "Through the Alaska Gold Diggings," *Alaska Magazine* 43 (March, 1977), 32–34; 60–62.

Arizona

Important Dates

1870 – The census listed twenty-six African Americans.

1880s – African-American "cowboys" during this decade included Isom Dart, a.k.a. "Cherokee Bill"; Tombstone's John Slaughter Swain, known as "Nigger Jim"; and Nat Love, famous as "Deadwood Dick."

1912 – An African-American population was established in Phoenix, Tucson, Flagstaff, and Sufford.

State Archives

Arizona State Library, Archives and Public Records
1700 W. Washington Street
Phoenix, AZ 85007
http://www.dlapr.lib.az.us/

Census Records

Federal Census Records

1860 (see New Mexico); 1870–1880, 1900–1930 (DNA); 1870–1880 (AzML, Az)

Mortality Schedules

1870, 1880 (DNA, DNDAR)

Special Census

Territorial Census, Other Territorial Censuses: 1864, 1866, 1867, 1869, 1872, 1874, 1876, 1882 (all counties are not represented in each census) (DNA, Az)

County Great Registers (voting registers) 1884–1911 (all counties are not represented in each of the years). Gives name, year, place of birth, and often occupation. Later Great Registers give physical descriptions of the individual (Located at Arizona State Library, Archives and Public Records (DLAP)

State and County Records

Birth-Marriage-Divorce-Death Records

Arizona State Vital Records Office
Arizona Department of Health Services
P.O. Box 3887
Phoenix, AZ 85030-3887
http://www.hs.state.az.us/vitalrcd/index.htm

Arizona started recording birth and death records in 1909. Marriages and divorces are still recorded in the county where the event took place.

Newspapers

The Phoenix Tribune, first black newspaper in Arizona, began publication in 1918.

Manuscript Sources: Personal Papers, Slave Records, and Diaries

The Arizona Pioneers Historical Society in Tucson has a limited selection of materials on black pioneers, including the following:

Culin, Beppie. Papers, 1850–1900 (AzTP)
　　　　Over 324 items of correspondence regarding bills of sale for slaves. MS 61–3576

Internet Resources

The University of Arizona has information on the following special topics listed on its web page *In the Steps of Esteban: Tucsons's African American Heritage* (**http://www.library.arizona.edu/images/afamer/**

homepage.html): A brief history of the early settlers; African-American soldiers; Dunbar School and educational opportunities; biographies and oral histories of pioneers, educators, military personnel, and members of the medical and legal professions, as well as other occupations; African Americans in aviation in Arizona; African-American churches in Tucson; African-American settlers in Tucson; African Americans of Tucson, past and present; a bibliography about African-American heritage in Arizona; and an exhibit section.

Research Contacts

The web site sponsored by the University of Arizona focusing on African Americans (**http://www.library.arizona.edu/images/afamer/homepage.html**) provides abundant resources for research in the state.

Bibliography

Harris, Richard E. *The First 100 Years: A History of Arizona Blacks.* Apache Junction, Ariz.: Relmo Publishers, 1983.

Katz, William L. *The Black West: A Documentary History of African American Westward Expansion of U.S.* New York: Simon and Schuster Trade Paperbacks, 1996.

_____. *Black People Who Made the Old West.* Trenton, N.J.: Africa World Press, Inc., 1992.

Leckie, William. *The Buffalo Soldiers: A Narrative of the Negro Calvary in the West.* Norman: University of Oklahoma, 1967.

Nimmons, Robert Kim. "Arizona's Forgotten Past: The Negro in Arizona, 1539–1965," (Master's Thesis, Northern Arizona University, 1971).

Smith, Gloria L. *Black Americana in Arizona.* Tucson: G. Smith, 1977.

Arkansas

Important Dates

1719 – John Law, a financier, colonized the Post of Arkansas with some 2,000 white immigrants from Germany and 300 enslaved Africans most recently from Old Biloxi, Mississippi, but originally from Guinea.

1771 – There were only sixteen African Americans living in Arkansas.

1803 – The Post of Arkansas had 107 African-American slaves and two free African Americans.

1810 – Only 287 slaves and five free blacks were listed as residents in the state. Conceivably many of them were descendants of the surviving original sixteen.

1820 – During the period 1820–30, the slave population increased markedly, with a corresponding increase in the white population. The slaves came from Alabama, Tennessee, Mississippi, and other states east of the Mississippi River. Most were settled along the river where, by the 1850 census, the number of slaves was greater than the white population of the state.

1840 – There were 19,935 slaves in Arkansas.

1877 – The rise of solid black middle class was accompanied by the establishment of churches, colleges, and private clubs.

State Archives

Arkansas History Commission
One Capitol Mall
Little Rock, AR 72201
http://www.ark-ives.com/

The Arkansas History Commission, the official state archives, is a research facility for those interested in researching various aspects of Arkansas history. The records listed below can be located there and illustrate the type of African-American records the researcher will encounter in the state.

Census Records

Federal Census Records

1830–1880; 1900–1930 (DNA, Ar-Hi)

Mortality Records

1850–1880 (Ar-Hi)

Slave Schedules

1850, 1860

Special Census

A sheriff's census was taken for some parts of Arkansas Territory in 1823 and 1829.

State and County Records

Birth-Marriage-Divorce-Death Records

Arkansas Department of Health
Division of Vital Records
4815 West Markham Street
Little Rock, Arkansas 72205-3867
http://www.healthyarkansas.com/

Arkansas began recording birth and death records statewide in 1914. Marriage records are recorded by the County Clerk for the county in which the license was granted. The Arkansas Department of Health has marriage records for the counties beginning in 1917. Some earlier birth, marriage, and death records may be located in the county clerk or circuit court office, along with divorce records.

Other State and County Records

Selected records from 1797–1950 are available from all Arkansas counties, including marriages, deeds, Circuit and Chancery Court records, tax records (both personal property and real estate), probate records (wills, guardianships, executors, and letters of administration), and some naturalization records. Inventories are available in the Research Room of the Arkansas History Commission.

Cemetery and Church Records

Some of Arkansas's church records are located at the Arkansas History Commission. They consist of organizational records and records of individual churches of various denominations. There are, in addition, cemetery records from all seventy-five counties of Arkansas, although those for some counties are more complete than others.

Military Records

An extensive collection of military records at the Arkansas History Commission includes Arkansas Civil War service and Confederate pension files; information about Arkansas soldiers in the Mexican War, the Spanish-American War, and the First World War; and various indexes to service in the American Revolution, the War of 1812, Indian wars, and the U.S. regular army.

Newspapers

Among the newspapers in the Arkansas History Commission's collection is the *Arkansas Mansion* (Little Rock)—1884–1887 Weekly Holdings: June 1883 to April 1884.

Manuscript Sources: Personal Papers, Slave Records, and Diaries

Brown, John, 1821–1865 (ArU)
Discusses experience as a lawyer and plantation owner in Arkansas.
Gulley, L.C. (Ar–Hi)
Discusses freedmen with whom he had dealings.
Woodruff, William Edward, 1820–82 (Ar–Hi)
Includes slave indentures. MS 68–527

Internet Resources

The *Arkansas/Oklahoma Funeral Records & Obituaries* web site is an example of the growing number of such records on the web (**http:// www.angelfire.com/ar/freedmen/fnrlrec.html**). These records provide information for family researchers and historians who are looking for information about death records and funeral programs. Many of the records come from Ft. Smith, Arkansas records, obituaries, and funeral programs.

A list of Arkansas African Americans in the state legislature during the period of 1868 to 1986 has been entered on the web by the African-American Genealogical Society of Northern California. See **http:// www.aagsnc.org/**.

Further examples of Arkansas resources concerning African Americans that can be found on the Internet are federal census slave schedules and federal census/black household schedules for Greene, Marion, Pike, and Ft. Smith counties (**http://www.afrigeneas.com/aacensus/ar/**), and Greene County, Arkansas newspaper death notices (**http://www.rootsweb.com/ ~usgenweb**).

In addition, the ArkansasGenWeb project (**http://www.rootsweb.com/ ~argenweb/**) includes land records (Bureau of Land Management homestead and bounty land records). A statewide state archives index is being developed for all Arkansas counties that includes a biography project, census project, land records, marriage project, and family group sheet project.

Research Contacts

Arkansas Humanities Resource Center
10816 Executive Center Drive, Suite 310
Little Rock, AR 72211-4383
http://www.arkhums.org/

This organization develops exhibits pertaining to African-American studies, including the extensive traveling exhibit titled "Persistence of the Spirit," and hosts a web site (**http://www.aristotle.net/persistence/**) devoted to the African-American experience in Arkansas. The web site contains resources, historical perspectives, photos, and history links to assist the researcher in Arkansas.

Bibliography

Patterson, Ruth Polk. *The Seed of Sally Good'n: A Black Family of Arkansas, 1833–1953*. Lexington: University Press of Kentucky, 1996.

Taylor, Orville W. *Negro Slavery in Arkansas*. Durham, N.C.: Duke University Press, 1958.

Tucker, David A. *Arkansas: A People and Their Reputation*. Memphis, Tenn.: Memphis State University Press, 1985.

Whayne, Jeannie, and Willard Gatewood, eds. *The Arkansas Delta: Land of Paradox*. Fayetteville: University of Arkansas Press, 1996.

California

Important Dates

1850 – On September 9th, 1850 California became the 35th state to join the Union, placing it under federal laws relating to slavery. Before 1850, fewer than a dozen African Americans lived in the state. The census of 1850 recorded only 962 people of color out of a total population of 75,000. By 1852, that number had increased to 2,200.

1849 – African Americans began to arrive in California in search of gold.

1860 – The African-American population was 4,086, with most settled in the gold regions around the middle-fork of the American River. Only four counties in the entire state had more than 100 free African Americans in residence in 1860.

State Archives

California State Archives
1020 O Street
Sacramento, CA 95814
http://www.ss.ca.gov/archives/archives_e.htm

The collection includes a broad array of materials related to California residents and their relationship to governmental processes. Family history research records include county land and probate records, professional licenses and Folsom Prison and National Guard records. The state archives also houses the genealogy library of the Root Cellar–Sacramento Genealogical Society, which is open to the public and staffed by volunteers several days each week.

Census Records

Federal Census Records

1850–1880; 1900–1930 (DNA, CU, COG, C, CSfGS, CSmH, and many other public and college libraries)

Mortality Records

1850–1880 (C)

Special Census

1897–1941 (various years), located at California State Archives
1852, also available at the Family History Library in Salt Lake City, Utah
Los Angeles Black Voters, 1892, 1896, 1898: lists adult black males, with maps indicating voters' homes, and a card file index with occupational and residential changes for 1888, 1890, 1897, and 1905 (CLCM)

State and County Records

Birth-Marriage-Divorce-Death Records

California Department of Health Services
Office of Vital Records
304 "S" Street   *Mailing Address*: P.O. Box 730241,
Sacramento, CA 95814   Sacramento, CA 94244-0241
http://www.dhs.cahwnet.gov/hisp/chs/OVR/Ordercert.htm

The web site for the state Office of Vital Records has a Directory of Local Registrars with detailed information about obtaining county records.

Cemetery and Church Records

The challenges of locating cemetery and church records in a large and populated state can be daunting. Many local genealogical and historical societies and county web sites have these kinds of records (try **http://www.rootsweb.com** and **http://www.CAGenWeb.com**). There are also other interesting web projects; see, for example, **http:// www.interment.net/us/ca/**.

Military

Military Records 1850–1942 (C–Ar)
> Includes organization papers, correspondence, election of muster rolls, loyalty oaths, and invoices relating to Independent Militia Units, Indian wars, Civil War, Spanish-American War, World War I and II. Name index available for Civil War Volunteers, 1861–1867

Grabill, Levi. Papers, 1861–92 (CSmH)
> Grabill was Captain of the 22d U.S. Colored Infantry. The collection includes pocket diaries, 1861 and 1865. MS 71–1060

Hooker, Joseph. Military Papers, 1861–64 (CSmH)
> Includes information on freed slaves. MS 68–359

Shaffer, William Rufus. Papers, 1863–1904 (CSt)
> Shaffer was commander of the 17th U.S. Colored Infantry. His papers include letters and broadsides about the Spanish-American War.

Civil War and Military Collection, 1851–69 (CSt)
> Letters and diaries of several members of Colored Troop regiments.

Alexander Collection, 1848–1939 (CSmH)
> Papers of a freedman and his son (graduate of West Point). Included is a journal on an 1888 march with a cavalry troop.

Newspapers

Elevator (San Francisco). April 6, 1865, to 1904? Weekly. Holdings: 1865–98 (incomplete); CChiS, CLS, CSdS, CSS, CtY, CU, CU-B, DLC, InNd, IU, KH, MB, MdBJ, NcU, WHi.

Pacific Appeal (San Francisco). 1862–80. Weekly. Holdings: 1862–80 CSdS, CSfSt CsmarP, CU, CU-B, DLC, FTaSU, KH, LU-NO, MdBMC, MiKW, TNF, WHi

Manuscript Sources: Personal Papers, Slave Records, and Diaries

California Supreme Court Papers (C-Ar)
> Topics covered include status of black slaves, habeas corpus rights of blacks, criminal cases, and school segregation.

Sacramento District and County Court Papers (C-Ar)
  Cases involving slavery and servitude.
King, Martin Luther, Jr., Collection (CSf)
  Regional black newspapers, family papers, organizational files, and oral history recordings with San Francisco blacks
Prison Records 1850–1945 (C-Ar)
  Includes San Quentin and Folsom inmate prison registers; photographs, commitment papers, inmate data files (samples only), and pardon files. Prison registers have name indexes, 1850–1930.

Internet Resources

An excellent Internet resource with information and links to census records, military records and other records was developed by the African American Genealogical Society of Northern California (see below for contact information).

Research Contacts

African American Genealogical Society of Northern California
P.O. Box 27485
Oakland, CA 94602
http://www.aagsnc.org/

Bibliography

Beasley, Delilah L. *The Negro Trailblazers of California*. New York: Negro University Press, 1969.
  A compilation of records from the California Archives in the Bancroft Library at the University of California, in Berkeley, includes diaries, old papers, and conversations of old pioneers in the state of California. Gives many hundreds of names of blacks in California from the pioneer period to the late nineteenth century.

Bowman, Alan P. *Index to the 1850 Census of California*. Baltimore: Genealogical Publishing Co., 1972.
  Lists blacks who were heads of family or living in households where the head had a different surname. The original census schedules must be consulted for additional information.

Broussard, Albert S. "Slavery in California Revisited: The Fate of a Kentucky Slave in Gold Rush California," *The Pacific Historian* 29:1 (Spring 1985):17–21.

Bunch, Lonnie. *Black Angelenos: The Afro-American in Los Angeles, 1850–1950.* Los Angeles: California Afro-American Museum, 1988.

Daniels, Douglas Henry. *Pioneer Urbanites: A Social and Cultural History of Black San Francisco.* Philadelphia: Temple University Press, 1980.

Edwards, Malcolm. "The War of Complexional Distinction: Blacks in Gold Rush California and British Columbia," *California Historical Quarterly* 66:1 (Spring 1977): 34–45.

Fisher, James Adolphus. *A History of the Political and Social Development of the Black Community in California, 1850–1950* (Ph.D. diss., State University of New York at Stony Brook, 1972).

Goode, Kenneth G. *California's Black Pioneers: A Brief Historical Survey.* Santa Barbara, Calif.: McNally & Loftin Publishers, 1974.

_____. "The Negro in Gold Rush California." *Journal of Negro History* 49 (April 1964): 84–98.

Hayden, Dolores. "Biddy Mason's Los Angeles, 1856–1891," *California History* 68:3 (Fall 1989): 86–99.

Lapp, Rudolph M. *Afro-Americans in California.* Florence, Ky.: Thomson Learning Co., 1987.

_____. *Blacks In Gold Rush California.* New Haven, Conn.: Yale University Press, 1995.

Wheeler, B. Gordon. *Black California: A History of African-Americans in the Golden State.* New York: Hippocrene Books, Inc., 1992.

Colorado

Important Dates

1776 – One of the earliest recorded instances of African Americans in what became Colorado.

1859 – A group of European-Americans from Georgia brought enslaved African Americans to Colorado to work in gold mines around Pike's Peak.

1860 – First census of population was conducted in the new territory; free African Americans numbered 46 persons, and increased to 456 by 1870.

State Archives

Colorado State Archives
1313 Sherman Street, 1B-20
Denver, CO 80203
http://www.archives.state.co.us/

Colorado State Archives is the repository for historical and contemporary records related to state and local governments, including court records, such as probate, criminal and civil cases; land records; military records; and some vital statistics. See the section of the Archives web site on family history materials for a comprehensive description of sources and services: **http://www.archives.state.co.us/geneal.html**.

Census Records

Federal Census Records

1860–1880, 1885, and 1900–1930 (DNA); 1860–1880; 1900–1920 (CoD); 1860–1880; 1900–1920 and 1885 (CoU)

Mortality Records

1870–80 and 1885 (DNA); 1870–80 (DNDAR)

Special Census

Colorado School Census: 1885

State and County Records

Birth-Marriage-Divorce-Death Records

Colorado State Vital Records Office
Colorado Dept of Health
4300 Cherry Creek Drive South
Denver, CO 80246-1530
http://www.cdphe.state.co.us/hs/certs.asp

The Vital Records Office and Colorado State Archives web sites give the location, dates of availability, and ordering information for birth, marriage, divorce, and death records in the state. The agency holds current records, while the Colorado State Archives holds earlier ones.

County Records

Each county's records are available in the county seat. The Colorado State Archives also has an extensive collection of county sources.

Newspapers

Denver Star. 1889—Weekly. Holdings: January 27, 1900; December 10, 1910 to January 3, 1914; Whi. November 23, 1912 to October 1918; CoHi.

Colorado Statesman originals can be found in the Western History/ Genealogy Department (WIUG) Denver Public Library.

The Stephen H. Hart Library of the Colorado Historical Society at 1300 Broadway, Denver, Colorado has an extensive Colorado Newspaper Project, a microfiche collection that catalogs some 2,700 titles of Colorado newspapers from 1859 to 1991.

Manuscript Sources: Personal Papers, Slave Records, and Diaries

Atkins, James A., 1890–1968 (CoHi)
    Pioneer black educator's personal papers. MS 74–83
Lewis, Junius R. Papers (CoHi)
    A Boulder County, Colorado, black miner. MS 71–1592

The Hart Library of the Colorado Historical Society has materials related to contributions African Americans have made to Colorado's growth, as well as the Works Progress Administration papers from 1930–35, containing unpublished interviews with early black pioneers.

Internet Resources

Information available on the Internet for African-American families in Colorado includes Deborah R. Hollis' "Census Schedules and Black Genealogical Research: One Family's Experience." As an Assistant Professor/State & Foreign Documents Librarian University Libraries, University of Colorado at Boulder, Hollis explores her own family and illustrates the use of census and other records in recreating a history of the family.

The Colorado State Archives web site (see address on page 79) includes a wide variety of indexes or records online, such as the following:

City Directories (1866–1975)
    Colorado Statewide Marriage and Divorce Index (1890–1939; 1975–1998)
    Denver Birth and Death Records (pre-1900 Only)
    Divorce Court Cases (availability and date span varies by county, and court and case)
    Gilpin County Marriage Index (1864–1944)
    School Records—including teacher lists and school pupil census lists for many counties

Research Contacts

Denver Public Library
Western History/Genealogy Department
10 W. 14th Avenue Parkway
Denver, CO 80204

The Denver Library holdings include U.S. census schedules, slave schedules, some passenger lists, and an extensive genealogy reference collection. It has free, useful guides such as *Genealogy: Beginners Guide*; *African-American Genealogy; Researching Your Native-American Ancestry*; and *Hispanic Genealogy Guide*.

Black American West Museum and Heritage Center
3091 California Street
Denver, CO 80205
http://www.coax.net/people/lwf/bawmus.htm

Documents, memorabilia, and artifacts related to African Americans throughout the West.

Black Genealogy Search Group
P.O. Box 40674
Denver, CO 80204-0674
http://www.coax.net/people/lwf/bgsg_den.htm

Meets at Ford-Warren Branch Library, 2825 High Street, Denver, Colorado. Web site provides information about its work.

Bibliography

Abbott, Carl, Stephen L. Leonard, and David McComb. *Colorado: A History of the Centennial State*. Rev. ed. Boulder, Colo.: Colorado Associated University Press, 1982.

Berwanger, Eugene H. *The Frontier Against Slavery: Western Anti-Negro Prejudice and the Slavery Extension Controversy*. Ann Arbor, Mich.: Books on Demand, 1967.

Davis, Lenwood G. *Blacks in the American West: A Working Bibliography*. Thousand Oaks, Calif.: Sage Publications, Incorporated, 1976.

Harvey, James R. "Negroes in Colorado." *Colorado Magazine* 26. (July 1949) 165–176.

Stewart, Paul, and Wallace Y. Ponce. *Black Cowboys*. Broomfield, Colo.: Phillips Publishing, Incorporated, 1986.

Wayne, George H. "Negro Migration and Colonization in Colorado 1870–1930." *Journal of the West*. (January, 1976) 102–140.

Connecticut

Important Dates

1679 – The first Africans arrived.

1790 – The African-American population was 5,473.

1820 – Less than 100 slaves were living in Connecticut because of the gradual emancipation law.

1830 – The African-American population reached 30,000.

State Archives

Connecticut State Library
231 Capitol Avenue
Hartford, CT 06106
http://www.cslib.org/archives.htm

The Connecticut State Library has housed Connecticut's governmental archives since 1855. The Library's extensive collection of vital records, newspapers, cemeteries, town records, and family records make it an essential repository for research on all of Connecticut's historic and present residents. Descriptions of resources for this state all lead back to the Connecticut State Library.

Census Records

Federal Census Records

1790–1880; 1900–1930 (DNA, Ct)
The Connecticut State Library's Connecticut Census Index, 1790–1850, covers the U.S. census for Connecticut, 1790–1850 (excluding New London County in 1790). It is an index of heads of households, 1790–1840, and all individuals for 1850.

Mortality Records

1850–1880 (Ct, DNA)

State and County Records

Birth-Marriage-Divorce-Death Records

Connecticut State Vital Records Office
Department of Public Health
410 Capitol Avenue
Hartford, CT 06134-0308
http://www.dph.state.ct.us/OPPE/hpvital.htm

Vital records in Connecticut are filed by town. The state maintains records from 1897.

Town and County Records

Records documenting the sale and ownership of land also document the sale, purchase, manumission, and emancipation of slaves, who were considered personal property. There is no statewide index to Connecticut land records, but general indexes to grantors and grantees are available for most towns. For suggestions on use of land records in genealogical research in Connecticut, see **http://www.cslib.org/landrec.htm**.

Land Records

An example of the type of information about blacks that can be found in land records is as follows:

Negro, Alpheus, Emancipated from John & Benj. Moseley, 31 Oct. 1808.
Glastonbury Land Records, Volume 15, page 413.

General Assembly Records

The following are located at the Connecticut State Library in Hartford:

Box 7, doc. 56. Peter White, an African by birth, late of Granby, died owning $200–$300 of real estate in Granby, had a wife "de facto" and a daughter Rany White. She seeks to inherit although illegitimate. Granted.

RG 2, General Assembly Papers, Rejected Bills.

Box 2, doc. 45 & 46. Petitions of Bias Stanley and William Lanson, both of New Haven and men of color. Both own comfortable homes to qualify them as voters relied on 1639 law that all inhabitants of 21 yrs. & with requisite property would be admitted as voters. Objecting to Connecticut State law of 1814 that added "white" to requirements. Seek exemption from all taxes for blacks if they are denied the right to vote.

Box 4, doc. 5. Petition by free persons of color in Norwich & New London against paying poll tax when they can't vote. Signed by Josiah Cornell, William Laws, William Harris, Deppard Billings, Ira Forset, Olney M. Douglass, Anthony Church, Thomas Hamilton, Joseph Facy, and John Meads.

Cemetery and Church Records

See the Connecticut State Library web page (**http://www.cslib.org/archives.htm**) for extensive information of statewide cemetery index and church records.

Military Records

Marshall, Henry Grimes. Letters, 1862–65 (MiU)
Marshall was the captain of the 29th Connecticut Volunteers, black regiment. MS 63–226 RG 12

Records of the State Library, War Records Department
Contains lists and other information about Connecticut members of the armed forces, 1776–1946; and men and women who served in the Revolution, the War of 1812, the Mexican War, the Civil War, the Spanish-American War, the Mexican Border Service, World War and I and World War II; plus extracts from the 1840 census of Revolutionary and military service pensioners.

RG 13, Records of the Military Department. Includes records pertaining to the 29th, 30th, and 31st Connecticut Regiments, which were black Civil War regiments, and the post-Civil War black Connecticut National Guard units, such as the Fifth Independent Battalion and the First and Second Separate Companies.

Newspapers

The *Connecticut Gazette* (New London) and the *Connecticut Courant* (Hartford) contain a considerable amount of genealogical material. Copies are held at the Connecticut State Library (see also their listings below).

Christian Freeman (Hartford). January 1843 to December 25, 1845. Weekly. Continues *Charter Oak*. Holdings: 1843–45; CtU, NIC, WHi.

Connecticut Courant (Hartford). November 26, 1764, to October 29, 1914. Weekly, semi-weekly. Subtitle varies. Holdings: 1764–1820; CFS, CNoS, CSdS, CSmH, CSt, CtY, CU.

Connecticut Gazette (New London). December 17, 1773, to February 26, 1823. Weekly. Subtitle varies. Holdings: 1773–1823; CU, ICU, LU-NO, MB, MBAt, MdBJ, MeU, NbOU, NcGrE, OKentU, OkS, OU, PBL, PEsS, PPiU, Readex, RPB, ScU, TrC.

The State Library holds an extensive collection of Connecticut newspapers in either original format or on microfilm. Important indexes include the following:

Hale Collection of Newspaper Marriage and Death Notices, ca. 1750–1865:

This Works Progress Administration project abstracted marriage and death notices from the 90 earliest newspapers published in Connecticut from about 1750 to about 1865. The index entries are arranged alphabetically by surname, with a "No Surname" section at the end that lists many blacks, Native Americans, and mulattos.

Manuscript Sources: Personal Papers, Slave Records, and Diaries

The manuscript collections at the Connecticut State Library and the Connecticut Historical Society contain extensive town records, correspondence, diaries, account books, and a variety of other useful material. The account books are of particular importance, for they frequently contain information not available elsewhere.

Donnon, Elizabeth. Papers, 1806–63 (CtU)
> Manuscript notes taken from ships' logs, etc. These notes were mostly used in her book on the slave trade.

Hempstead, Stephen. Papers, 1754–1927 (MoHistSoc)
Son of Joshua Hempstead of New London, Connecticut. Lists occupations of slaves and those who migrated to Missouri with him. MS 68–1287. See also the Hempstead papers at the Missouri State Archives.

Slavery Records*

A sample of items found at the Connecticut State Library include the following:

Adams, Eliphalet. Bill of sale or indenture made by Eliphalet Adams of New London, Connecticut to Joseph and Jonathan Trumble of Lebanon, Connecticut, whereby he sells his mulatto girl, Flora, a slave for life, May 12, 1736 [call number Main Vault 326 Ad15].

Caples, J. A., comp. Memoirs of the Caples family, history and description of Lyme, Connecticut, scrapbook of poems, death notices, Grassy Hill Congregational Church (blacks) [call number Main Vault 974.62 L89 ca].

Law, Lyman. Certificate by Lyman Law, Notary Public at New London, Connecticut, showing that Caesar Shaw (free Negro), mariner on board sloop *Betsy*, declares that he was born Feb. 10, 1760, in New London, Conn., and has a wife and family living in New London and that he is an inhabitant thereof and a citizen of the United States, Dec. 30, 1795 [call number Main Vault 920 Sh52L].

Powell, L. H. Bill-of-sale made by L. H. Powell to Hopkins Nowlin for the sale of Sarah, a slave, 16 years of age, for life, Mar. 22, 1850 [call number Main Vault 326 P3].

New London County. Certificate of emancipation of Robert Jones, Negro, requested by him and applied for by his masters, Charles A. and George R. Lewis. Dated New London, May 8, 1827, and subscribed by Jirah Isham and Ebenezer Learned, justices of peace [call number Main Vault 326 N46].

Trumbull Papers. Official Connecticut colonial papers, ca. 1631–1784, collected by Governor Jonathan Trumbull under instruction of the Connecticut General Assembly [call number Main Vault 974.6 fT76]. Check the slip index under the headings "Negroes"

---

* Beverly L. Naylor, Librarian, History and Genealogy Unit, Connecticut State Library assisted in developing information in this chapter.

and "Slavery," and the names of individuals and towns. A sample entry includes the Negroes Petition by negro servants of Hartford for their freedom, Oct. 1780. Volume XIII, doc. 286a-d.

Internet Resources

See **http://www.cslib.org/handg.htm**, under "Collections," for the Connecticut State Library's listing of history and genealogy resources. Also see **http://www.cslib.org/blagen.htm** for *A Research Guide to African-American Genealogical Resources.*

Research Contacts

In addition to the collections at the Connecticut State Library, the Bridgeport Public Library (925 Broad Street, Bridgeport, CT 06604, **http://bridgeport.lib.ct.us/bpl/**) has a newspaper collection and a large historical collection covering local, state, and ethnic group history for the area.

Bibliography*

"Augustus Washington, Black Daguerreotypist of Hartford." *Connecticut Historical Society Bulletin* 39 (January 1974) 1:14–19.

Andrews, Charles M. "Slavery in Connecticut." *Magazine of American History* 21 (May 1899) 5:422–23.

Bailey, Frederic William. *Early Connecticut Marriages: As Found on Ancient Church Records Prior to 1800.* Baltimore: Genealogical Publishing Co., 1997.
Black marriages are included in this listing.

Barnes, Barbara A. "Venture Smith's Family." Unpublished paper "submitted to the faculty of Wesleyan University in partial fulfillment of the requirements for the degree of Certificate of Advanced Study, March 1, 1996."

Beach, E. Merrill. *From Valley Forge to Freedom.* Chester: Globe Pequot Press, 1982.
The story of Nero Hawley, of Trumbull, who served with General George Washington at Valley Forge.

---

* Beverly L. Naylor, Librarian, History and Genealogy Unit, Connecticut State Library assisted in developing information in this chapter.

Beeching, Barbara J. "The Primus Papers: An Introduction to Hartford's Nineteenth Century Black Community" (Master's thesis, Trinity College, 1995).

Beeching, Barbara J. "African-Americans and Native Americans in Hartford, 1636–1800: Antecedents of Hartford's Nineteenth Century Black Community" (unpublished paper "submitted to Professor Pfeiffer, Social Studies 637," Trinity College, 1993).

Bontemps, Arna, ed. *Five Black Lives: The Autobiographies of Venture Smith, James Mars, William Grimes, The Rev. G. W. Offley, & James L. Smith.* Hanover, N.H.: University Press of New England, 1987.
Autobiographies of ex-slaves living in Connecticut between 1729 and 1870.

Brown, Barbara W., and James M. Rose. *Black Roots in Southeastern Connecticut, 1650–1900.* Gale Genealogical and Local History Series, Volume 8. Detroit: Gale Research Co., 1979. Reprint, New London: New London Historical Society, 2001.
An alphabetical listing of African Americans and related Native and European Americans in the records of Southeastern Connecticut.

Catterall, Helen T. *Judicial Cases Concerning American Slavery and the Negro.* Carnegie Institution of Washington, Publication No. 374. 5 vols. Washington: Carnegie Publications, 1926–37. Reprint, Buffalo: William S. Hein and Company, Incorporated, 1998.
Lists and discusses fifty cases regarding slaves or slavery that were decided in the Connecticut Supreme Court of Errors, 1702–1873.

Collier, Christopher, with Bonnie Collier. *The Literature of Connecticut History.* Middletown, Conn.: Connecticut Humanities Council, 1983. See pages 242–251, "Slavery and the Black Experience."

Fowler, William Chauncey. *Local Law in Massachusetts and Connecticut.* Manchester, Mass.: Ayer Company Publishers, 1977.

Greene, Lorenzo Johnston. *The Negro in Colonial New England, 1620–1776.* Temecula, Calif.: Reprint Services Corporation, 1993.
Excellent background reading and bibliography for blacks tracing New England ancestry.

Hodges, Graham Russell, Susan H. Cook, and Alan H. Brown, eds. *The Black Loyalist Directory: African-Americans in Exile After the American Revolution.* New York: Garland Publishing Incorporated, 1995.
Includes manumission certificates in Wethersfield records. Lists 3,000 African Americans who left New York for Nova Scotia, noting their origins, age, gender, and former owners.

Johnson, Charles S. *The Negro Population of Hartford, Connecticut.* New York: Department of Research and Investigations of the National Urban League, 1921.

Johnson, Charles S. "The Negro Population of Waterbury, Connecticut." *Opportunity: A Journal of Negro Life* 1 (Oct. 1923) 10: 298–302, 1 (Nov. 1923) 11: 338–342.

Mead, Jeffrey B. *Chains Unbound: Slave Emancipations in the Town of Greenwich, Connecticut.* Baltimore: Gateway Press, 1995.

"Minority Military Service, Connecticut, 1775–1783." Washington: National Society Daughters of the American Revolution, 1988.

Mitchell, Mary Hewitt. "Slavery in Connecticut and Especially in New Haven." *Papers of the New Haven Colony Historical Society* 10 (1951): 286–312.

Nason, Mary L. *African-Americans in Simsbury, 1725–1925.* M. L. Nason, 1995.

Newton, Alexander H. *Out of the Briars.* Manchester: Ayer Company Publishers, Incorporated, 1977.

Pasay, Marcella Houle. *Full Circle: A Directory of Native and African-Americans in Windham County, CT, 1650–1900.* Bowie, Md.: Heritage Books, 2002.

Ritter, Kathy A. *Apprentices of Connecticut, 1637–1900.* Provo: Ancestry Pub., 1986.

Rose, James M., and Barbara Brown. *Tapestry: A Living History of the Black Family in Southeastern Connecticut.* New London County Historical Society, 1979.
A historical narrative gathered from *Black Roots in Southeastern Connecticut.*

Saunders, Ernest. *Blacks in the Connecticut National Guard: a Pictorial and Chronological History, 1870 to 1919.* New Haven: Afro-American Historical Society.

Steiner, Bernard Christian. *History of Slavery in Connecticut.* 1893. Reprint, New York: Johnson Reprint Corp., 1973.

Tobey, Ilene. *Searching Black Genealogy.* Hartford: Connecticut State Library, 1989.

Trapp, Patricia A. "Silent Voices and Forgotten Footsteps: A Chronicle of the Early Black Culture of Glastonbury, 1693–1860" (Master's thesis, Wesleyan University, 1996).

Warner, Robert Austin. *New Haven Negroes, a Social History.* Reprint, Ayer Company Publishers, Incorporated, 1970.
Excellent book on blacks in this area. A "must" reading for fine genealogical leads.

Weld, Ralph Foster. *Slavery in Connecticut.* Tercentenary Pamphlet Series, No. 37. New Haven: Published for the Tercentenary Commission by the Yale University Press, 1935.

White, David O. "Addie Brown's Hartford." Connecticut Historical Society *Bulletin* 41 (April 1976) 2: 56–64.

Delaware

Important Dates

1638 – Swedes established the first permanent European settlement in Delaware at Fort Christina.

1763 – Slaves made up almost 25 percent of Delaware's population.

1775–1810 – A strong anti-slavery movement led to a Quaker and Methodist sweep through Delaware resulting in a number of manumissions.

1860 – Many African Americans were still enslaved.

1865 – The Thirteenth Amendment brought an end to slavery in the state.

State Archives

Delaware Public Archives
121 Duke of York Street
Dover, DE 19901
http://www.state.de.us/sos/dpa/

Delaware Public Archives' web site provides an excellent guide to its digital and paper collections.

Census Records

Federal Census Records

1790–1880; 1900–1930 (DNA, De-Ar)

Mortality Records

1850–1880 (De-Ar)

Slave Schedules

1850, 1860

State and County Records

Birth-Marriage-Divorce-Death Records

Delaware State Vital Records Office
Office of Vital Statistics
Division of Public Health
P.O. Box 637
Dover, DE 19903
http://www.deph.org/vs.htm

Statewide recording of vital records began in 1913. Birth records older than seventy-two years and marriage and death records older than forty years are available at the Delaware Public Archives. Newer records are available from the Vital Records Office.

Other State and County Records

As in all geographic areas, various records that document vital events were kept before the mandatory recording of vital records. The Delaware Public Archives web site has an extensive list of those sources for Delaware. In addition, the Archives is a central repository for research in all of Delaware's county records, such as land, probate, court, tax, and survey. Manumissions can also be found among these records.

Cemetery and Church Records

The Delaware Public Archives has digital images of a large number of church records, as well as coroner reports. To locate the actual records for churches and cemeteries, try consulting **http://www.rootsweb.com/ ~degenweb/**.

Military Records

Friends of the African Union Church Cemetery maintain a web site at **http://www.magpage.com/~33dny/friends.htm**, with a listing of "Colored Troops" from Delaware who served in the Civil War. The site also includes photographs of grave sites of those buried in the cemetery.

Newspapers

Advance (Wilmington). 1899–1901? Weekly. Holdings: September 22, 1900; CSdS, CSS, CU, DeWI, DLC, FTaSU, LU-NO, McP, MdBMC, MiKW, TNF.

The University of Delaware Newspaper Project recently completed a project to microfilm and make available to participating Delaware libraries the microfilm copies of historically important Delaware newspapers. In addition to the *Advance*, three other papers specifically dealing with African-American life and news—*The Delaware Abolitionist*, *Wilmington Herald Times,* and *The Delaware Reporter*—were also included in this project. See **http://www2.lib.udel.edu/new/newsprjt.htm** for more information.

Manuscript Sources: Personal Papers, Slave Records, and Diaries

African School Society. Papers, 1809–1916 (DeH)
> This collection from Wilmington organizations includes seven volumes of memos and records.

Reese, Ann. Papers, 1715–1877 (De-Ar)
> This collection of documents includes land records, deeds, apprenticeships, indentures, and manumissions. MS 64–213

The Delaware Public Archives maintains a library of Delawareana that includes books, genealogies, pamphlets, maps, newspaper clippings, microfilm, photographs, motion pictures, slides, and sound recordings. Research is needed to determine how these sources benefit researchers of African-American families.

Internet Resources

A History of African Americans of Delaware and Maryland's Eastern Shore, edited by Carole C. Marks, can be accessed online at **http://www.udel.edu/BlackHistory/**.

Research Contacts

The Historical Society of Delaware
505 Market Street
Wilmington, DE 19801
http://www.hsd.org/

See the Society's guide to genealogical research in Delaware, available on the Internet at **http://www.hsd.org/gengd.htm**.

The University of Delaware, Morris Library
Special Collections
Newark, DE 19717

The University of Delaware's library contains holdings and bibliographic materials on African-American related topics; see, for example, "The Underground Railroad in Delaware" at **http://www.lib.udel.edu/ud/spec/exhibits/undrgrnd.htm**.

Bibliography

One essential book to consult for Delaware is Paul Heinegg's *Free African Americans of Maryland and Delaware from the Colonial Period to 1810* (Baltimore: Genealogical Publishing Company, 2000). See also the following:

Dean, John Gary. "The Free Negro in Delaware: A Demographic and Economic Study, 1790–1865." (Master's thesis. University of Delaware, 1970).

Essah, Patience. "Slavery and Freedom in the First State: The History of Blacks in Delaware from the Colonial Period to 1863" (Ph.D. dissertation, U.C.L.A., 1983).

Hancock, Harold B. "Not Quite Men: The Free Negroes in Delaware in the 1830's." *Civil War History* (December 1971): 320–331.

Livesay, Harold C. "Delaware Negroes 1865–1915." *Delaware History* (October 1968): 87–123.

Munroe, John A. "The Negro in Delaware." *South Atlantic Quarterly* (Autumn 1957): 428–444.

Williams, William H. *Slavery & Freedom in Delaware, 1639–1865.* Wilmington, Del.: Scholarly Resources, Inc., 1999.

District of Columbia

Important Dates

1791 – District of Columbia created. African Americans were the largest population group. Benjamin Banneker helped survey land for the planned city.

1807 – Former slaves George Bell, Moses Liverpool, and Nicholas Franklin established a school.

1860–65 – This time period witnessed the growth of the African-American middle class.

1863 – Several thousand African Americans volunteered for the Union Army.

1867 – Howard University was established with the support of the Freedmen's Bureau.

State Archives

National Archives and Records Administration
700 Pennsylvania Avenue, N.W.
Washington, DC 20408
**http://www.archives.gov/research_room/federal_records_guide/
district_of_columbia_rg351.html**

The National Archives houses materials from all states and the District of Columbia.

Office of Public Records Management, District of Columbia
Archives Division
1300 Naylor Court, N.W.
Washington, DC 20001
http://os.dc.gov/archives/services/index.shtm

This is the agency charged with maintaining the public records for the District, including vital records, wills and probates, land records, indentures, apprenticeship records, business incorporations, and all governmental records related to the District.

Census Records

Federal Census Records

1800–1880; 1890 (partial) 1900–1930 (DNA). See Maryland for 1790 census. Virginia 1790 is only partially extant.

Mortality Records

1850–1880 (DNA)

Slave Schedules

1850, 1860 (DNA)

State and County Records

Birth-Marriage-Divorce-Death Records

Vital Records Division
825 North Capitol Street, N.E., First Floor
Washington, DC 20002
http://dchealth.dc.gov/services/vital_records/index.shtm

The web site includes a comprehensive description of the categories and dates of vital records related to the District of Columbia and how to obtain them.

Cemetery and Church Records

Clarke, Nina Honemond. *History of the Nineteenth-Century Black Churches in Maryland and Washington, D.C.* New York: Vantage Press, 1983.

Sluby, Paul E., Sr. *Mt. Zion Cemetery, Washington, D.C. Brief History and Interments.* Washington, D.C.: Columbian Harmony Society Publication, 1984.

_____. *Woodlawn Cemetery: Washington, D.C. History and Inscriptions.* Washington, D.C.: Columbian Harmony Society Publication, 1984.

Newspapers

Washington Bee. June 3, 1882, to July 1884, Weekly. Continued by *Washington Bee* (see below). Holdings: 1882–84; CSdS, CtY, CU, DLC, ICU, MB, MdBJ, MnU, MoJcL, MoSW, NcU, NhD, TNF, TxFS, ViW, WHi.

Colored American. 1893–1904? Weekly. Holdings: August 11, 1894; March 12, 1898, to November 12, 1904 (incomplete); CSS, CtY, CU, DLC, FTaSU, ICU, MdBJ, MnU, MoSW, NcU, NjP, TNF, WHi.

New Era. January 13, to September 1, 1870. Weekly. Continued by *New National Era* (see below). Holdings: January to September 1870; DLC, ICU, MnU, NhD, NRU, WHi.

New National Era. September 8, 1870, to April 10, 1873. Weekly. Continues *New Era* (see preceding entry); continued by *New National Era and Citizen* (next entry). Holdings. 1870–73; DLC, ICU, MnU, NhD, NHi,-NRU, WHi.

New National Era and Citizen. April 17, 1873 to October 22, 1874. Weekly. Continues *New National Era* (see above). Holdings: 1873–74 (incomplete); DLC, ICU, MnU, NhD, NM, NRU, WHi.

People's Advocate. 1879?–1884? Weekly. Holdings: April 19, 1879, to April 12, 1884; CSdS, CtY, CU, DLC, MB, MdBJ, MnU, NcU, NhD, NjP, TNF, WHi.

Washington Bee. August 1884 to January 21, 1922. Weekly. Holdings: 1884–1922 (incomplete); CSdS, CtY, CU, DLC, FTaSU, ICU InNcl, MD, MdBJ, MnU, MoJcL, MoSW, NcU, NhD, TNF, TxFS, ViW, WHi.

Manuscript Resources: Personal Papers, Slave Records, and Diaries

The Library of Congress, Manuscript Division
Room LM101, James Madison Building
101 Independence Avenue, S.E.
Washington, DC 20540-4680

The Library of Congress houses the Slave Narrative Collection of the Federal Writers Project (**http://memory.loc.gov/ammem/snhtml/ snhome.html**), as well as more than 5,000 items appropriate to African-

American genealogy in its manuscript and personal papers collections. The following are examples of its holdings:

Accounts Book Collection
African Colonization Society lists of immigrants
NAACP and National Urban League papers
Slave papers with appraisal, mortgages, birth certificates, and emancipation certificates.

See also these two resources:

Fleetwood, Christian Abraham. Papers, 1797–1945 (DLC)
    Diaries, correspondence, legal documents, genealogical records, photos, and scrapbook of a free black soldier and civic leader. MS 60–3194
Peabody, George Foster, 1830–57 (MSaE)
    Extensive slave trading records for Massachusetts, Washington, D.C., and Maryland.

Internet Resources

District of Columbia Public Library
901 G Street, N.W.
Washington, DC 20001
http://www.dclibrary.org/

A searchable catalog online includes local materials and locations of various branches of the library. An online project is the Black Renaissance in Washington, D.C., 1920–1930s, with biographies, time line, and links to other sources; see **http://www.dclibrary.org/blkren/ index.html**.

Research Contacts

Afro-American Historical and Genealogical Society (AAHGS)
P.O. Box 73086
Washington, DC 20056-3086
http://www.rootsweb.com/~mdaahgs/

Founded by James Dent Walker, the society is dedicated to the preservation of history, genealogy, and culture of those with African ancestry. Local organizations assist in the collection and dissemination of African-American historical materials.

Daughters of the American Revolution Library [The DAR Library]
1776 D Street, N.W.
Washington, DC 20006-5392
http://www.dar.org/library/default.html

Over 150,000 volumes dealing with family history research and sources are maintained by this extensive library. An online catalog, organized by both state and subject area is available at **http://www.dar.org/library/onlinlib.html**.

Bibliography

Johnston, Allan John. *Surviving Freedom: The Black Community of Washington, D.C., 1860–1880.* New York: Garland Publishing, Inc., 1993.

Provine, Dorothy. *District of Columbia Free Negro Registers 1821–1861.* Bowie, Md.: Heritage Books, Incorporated, 1996. This book contains abstracts of official registrations of free status of non-slave African-American residents of antebellum Washington, D.C.

Schaefer, Christina K. *The Center: A Guide to Genealogical Research in the National Capital Area.* Baltimore: Genealogical Publishing Company, 1996. The aim of this book is to identify those resources in the Washington, D.C. area that will aid family historians in tracing their ancestors (the National Archives, Library of Congress, the DAR Library, the National Genealogical Society, and many more).

"The Negro in Washington." In *Washington, City and Capitol.* Washington, D.C., 1937, pp. 68–90.

Washington Chapter, Daughters of the American Revolution. *Lest We Forget: A Guide to Genealogical Research in the Nation's Capital.* Washington: Daughters of the American Revolution, 1989.

Florida

Important Dates

1565 – African Americans lived in St. Augustine, shortly after its discovery by Spain.

1763 – Spain surrendered Florida and practically all its inhabitants, including at least six hundred slaves and twenty-three free African Americans, to the English.

1838 – Free African Americans helped found Jacksonville's First Bethel Baptist Church.

1860 – The free African-American population was 932.

1866 – The Freedmen's Bureau established sixty-five African-American schools.

1867 – Congress dissolved Florida's government and granted African-American males the right to vote.

State Archives

Florida State Archives
R. A. Gray Building (M.S. 9A)
500 S. Bronough Street
Tallahassee, FL 32399-0250
http://dlis.dos.state.fl.us/barm/fsa.html

The Black Experience: A Guide to Afro-American Resources in the Florida State Archives is a downloadable document from the Archives web site. It provides information on state government records, manuscripts, and photographs housed in the Florida State Archives that relate to the history of African Americans in Florida. While the guide was up-to-date when revised in 1991, additional records have been acquired by the Archives. Included in the Manuscript Collections chapter are slave books, bills of sale for slaves, church membership rosters, baptisms, marriage records, and other African-American sources, including photographs. Another chapter focuses on sources found in the Florida Collection of the State Library. Further information can be found in several publications relating to African-American history, including *The Negro in the Reconstruction of Florida, 1865–1877*; *Elm City: a Negro Community*; *Black Tampa: the Roots of a People*; as well as in various county histories with chapters on African-American communities.

Census Records

Federal Census Records

1830–1880; 1900–1930 (DNA, FM, FTaSU, F-Ar)

Mortality Records

1885 (DNA)

Slave Schedules

1850, 1860

Special Census

1825, 1855, 1866, 1867, 1875, 1935, and 1945, state census (DNA, F-Ar; schedules for some years are also available at other libraries in the state).

Voter Registration Rolls, 1868 (Series 98) (F-Ar)

Most volumes list voter's name, race, time of residence in county and state, place of nativity, naturalization (where, when, and how), and date of registration.

State and County Records

Birth-Marriage-Divorce-Death Records

Florida State Vital Records Office
P.O. Box 210
1217 Pearl Street
Jacksonville, FL 32231
http://www.doh.state.fl.us/planning_eval/vital_statistics/index.html

Cemetery and Church Records

The Florida State Archives (**http://dlis.dos.state.fl.us/barm/fsa.html**) now has its archival collection catalog online. Using the search feature on that site, you can determine what records are available in that collection. Following are some examples of what information you will find here:

Blessed Sacrament Catholic Church (Tallahassee) Records 1847–1878: 1908–1941, 1 microfilm roll M74–021. Collection includes a register, with names of blacks baptized from 1851 to 1864.

Catholic Church (St. Augustine) Parish Records 1594–1763, 7 microfilm rolls M72–10. These parish records for the period 1594–1763 include baptisms, marriages, burials, and confirmations. Also listed are burials and baptisms of free African-American slaves, and persons of "mixed bloods."

Richardson Family Bible, 1811, 1 volume M87–007. Family Bible, containing birth, death, and marriage records of Richardson's descendants, and also some birth and death records of slaves owned by the Richardson family.

St. Michael's Catholic Church (Pensacola) Parish Records, 1811–1956, 4 microfilm rolls M74–005. Restricted records of the Pensacola (Escambia County) church include baptisms, marriages, burials, and confirmations. Of particular interest are records of baptisms of blacks from 1817–1882 (microfilm).

Swilley's Funeral Home Records, 1959–1970, 2 microfilm rolls M79–182. (F-Ar)

Trinity United Methodist Church (Tallahassee) Records 1836–1954, 2 microfilm rolls M74-023 (a "colored" church)

Military Records

See the Florida State Archives and its web site (**http://dlis.dos.state.fl.us/barm/fsa.html**).

Newspapers

Florida Evangelist (Jacksonville). 1896–1902. Weekly. Holdings: January 20, 1900; CSdS, CSS, CU, DLC, FTaSU, LU-NO, MdBMC, MiKW, TNF, WHi.

Florida Sentinel (Pensacola). 1887–1913. Weekly. Holdings: January 26, 1900; CSdS, CSS, CU, DLC, FTaSU, LU-NO, MdBMC, MiKW, TNF, WHi.

Manuscript Sources: Personal Papers and Slavery Records

Columbia County—List of Slave Owners, 1850 (G-Ar)
Jefferson County Plantation Records (FTaSU)
 Includes Bunker Hill, Nacossa, Freelawn, and Mt. Vernon plantation records.
Owsley Charts (T)
 Charts from 1840–60 of land, slaves, etc., for all counties from the federal census schedules.
Weedon and Whitehurst Family Papers, #4057, 1824–1869; 1932–1966 (NcU)
 Bills of sale for slaves: St. Augustine, Florida: Activities in Liberia.

Internet Resources

The Florida State Archives has a searchable database on its web site (**http://dlis.dos.state.fl.us/barm/fsa.html**), as well as indexes and guides to its collection. The Florida Confederate Pension Application Files online provides some information on slave owners; see **http://dlis.dos.state.fl.us/barm/Pensionfiles.html**.

Florida African American Roots web site (**http://www.rootsweb.com/~flafram/home.html**) has a detailed time line of African-American history in the state and search links to helpful sources.

Research Contacts

See Florida African American Roots web site above.

Bibliography

Colburn, David R., and Jane L. Landers, ed. *The African-American Heritage of Florida.* Gainesville, Fla.: University of Florida Press, 1995.

Includes an introduction by David Colburn and an impressive array of essays on African-American history and experience in the state.

Evans, Arthur B. *Pearl City, Florida: A Black Community Remembers.* Boca Raton, Fla., 1980.

Jones, George Noble. *Florida Plantation Records from the Papers of George Jones.* Edited by Ulrich Bonnell Phillips and James David Glunt. St. Louis: Missouri Historical Society, 1927. Reprint, New York: B. Franklin, 1971.
Excellent background reading and guide to Florida plantations.

Landers, Jane. *Black Society in Spanish Florida.* Contributor, Peter H. Wood. Champaign-Urbana, Ill.: University of Illinois Press, 1999.
Chronicles Mose, an 18th-century free black town on the periphery of St. Augustine. Discusses black religious life, lives of black women. Includes militia records, slave records, land grants to free blacks, slave imports data. (See also other books by Landers.)

McDonough, Gary W., ed. *The Florida Negro: A Federal Writers' Project Legacy.* Jackson, Mi., 1993.

Otto, John Solomon. *Cannon's Point Plantation, 1794–1860: Living Conditions and Status Patterns in the Old South.* Orlando, Fl.: Academic Press, Inc., 1984.

Robie, Diane C. *Searching in Florida: A Reference Guide to Public & Private Records.* Costa Mesa, Calif.: ISC Publications, 1982.

Smith, Julia Floyd. *Slavery & Plantation Growth in Antebellum Florida, 1821–1860.* Reprint, Ann Arbor: Books on Demand, 1973.
Good background material, including bibliography.

Georgia

Important Dates

1751 – Georgia officially became a slave society.

1776 – Over 15,000 slaves lived in Georgia.

1872 – Political reconstruction came to an end.

1890 – The Legislature established Georgia Normal and Industrial Institute in Savannah (now Savannah State College) as Georgia's black land grant school.

State Archives

Georgia Department of Archives and History
5800 Jonesboro Road
Morrow, GA 30260-1101
http://www.sos.state.ga.us/archives/

Operating under the Georgia Secretary of State, this agency is the repository for both current and historical documents relating to Georgia's history and residents.

Census Records

Federal Census Records

1820–1880, 1890 (partial), 1900–1930 (DNA); 1830, 1850, 1880 (GU); 1820–1880, 1900–1920 (G-Ar)

Mortality Records

1850, 1860, 1870, 1880 (DNA, DNDAR)

111

Slave Schedules

1850, 1860 (DNA, DNDAR, G-Ar)

State and County Records

Birth-Marriage-Divorce-Death Records

Georgia Department of Human Resources
Vital Records Service
2600 Skyland Drive, N.E.
Atlanta, GA 30319-3640
http://health.state.ga.us/programs/vitalrecords/index.shtml

This state office maintains birth and death records since 1919, and marriage applications and licenses from 1952–1996. There is no state-wide index of divorce records. For those and all earlier vital records, check the individual county records for events in that county.

Voting Records

Reconstruction Registration Oath Books (1867): (RG 1-1-107) Lists name, date of registration, and county of residence. (G-Ar)

Reconstruction Returns of Voters (1867): (RG 1-1-108) Lists voter's number; date of registry; name; number and page in Oath Book; race; time of residence in state, county, and precinct within a year; nativity by state or county; naturalization (if any); and remarks (if any). (G-Ar)

Other State and County Records

The web site **http://www.sos.state.ga.us/archives/rs/gsrc.htm** identifies numerous record groups for African-American research in Georgia. These records are similar in nature to records available in most southern states and should be used not only as a guide for Georgia but also as an indication of what ought to be found in other southern states. This list of materials relating to African-American genealogical research is by no means definitive. It represents only those records on microfilm that specifically state that they concern African Americans (e.g., the marriage records listed are only those for African-American marriages). Counties not mentioned on the list may have kept similar records but interspersed them with European-American ones. An actual check of other microfilms will be necessary to determine the existence of other county records relating to African Americans. Some of these records can also be found on the Internet, and more are being entered every day.

The list of records that follows will give you an idea of what is available on microfilm from the Georgia Department of Archives and History:

Appling County: Free Persons of Color, 1843–56

Baker County: Marriages, 1905–25, 1925–43

Baldwin County: Free Persons of Color, 1932–64; Trials of Slaves, Inferior Court Minutes: 1812–38, 1812–26

Berrien County: Marriages, 1905–27, 1827–49

Bibb County: Marriages, 1828–39, 1865–74, 1874–82, 1882–88, 1888–97, 1892–95, 1895–99, 1899–1911, 1902–8, 1906–10, 1913–19, 1917–19, 1919–21, 1929, 1936, 1963, 1964; Index to Marriages, 1823–1963

Brooks County: Marriages, 1894–1904, 1904–13, 1911–25, 1924–37, 1937–49, 1949–66

Bryan County: Marriages, 1870–97

Bulloch County: Marriages, 1912–25, 1925–39, 1939–66, 1952–69

Burke County: Slave List, 1798 (Second District C)

Butts County: Marriages, 1882–1903, 1903–29, 1929–48

Camden County: Affidavits of Persons Bringing Slaves into Georgia, 1818–47; Affidavits of Persons Bringing Slaves into Georgia, 1818–47 (Superior Court); Free Persons of Color, 1819–43; Marriages, 1931–49, 1949–52

Campbell County: Marriages, 1898–1928

Carroll County: Marriages, 1892–1906

Chatham County: Free Persons of Color, 1780–1865, 1837–49, 1861–64, 1826–36 (some also at GHS); List of Negroes Freed (Superior Court) (compiled by General Robert J. Travis)

Chatooga County: Free Persons of Color, 1847–62; Marriages 1909–16, 1916–43, 1943–56

Clay County: Indentures for Free Persons of Color, 1866–67; Marriages, 1906–18, 1922–33

Clinch County: Marriages, 1922–65

Colquitt County: Marriages, 1942–46, 1946–50, 1950–62, 1962–67

Columbia County: Affidavits of Persons Bringing Slaves into Georgia, 1818–35; Free Persons of Color, 1819–36; Marriages, 1914–43; 1943–52

Coweta County: Index to Marriages, 1827–1966

Crawford County: Marriages, 1909–43

Decatur County: Voters Registration (Superior Court), 1902

DeKalb County: Marriages, 1893–1908

Dodge County: Marriages, 1893–1940, 1905–19, 1919–37, 1937–52, 1952–66; Index to Marriages, 1871–1958

Dooly County: Marriages, 1852–75, 1868–90, 1890–99, 1899–1908

Douglas County: Marriages, 1894–1941

Elbert County: Affidavits of Persons Bringing Slaves into Georgia, Volume A, 1822–47; Free Persons of Color, 1819–59; Marriages, 1882–91, 1898–1909; Slave Trials, 1837–49

Emanuel County: Free Persons of Color, 1855; Marriages, 1905–17, 1917–33, 1933–47, 1948–61, 1952–61

Fayette County: Superintendent of Schools, School Census, 1928, 1933, 1938

Forsyth County: Marriages, 1895–1900

Franklin County: Importation of Slaves, 1818–1938

Fulton County: Marriages, 1866–78, 1878–84, 1884–89, 1889–93, 1893–96, 1896–1900, 1900–1902

Glascock County: Marriages, 1871–1920, 1921–45, 1945–66

Glynn County: Marriages, 1898–1905, 1905–18

Gordon County: Marriages, 1908–65

Greene County: Marriages, 1866–75, 1875–77, 1878–83

Hall County: Marriages, 1866–1900, 1900–1920, 1920–53

Hancock County: Free Persons of Color, 1855–62; Slave Trials, 1834–50 (Inferior Court)

Harris County: Marriages, 1859–72, 1870–83, 1890–1923

Hart County: Marriages, 1867–99, 1899–1923

Henry County: Marriages, 1851–85, 1881–92, 1885–1916, 1916–33; Index to Marriages, 1821–1939

Houston County: Licenses to Sell Spiritous Liquor to Free Persons of Color, 1834–62

Irwin County: Marriages, 1854–74, 1904–17, 1917–54

Jackson County: Affidavits of Persons Bringing Slaves into Georgia, 1818–30; Marriages, 1895–1911

Jefferson County: Free Persons of Color, 1818, 1820–22, 1840–59; Marriages, 1866–90, 1899–1917, 1918–30, 1929–58, 1942–56

Johnson County: Marriages, 1907–28, 1928–52, 1952–66

Jones County: Index to Slave Deeds (Superior Court), Grantor and Grantee, 1791–1864

Laurens County: Marriages, 1897–1907, 1907–15, 1915–33, 1921–29

Lee County: Marriages, 1867–1905

Liberty County: Bonds of Apprenticeship, 1866–73; Free Persons of Color, 1852–64; Marriages, 1819–96, 1897–1909, 1909–37, 1936–56, 1867–72

Lincoln County: Docket of Slaves Indicted for Capital Crimes, 1814–38 (Inferior Court); Free Persons of Color, 1819–63; Marriages, 1866–75, 1875–84, 1884–96, 1896–1925, 1925–68; Index to Marriages, 1866–1939

Lowndes County: Marriages, 1904–10, 1909–16, 1916–21, 1921–29, 1925–34

Lumpkin County: Free Persons of Color, 1848–64

McDuffie County: Voters Register (Ordinary), 1886–94

Marion County: Voters List, 1898, 1900, 1903, 1906 (Superior Court)

Meriwether County: Superintendent of Schools, School Census, 1898, 1903, 1913

Miller County: Marriages, 1939–53, 1965–66

Mitchell County: Marriages, 1909–17, 1915–24, 1924–35, 1935–43, 1943–52

Montgomery County: Marriages, 1893–1946

Morgan County: Marriages, 1866–91, 1891–1904; Slave Register (Ordinary), 1818–24; Tax Digests, 1890–1910, 1895

Oconee County: Marriages, 1932–66

Oglethorpe County: Marriages, 1873–94, 1897–1908; Marriage Licenses Issued to Freedmen, 1865–73

Polk County: Marriages, 1917–19 and 1928, 1916–47, 1947–65

Pulaski County: Free Persons of Color, 1840–65; Marriages, 1894–1910, 1910–19; Slave Records (Ordinary), dates not stated

Putnam County: Trials of Slaves, 1813–43

Richmond County: Slave Requisition, 1818–20, 1822–30, 1835–37 (Superior Court)

Rockdale County: Marriages, 1891–1902

Screven County: Docket for Trials of Slaves and the Free Persons of Color, 1844–48 (Inferior Court)

Spalding County: Marriages, 1893–98, 1898–1903, 1903–10, 1910–17, 1917–23, 1923–34, 1933–42, 1942–51, 1951–52

Sumter County: Marriages, 1888–97; Voters Register, 1909, 1911–13

Taliaferro County: Free Persons of Color, 1796–1865, Book A; Free Persons of Color, 1829–64, Books A and B; Marriages, 1866–

1929, 1875–1905; Trials of Free Persons of Color, Book A, 1857–58

Tattnall County: Marriages, 1866–72, 1910–50

Terrell County: Marriages, 1869–88, 1888–1906; Voters Registration, 1895–1909

Thomas County: Free Persons of Color, 1858–62; Marriages, 1868–74

Troup County: Marriages, 1892–1908

Upson County: Marriages, 1866–76, 1893–1908

Walton County: Marriages, 1896–1908, 1905–19

Warren County: Free Persons of Color, 1844–63; Marriages, 1888–1902; Slave Owner's List, 1798 (Superior Court)

Wayne County: Marriages, 1907–55

Webster County: Marriages, 1914–61

City Records

Atlanta

Tax Digest; includes Negro property for all of Fulton County, 1890.

Milledgeville Census, 1911; contains name, age, color, residence, and remarks (G-Ar)

Treasurer: Tax Digests, 1859–67; 1869 lists African-American tax-payers.

Savannah

Free Persons of Color Register, 1817–29; 1860–63 (G-Ar; GHi)

Apprentice/Indenture Records:

These registers primarily document freedmen. The information available gives the names of the persons being apprenticed or indentured, the person to whom they are bound, and sometimes family information or place of origin. In some cases, the registers may indicate former slavery relationships. They can be found in either the Ordinary (Probate) Court or Superior Court records for the thirty-four counties: Baldwin, Campbell, Carroll, Chatham, Chattooga, Cherokee, Clay, Clinch, Coweta, Dooly, Glascock, Haralson, Jackson, Laurens, Liberty, Lincoln, Madison, McDuffie, Meriwether, Mitchell, Monroe, Morgan, Oglethorpe, Polk, Pulaski, Putnam, Sumter, Taliaferro, Terrell, Thomas, Washington, Webster, Whitfield, and Wilkes.

Cemetery and Church Records

Cemeteries

Baldwin County (G-Ar)
Central State Hospital Cemetery Records, 1880–1951. Negro: male and female, name, date of burial, grave number, section number, and remarks.
Chatham County (G-Ar)
Laurel Grove Cemetery Records. Records include deaths, burials, and title to lots, 1852–1942; not indexed.
Sumter County (G-Ar)
Oak Grove Cemetery Records, 1903–59; indexed.
Thomas County (G-Ar)
Old Negro Cemetery. Transcribed records, histories, loose notes related to the cemetery.

Church Records

The following church records are in the Georgia Department of Archives and History:

Baptist

First Baptist Church for the Colored, Macon, Bibb County
Jordan Grove Baptist Church, Lee County Palmyra District
Sandy Creek Baptist Church, Morgan County. Minutes and membership rolls, 1808–66, 1905–50
Bethlehem Baptist Church, Appalachee, Morgan County. Minutes, 1859–96.

Episcopal

St. Anthanasius Episcopal Church, Brunswick, Camden County. Records include the monthly publication *WORTH* and a short sketch of the church, 1915–24; the will of Mary Rhinelander King of New York, with bequest to the church is also included.
Bartholomew's Episcopal Church, Chatham Country. There are records of baptisms, marriages, burials, and memberships, 1877–1925.

Methodist

Bethel Methodist Church, Screven County. Records contain appointments and list of members, 1836–78.

Presbyterian

Hebron Presbyterian Church, Banks County. Church records, 1847–84.

Independent Presbyterian Church, Chatham County. Minutes of First African Sabbath School, 1826–39; colored Sunday School, 1844; colored marriages and members, 1829–87.

New Hope Presbyterian Church, Madison County. Minutes, 1838–61; church history, 1788–1838; baptisms, marriages, and members, 1849–59.

Military Records

U.S. Adjutant General Records (G-Ar).

The Negro in the Military Service of the U.S. 1639–1886. (G-Ar). Seven volumes of materials, including employment, civil status, battles, and treatment and exchange of prisoners.

Confederate record: An official request for use of the slave of J. J. Jones of Burke County from C.S. Engineering Department, Office Enrollment of Slaves, Savannah, December 9, 1836.

"Military Impressment of Negroes for the Defense of Georgia," Two forms filed by estate of S. A. Jones for use of slaves, August 5, 1862.

Record Group 109, "War Department Collection of Confederate Records (DNA)." Medical Department, Ordinance: Macon records of slaves hired, letters to owners, and returns for work done by African-American laborers, carpenters, and bricklayers.

Newspapers

Loyal Georgia (Augusta). January 13, 1866 to 1868. Weekly. Holdings: 1866–68; CSdS, CSS, WHi.

Savannah Tribune. 1875 to September 24, 1960. Weekly. Holdings: December 4, 1875; 1889; December 1891 to 1943; ATT, DHU, DLC, GAU, MH, MoJcL, NN, OCI, OkentU, TNF, ViHal, WHi. December 4, 1875, to December 25, 1924; Cty, CU. October 23, 1886, to December 15, 1888; GSSC, CU.

Savannah Weekly Echo. 1879–84. Weekly. Holdings: 1883–84; CSdS, CSS, CU, DLC, FTaSU, LU-NO, MdBMC, MiKW, TNF, WHi.

Manuscript Sources: Personal Papers, Slave Records, and Diaries

Allen, Eliza A., 1841–63 (G-Ar)
> Personal correspondence and business papers, Burke County plantation.

Anderson, Edward Clifford. Papers, 1813–82 (NcU)
> Includes miscellaneous plantation and slave records of Savannah. MS 64-389

Berrien, John McPherson, 1781–1856 (G-Ar)
> Conditions of slaves.

Cameron Family Papers, 1739–1929 (NcU)
> Contains some slave registers for a planter of Orange county and Raleigh. MS 64-445

Cooper, Mrs. Mark, 1790 (G-Ar)
> Includes deed for slave Reuben Payne to Thomas Cooper.

Cooper, Mark Anthony, 1794–1875 (G-Ar)
> Includes deeds, warrants, grants, and slave deeds.

Cowan, Mrs. F. B., 1837 (G-Ar)
> Includes receipts of slave, December 1, 1837, Franklin County.

Greene, Richard Appling (G-Ar)
> Lists of slaves owned in Macon County.

Jones, John J. 1835–65 (G-Ar)
> Includes records relative to slavery.

Jones, William B., M.D. (G-Ar)
> Includes bills of slave sales.

King, Parrington (G-Ar)
> Includes deeds, receipts, and bills of sale of slaves, from Darien and Roswell, Georgia

Maye Collection (G-Ar)
> Includes 1844 bill of sale for a slave, signed by Joseph and E.O. Forbes and Isaac Tull.

Nephew, James. (G-Ar)
> Includes deeds for land and slaves, McIntosh County.

Orr, James M. (G-Ar)
> Includes bills of sale for slaves, Gwinnett County.

Turner, Daniel. (G-Ar)
  Includes economic, social, and political conditions related to slavery. Turner was a physician at St. Mary's, 1805–08.
Yancy, D. C. Account Book for Coosa River Plantation, 1853–66 (G-Ar)
  These records are from Cherokee County, Alabama, and Blue Spring Plantation in Dougherty County, Georgia. Includes births and deaths of slaves, and accounts of freedmen working, 1865–66.

In addition, the Georgia Historical Society in Savannah has the following:

Bills of Sale, miscellaneous.
Plantation Records for Argyle, 1828–31; papers of Beverly Berwick, 1874–76; papers from the Telfair Family Plantation, 1794–1864.
Slave Importation Register and/or Lists of Slaves/Slave owners
  Affidavits of persons bringing slaves into the state, as well as lists of slaves and slave owners, are available in twelve counties: Georgia: Camden, Columbia, Elbert, Franklin, Jackson, Jones, Morgan, Oglethorpe, Pulaski, Richmond, Warren, and Wilkes.

Family Papers

The family papers listed below can be found at the Wilson Library, University of North Carolina. The annotations below were taken from the Library's extensive web site.

Edward Clifford Anderson Papers, #3602, 1813–1882.
  Family letters and assorted volumes of Anderson, U.S. Navy officer, Confederate officer, planter, politician, and businessman of Savannah, Georgia. Correspondence covers various topics including African-American Union soldiers (1863) and African Americans living in Savannah (1868). Manuscript volumes include slave papers that document slave births and deaths (1817–1866) and records of blankets and shoes distributed to slaves (1853–1866).
Arnold and Screvan Family Papers, #3419, 1762–1903.
  Papers of members of the Arnold family of Providence, Rhode Island, and Bayou County, Georgia, and of the Screvan family of Savannah, Georgia. The collection contains business and family correspondence, financial and legal writings, farm journals, and genealogical information. Papers include instructions on the management of slaves in Georgia (1832–1861), medical bills for treatment of slaves (1762–1826), and slave lists (1811–1869).

David Crenshaw Barrow Papers, #1251, 1834–1893.
> Correspondence and other papers of Barrow and members of his family of Lexington, Georgia. The collection includes slave bills of sale and a receipt from a jailor for a runaway slave (1850). Correspondence, generally relating to Barrow's plantations in various parts of Georgia, discusses preaching to slaves (1859); slave insurrections and runaways (1860–1865); promises made to slaves concerning the percentage of crops they would receive; efforts to keep slaves out of Sherman's path (1865); attempts to raise slave troops and an advisement against the use of slave soldiers in the Confederacy (1865); an agreement with "Tillman, a freedman" for labor (1865); and voting.

Diaries

Allen, Eliza Harriet (Arnold), 1831, 1837, 1841, 1841 (RHi). Records visits on brother's Savannah plantation.

Barrow, Clara Elizabeth, 1869, 1875 (GU). Records Oglethorpe County, Milledgeville, and Americus daily life.

Barrow, Col. David Crenshaw, 1847–49, 1851–52, 1856–58, 1863, 1876, 1879 (GU). An Oglethorpe County plantation diary. MS 64–219

Cooper, James Hamilton, 1839–54 (NcU). A Hopeton Plantation journal, Glynn County.

Dickey, William J., 1858–59, 1879–80, 1884–89 (GU). Thomas County plantation diary.

Lumpkin, Wilson, 1838–63 (GHi). Births and deaths of slaves are listed.

Parker, William Foster, 1859–60 (GHi). A Savannah slave dealer's journal.

Ravenel, Miss, 1865 (GHi). Describes plantation conditions.

Ravenel, Henry, Jr., 1806–22 (GHi). This diary lists blacks inherited and their descendants (1780–1820).

Ravenel, Dr. Henry, 1830–32 (GHi). Records slave births, 1809–29.

Ravenel, Thomas Porcher, 1845–1903 (GHi). Describes plantation life.

Richardson, Gilbert M. 1860–61 (GHi). A Lumpkin plantation diary.

Spratlin, James A., 1866 (GHi). An Oglethorpe County overseer's record.

Internet Resources

The following resources on the Internet will help lead to source material in Georgia:

Georgia's Slave Population in Legal Records: Where and How to Look (**http://www.rootsweb.com/~gapike/slave.htm**). An excellent introduction by David E. Paterson of courthouse resources and how to use them to research African-American ancestry in Georgia.

African-American Resources at the Georgia Department of Archives and History (**http://www.sos.state.ga.us/archives/rs/gsrc.htm**) has a very helpful slave research checklist for Georgia.

Research Contacts

Georgia Historical Society
501 Whitaker Street
Savannah, GA 31401
http://www.georgiahistory.com/

The University of Georgia also has a helpful web site (**http://www. cviog.uga.edu/Projects/gainfo/gahist.htm**) for all periods and aspects of Georgia history.

Bibliography

Alexander, Adele Logan. *Ambiguous Lives: Free Women of Color in Rural Georgia, 1789–1879.* Fayetteville: University of Arkansas Press, 1992.

Austin, Jeannette Holland. *Fayette County, Georgia, Probate Records: Annul Returns, Inventories, Sales, & Bonds, 1845–1897.* Roswell, Ga.: Wolfe Pub., 1996.

Cox, Jack F. *The 1850 Census of Georgia Slave Owners.* Baltimore: Clearfield Company, 2000.
Covers 37,000 slave owners. Very valuable when locating free and slave ancestors on the plantation.

Davis, Robert Scott. *Research in Georgia: With a Special Emphasis Upon the Georgia Department of Archives & History.* Greenville, S.C.: Southern Historical Press, 1991.

Hancock, Mary. *Cobb County, Georgia Marriages White 1865–1937, Colored 1865–1966.* Marietta, Ga.: Cobb County Genealogical Society, Inc., 1995.

Miller, Randall M., ed. *Dear Master: Letters of a Slave Family.* Athens: University of Georgia Press, 1990.

Mills, William A. *Houston County, Georgia Administrators & Guardians Bond Abstracts, 1852–1870.* Perry, Ga.: W.A. Mills, 1998.

Perdue, Robert. *The Negro in Savannah, 1865–1900.* Fort Lauderdale, Fla.: Exposition-Phoenix Press, Inc., 1973.
Gives a good general history of African Americans in Savannah and lists a number of names of free African Americans. Also contains a good account of migrations into and out of the city. Good bibliography, pages 142–53.

Phillips, Ulrich B. *Plantation and Frontier 1649–1863.* New York: Burt Franklin Publisher, 1969.
Contains a record of names of African Americans on the Gourie and East Heritage estates, which were operated on one plantation on Argyle Island in the Savannah River in Georgia (1, 134). This work also has an official register of free persons "of color" in Richmond County, Georgia, in 1819 (11, 143).

Ray, David Thornton, ed. *African-American Marriage Records: Hart County, Georgia.* Hartwell, Ga.: Savannah River Valley Genealogical Society, 1994.

Turner, Freda R. *Henry County, Georgia, 1821–1894: Marriage, Colored/Freedman Record of Sales, Inventory and Wills.* Roswell, Ga.: Wolfe Pub., 1995.

Wallace, Laura Singleton. *History of Ware County (GA).* Reprint. Salem, Mass.: Higginson Book Company, 1997.

Wood, Betty. *Slavery in Colonial Georgia, 1730–1773.* Athens: University of Georgia, 1984.

Hawaii

Important Dates

1813 – Anthony D. Allen, an ex-slave came to the island of Oahu from New York. In 1813 he married a Hawaiian woman and had three children. He was granted six acres of land in Waikiki, where he established a boardinghouse, as well as the first hospital for American seaman in Pawa'a. The land he owned is now the site of Oahu's Washington Intermediate School.

1821 – The earliest settlers of African ancestry arrived in Hawaii, then called the Sandwich Islands, well before this date.

1824 – Betsy Stockton, who was probably the first African-American woman on the Islands, helped to found the Lahainaluna School on Maui. The school was later used as a model by General Samuel Armstrong for the founding of Hampton Institute of Virginia.

1898 – Hawaii became United States territory and soon thereafter saw the arrival of African-American laborers and middle-class professionals.

1900 – The first federal census for the territory lists 233 African-American Hawaiians.

State Archives

Hawaii State Archives
Iolani Palace Grounds
478 South King Street
Honolulu, HI 96813
http://www.hawaii.gov/dags/archives/

The State Archives has over 10,000 cubic feet of material in its collections. The largest groups of government records are as follows:

Records of the Executive Branch. Contain minutes, correspondence, reports, plans, registers, certificates, and ledgers documenting activities of the executive branch agencies from 1840 to the present.

Legislative Records. Include bills, committee reports, journals, testimonies, petitions, messages, communications, and minutes from 1840 to present.

Judiciary Records. Cover 19th- and early-20th-century probate, divorce, criminal, civil, equity, law and admiralty case files, minute books, and wills.

Governor's Records. Over 483 collections of private papers, manuscripts, and records documenting the social, economic, civic or political history of Hawaii. It is not known what materials relevant to African-American genealogical information can be found within these holdings.

Census Records

Federal Census Records

1900–1930 (DNA) 1900–1920

State and County Records

Birth-Marriage-Divorce-Death Records

Vital Records Section
Office of Health Status Monitoring
P.O. Box 3378
Honolulu, HI 96801
http://www.state.hi.us/doh/records/

Microfilms of selected vital records indexes are available at the Hawaii State Library. Paper indexes of birth records (between 1896 and 1909) are in the custody of the Hawaii Department of Health, and available at Hamilton Library of the University of Hawaii at Manoa. All vital records seventy-five years and older in the custody of the Hawaii Department of Health have been microfilmed by the Genealogical Society of Utah and are available statewide through the LDS Family History Centers.

Bibliography

"Afro-Americans in Hawaii." Special issue. *Afro-Hawaii News* (February 1988).

Greer, R. A. "Blacks in Old Hawaii." *Honolulu* (November 1986)

Lee, Lloyd L. "A Brief Analysis of the Role and Status of the Negro in the Hawaiian Community." *American Sociological Review* (August 1948).

Nordyke, Eleanor C. "Blacks in Hawaii: A Demographic and Historical Perspective." *Hawaiian Journal of History* (1988).

Idaho

Important Dates

1804-1820s – African-American trappers and guides traversed the area.

1870 – Sixty African Americans, most of them miners, arrived in Idaho. The largest concentrations lived near Silver City in the southwest corner of the territory, and in Boise County.

1880 – Idaho had few African-American homesteaders.

1889 – Joseph and Laura Wells arrived in the Boville-Deary area from Asheville, North Carolina.

1890 – Idaho became a state; the African-American population was 201.

1910 – William King and family came from North Carolina to Northern Idaho to homestead near the Coeur d'Alene Indian Reservation.

State Archives

Idaho State Historical Society Library and Archives
450 N. Fourth Street
Boise, ID 83702
http://www.idahohistory.net/research.html

The Archives' holdings are extremely varied in subject, geographic area, and time period, and include historical and genealogical information in a wide variety of mediums, including manuscripts, state archives, books, periodicals, oral history interviews, motion picture films, videos, microfilm, and maps.

Census Records

Federal Census Records

1870–1880, 1900–1930 (DNA); 1870–1880, 1900–1920 (IdHi)

Mortality Records

1870–80 (IdHi)

State and County Records

Birth-Marriage-Divorce-Death Records

Idaho State Vital Records Office
Idaho Center for Vital Statistics
P.O. Box 83720
450 W. State Street
Boise, ID 83720
http://www2.state.id.us/dhw/vital_stats/appmenu.html

The state began recording vital events in 1911. Before that, vital records were kept on the county level. The state's vital records web site provides appropriate forms for requesting information.

Cemetery and Church Records

See the Idaho State Historical Society web site (**http://www. idahohistory.net/**) for information on cemetery records.

Newspapers

The Idaho State Historical Society Library and Archives web site (**http://www.idahohistory.net/research.html**) has a directory of indexed weekly and daily newspapers in the state.

Research Contacts

Idaho State Historical Society
1109 Main Street
Suite 250
Boise, ID 83702
http://www.idahohistory.net/

The Society's web site has an excellent time line for the state, guides to cemeteries, census records, and city directories.

Bibliography

Oliver, Mamie O. *Ebony: The Afro-American Presence in Idaho State History.* Boise, Id.: State Historical Society, 1990.

Mercier, Laurie, and Carole Simon-Smolinsk. *Idaho's Ethnic Heritage: Historical Overview.* 3 vols. Boise, Id.: Ethnic Heritage Project, 1990.

Illinois

Important Dates

1717 – Phillip Francis Renault brought 500 slaves from St. Dominique (later Haiti) to work in French Louisiana Territory's "Illinois Country."

1720 – The Director General of Mines for the Company of the Indies arrived with African slaves.

1763 – British took control of "Illinois Country." Six hundred African-American slaves, mostly house servants and laborers, lived on small farms along with a few free African Americans.

1800 – The 1800 census of the Indiana Territory, which encompassed the Illinois country, listed 135 slaves and 163 free persons of Mexican descent. By 1810 the Illinois Territory itself had 781 African-American residents,168 registered as slaves.

1807 – Slave owners with African Americans aged fifteen and older were permitted to bring them to Illinois, as long as the owners went before the clerk of the Court of Common Pleas and registered their slaves. Many of these records are still extant.

1812 – As of December 8, 1812, "free blacks and mulattoes" were required to register six months after they arrived in the state. Such records are still available.

1818 – Illinois, after admission into the Union, passed a constitution that forbade slavery, and provided for the end of slavery in mines by 1825. The General Assembly began enacting a series of laws known as the "black codes." These restrictive laws continued the practice of indentured servitude, denied legal protection to Mexican-Americans and required local governmental officials to maintain registers of indentured servants and free Negroes and mulattoes.

1820 – The 1820 federal census listed 917 slaves and 457 free African Americans.

1825 – African Americans began arriving in Illinois in great numbers with the influx of European-American settlers to the Northwest Territory.

1829 – Free African Americans were issued freedom certificates.

1840 – The 1840 census was the last one to record slaves in Illinois. For that year there were 331 slaves and 3,598 free African-Americans in Illinois.

State Archives

Illinois State Archives
Norton Building, Capitol Complex
Springfield, IL 62756
http://www.library.sos.state.il.us/departments/archives/archives.html

As the official repository in Illinois for state and local public records, the agency has an array of guides and databases available for research in person, by mail, and through the Internet. It does not hold manuscript, newspaper, or non-official sources.

Illinois has a system of regional centers set up for research in local records. The Illinois Regional Archives Depositories [IRAD] are located at universities throughout the state. For information about the IRAD system, see the web site above. Records are sorted by counties and then housed within the appropriate region. Records may relate to birth, death, marriage, divorce, real property, personal property, naturalizations, estates, school attendance, city council proceedings, minutes of towns and townships, voter registrations, court actions, paupers, and professions.

The locations of the Illinois Regional Archives Depositories are as follows:

Eastern Illinois University, Charleston, Illinois
Illinois State University, Normal, Illinois
Northeastern Illinois University, Chicago, Illinois
Northern Illinois University, DeKalb, Illinois
Southern Illinois University, Carbondale, Illinois
University of Illinois/Springfield, Springfield, Illinois
Western Illinois University, Macomb, Illinois

Census Records

Federal Census Records

1820–1880, 1900–1930 (DNA);1790–1880, 1900–1920 (I-Ar); numerous public and college libraries have schedules available for some years.

Mortality Records

1850–1880 (DNA, I-Ar)

Special Census

1818: Territorial Census (DNA)

Other Federal Records

The National Archives and Records Administration—Great Lakes Region (see below under "Research Contacts") holds the following federal records of interest to African-American research:

Records of the United States Court of Appeals
>Includes records of cases related to civil lawsuits, criminal prosecutions, and the naturalization of blacks from Canada and the Caribbean. RU 276

Records of the United States District Courts: Illinois 1819–1982
>Includes post-Civil War lawsuits of free blacks who were kidnapped and sold into slavery; admiralty cases documenting African Americans who worked on the Mississippi and Ohio River boats; cases involving the legal status of slaves captured on Confederate steamboats by Union naval forces at Cairo, Illinois; case records 1870–1880s of small business owners and everyday people. RG 21

State and County Records

Birth-Marriage-Divorce-Death Records

Illinois State Department of Public Health
Division of Vital Records
605 West Jefferson Street
Springfield, IL 62702-5097
http://www.idph.state.il.us/vital/vitalhome.htm

The Illinois State Archives marriage index on microfiche 1818–1900 is widely available in research libraries and on the Internet. Other city, county, and state vital record indexes widely available (including at the Chicago Heights [LDS] Family History Center in Chicago Heights, Illinois) are the following:

Chicago Birth Registers, 1871–1915
Chicago City Directories, 1844–1901
Cook County Birth Records Indexes, 1871–1916
Illinois, Cook County, Chicago Deaths, 1871–1933
Illinois, Cook County, Chicago, Delayed Birth Indexes, 1871–1948
Illinois, Cook County, Chicago, Index to Birth Corrections, 1871–1915
Illinois, Cook County, Marriage Indexes, 1871–1916
Illinois Death Record Indexes, 1871–1916, 1916–1938

Other State and County Records

Circuit Court Clerk of Cook County Archives
Richard J. Daley Center, Room 1113
Chicago, IL 60602

Records include probate cases, 1871–1963; administration of wills and estates, estates of minors, and incompetents; indexes for probates deceased, 1871–1967; minors, 1871–1976; incompetents, 1911–1976; wills, 1850–1993; docket books, 1871–present; law and chancery cases, 1871–1964; divorce cases, 1871–1982; criminal felony cases, 1871–1900, 1927–1983; county court cases, 1871–1964; County Division, 1964–present; adoption cases (closed) 1871–present; mental health cases (closed) 1871–present; juvenile cases (closed) 1899–1926 with gaps, 1926–1964 destroyed. Closed adoption cases can be opened by the presiding judge of Cook County Circuit Court, County Division; juvenile cases must have an order from the presiding judge of Cook County Circuit Court. Juvenile Division and mental health cases must have permission from the chief deputy clerk of the County Division. Records not readily available are the cases of the Municipal Court of Chicago, 1904–1964; the Municipal Department, Civil and Criminal Division, 1964–present; Law Division, 1964–present. These case records are routinely destroyed in accordance with Illinois statute.

Cemetery and Church Records

Cemeteries

Cemeteries with asterisks (*) are predominately African-American cemeteries. This does not include all cemeteries where African Americans are buried in Illinois. Records are maintained by individual cemeteries.

*Burr Oak Cemetery, 4400 West 127th Street, Alsip, IL 60658 records date from 1925.

Cedar Park Cemetery, 12540 South Halsted, Calumet Park, IL 60643; records are in the office and date from 1923.

Cook County Cemetery, 159th Street and Oak Park Avenue (Oak Forest grounds), closed in 1970. Records date from 1910–1968. Oak Forest Hospital Medical Records Department will search for records if a death certificate is provided.

Homewood Memorial Gardens, 600 Ridge Road, Homewood, IL 60430; records date from 1910.

*Lincoln Cemetery, 12300 South Kedzie, Alsip, IL 60455; records date from 1911 and are in the office.

Mount Glenwood Memory Gardens South, 18301 Glenwood-Thornton Road, Glenwood, IL 60425; records date from 1902.

Oakland Memory Lanes, 15200 Lincoln, Dalton, IL 60419; records date from 1860.

*Oak Hill Cemetery, 12300 Kedzie, Alsip, IL 60455.

Oak Woods Cemetery, 1035 East 67th Street, Chicago, IL 60637; records are available in the office.

*Restvale Cemetery, 117th and Laramie, Alsip, IL; records are at 176 West Adams, Suite 2210, Chicago, IL 60603; (312) 236-4077.

Tinley Park Mental Health Cemetery, closed in 1976, interments removed to Mantoee, Kankakee County, IL; write to Bremen Township Registrar, 6825 West 167th Street, Tinley Park, IL 60477.

Washington Memory Gardens, Halsted Street and Ridge Road, Romewood, IL 60430; write to the office at 701 Ridge Road, Homewood, IL 60430.

Church Records

The following church histories and miscellaneous papers are housed in the Vivian G. Harsh Research Collection at the Chicago Public

Library's Carter G. Woodson Regional Library (see "Research Contacts" below for contact information). The names of pastors, committees, organizations, and members are listed in these booklets.

Arnette Chapel A.M.E. Church. Chicago: Arnette Chapel, 1958.

Carter Temple C.M.B. Church anniversaries booklets and Sunday bulletins.

Grace Presbyterian Church Fifty-Seventh Anniversary Tea. Chicago: Grace Presbyterian Church, 1945.

Greater Metropolitan Missionary Baptist Church. Chicago: 1976.

Rev. Floyd D. Johnson Collection. Papers from the Foreign Mission Board, National Baptist Convention of American and Zion Temple Missionary Baptist Church, Chicago.

Quinn Chapel A.M.E. Church Centennial Celebration. Chicago: 1947, members and committees.

The following Catholic Church records are located at the Chicago Heights Family History Center (LDS), Chicago Heights, Illinois:

St. Elizabeth Catholic Church records, 1882–1905. Holy Angels Church, 1881–1930. Baptisms, confirmations, and marriages.

Immaculate Conception Parish, Kaskaskia, Randolph County, Ill., 1695–1844 (IC Hi). Baptisms, marriages, and deaths of blacks recorded.

St. Anne's Parish, St. Charles, 1721–65 (ICHi). Baptisms, marriages, and deaths of blacks recorded.

St. Joseph's Parish, Prairie du Pocher, 1761–99 (ICHi). Baptisms, marriages, and deaths of blacks recorded in French.

Military Records

Administrative Files on Civil War Companies and Regiments, 1861–1903.
    African Americans from Illinois who enrolled in other U. S. military units. RG 301.018 (I-Ar)

Griffin, John A. Papers, 1860–69 (IHi).
    Diary written in 1862–63 when Griffin was a private in Company D, 17th Illinois Infantry. Includes letters from soldiers in the 53d U.S. Colored Infantry.

Griffith, Dr. David J., 1862–64 (ICHi).
    Civil War medical records, reporting the care of black troops, and employment of black personnel.

Kendrick, John F. Papers, 1959 (ICHi).
>   Manuscript papers for *Midsummer Picnic of '98*. Describes and
>   evaluates work of Negro Troops of 24th U.S. Infantry and 8th
>   Illinois Infantry in Cuba.

Muster and Descriptive Rolls, 1861–1865.
>   Includes the roster of the 29th U. S. Colored Infantry. RG
>   301.020 (I-Ar)

Muster In Rolls, 1898–1899. RG 301.087. (I-Ar)
>   *Report Containing the Complete Muster Out Rolls of the Illinois
>   Volunteers Who Served in the Spanish-American War, 1898–
>   1899.* (I-Ar)

Spanish American War (1898–1899) *Muster Out Rolls 1878–1899*. RG
301.089 (I-Ar)

See, also, the Illinois State Archives web page at **http://www.library.
sos.state.il/departments/archives/archives.html**.

Newspapers

The Vivian G. Harsh Research Collection of Afro-American History
and Literature (see "Research Contacts") houses major national African-American newspapers in addition to those published in Illinois. The
collection, including twelve reels of the Negro Newspapers Miscellaneous Collection, is located at the Carter G. Woodson Regional Library
and includes the following:

Bilalian News, 1975–1981
Black Panther, 1972–1980
BroadAx, Chicago, 1895–1926
Chicago Daily Defender, 1909 to present
The Conservator, 1882, 1883, 1886
The Eagle
Illinois Record, Springfield, 1897–1899
Muhammad Speaks, 1960–1975
Muslim Journal, 1985–1986
The State Capital, Springfield, 1891–1892, 1899
The World, 1900

Manuscript Sources:
Personal Papers, Slave Records, and Diaries

Brotherhood of Sleeping Car Porters. Papers, 1925–69 (ICHi)
  Membership records and letters. MS 71–41
Hector Davis and Company Account Books, 1857–65 (ICHi)
  Richmond, Virginia, company, with superior ledgers of slave
  sales and food and doctor bills.
WPA Illinois Writers' Project (IC-H)
  Files for "The Negro in Illinois," including interviews with early
  black settlers conducted in 1938–40.

Internet Resources

The Illinois State Archives web page at **http://www.library. sos.state.il.us/departments/archives/databases.html** has several searchable online databases available. One valuable database is *Servitude and Emancipation Records (1722–1863)*, which has the following:

Edwards County—Servitude and Emancipation Records, 1815–1860
Gallatin County—Servitude Register, 1815–1839
Pope County—Servitude Register, 1816–1819
Randolph County—Record Book 1, 1736–1782; Deed Record J–M,
  1797–1815; Servitude and Emancipation Registers, 1809–1863;
  Kaskaskia Manuscripts, 1714–1816
St. Clair County—Registers of insinuations, 1737–1769; Records of
  Auctions of Charleville Estate, 1782; Deed Record A–C, 1790–
  1796 and 1800–1813; Servitude Register, 1805–1832; 1846–
  1863; Slaves Registration Files, 1807–1849; Emancipation
  Register, 1812–1843
Union County—Emancipation Register, 1833–1844

Research Contacts

Afro-American Historical and Genealogical Society–Patricia Liddell
Researchers
P.O. Box 438652
Chicago, IL 60643

Carter G. Woodson Regional Library of The Chicago Public Library
Vivian G. Harsh Research Collection of Afro-American History and
Literature
9525 S. Halsted Street
Chicago, IL 60628
http://www.chipublib.org/002branches/woodson/wnharsh.html

Newberry Library
60 West Walton Street
Chicago, IL 60610-7324
http://www.newberry.org/

A major resource for African Americans is the Pullman Company
archives at the Newberry Library, which includes records of the Pullman porters, busboys, attendants, cooks, conductors, administration, and
other employees; Record Group 60: central office records, insurance,
social security applications, porters application index and register, disability payment records, refined pension files, deceased employees, prior
service records.

Chicago Historical Society Library
1601 N. Clark Street
Chicago, IL 60614
http://www.chicagohs.org/

Large manuscript collection, including bills of sale (some in French),
marriage certificates, manumissions, and indentures.

The Illinois State Historical Library
Old State Capitol
Springfield, IL 62701-1507
http://www.state.il.us/hpa/lib/

An extensive collection of newspapers and audiovisual and research
materials, covering all aspects of Illinois history.

National Archives and Records Administration-Great Lakes Region
7358 S. Pulaski Road
Chicago, IL 60629
http://www.nara.gov/regional/chicago.html

Records available at NARA Great Lakes Region include Chicago City Directories: 1839, 1844, 1871, 1880, 1890, 1900, 1910 and 1917; Indexes to Rosters of Railway Postal Clerks, ca. 1883 to ca. 1902. M2077; and Registered Voters and Poll of 1888–1890: City of Chicago-Board of Election Commissioners, City of Chicago, Hyde Park and township of Lake.

Bibliography

Abstracts of Funeral Programs: 1938–1995, Patricia Liddell Researchers Collection, vols. 1–2. Chicago, 1995.
The organizations' Funeral Program Collection consists of over 2,500 funeral programs.

Chavers-Wright, Madrue. *The Guarantee. P. W. Chavers: Banker, Entrepreneur, Philanthropist in Chicago's Black Belt of the Twenties.* New York: Wright-Armistead, 1985.
Information on the Chavers' family, Baker, Bannister, Calloway and Pannell families and historical information on Chicago's early twentieth-century "black belt."

Chicago Edition Black's Blue Book. 1923–1924. (Newberry Library).

Colored People's Blue Book and Business Directory of Chicago, Illinois 1905. Chicago: Celebrity, 1905. (Newberry Library).

Davis, Elizabeth Lindsay. *The Story of the Illinois Federation of Colored Women's Clubs.* Chicago: Illinois Federation of Colored Women's Clubs, 1922.

Dorsey, James. *Up South: Blacks in Chicago's Suburbs.* Bristol, Ind.: Wyndham Hall Press, 1986.

Eisenberg, Marcia, comp. "Blacks in the 1850 Federal Census City of Chicago, Cook County, Illinois," *AAHGS Journal,* 6:1 (Spring 1985).

Furgel, Suzanne Kersten. "Blacks and Mulattoes in the First and Second Wards of Chicago, Illinois as Found in the 1860 Federal Census," *AAHGS Journal,* 6:3 (Fall 1985).

_____. "Blacks and Mulattoes in Wards Eight, Nine and Ten of Chicago, Cook County, Illinois, as Enumerated in the 1860 Federal Census," *AAHGS Journal,* 6:3 (Fall 1985).

Harris, Norman Dwight. *The History of Negro Servitude in Illinois and of Slavery Agitations in that State, 1719–1864.* Westport, Ct.: Greenwood Publishing Company, 1969.
This book starts by giving a background on the beginning of slavery in Illinois, reporting that on June 6, 1719, 500 slaves

arrived in Lower Louisiana from Guinea. Many of these slaves migrated up the Mississippi River with their masters to Illinois Territory. The book's footnoting is superior and gives excellent indications of location of records. Examples include bills of sale (p. 258) and registers of free Negroes for many counties (pp. 245–57), as well as numerous other sources on blacks. An essential book for research in Illinois.

Historical Registers of National Homes for Disabled Volunteer Soldiers, 1866–1938.
Records relating to Branch Homes in Dayton, Ohio; Danville, Illinois; Marion, Indiana; and Milwaukee, Wisconsin.

Howard, Robert P. *Illinois: A History of the Prairie State.* Grand Rapids, Mich.: William B. Eerdmans Publishing, 1992.

Husband, Lori. *Deaths in the Chicago Defender 1919–1920.* Park Forest, Ill.: Author, 1990.

_____. *World I Draftees: Districts 3, 4, 5 and 70.* Park Forest, Ill.: Author, 1990.

Marriage Book E, Fulton County, Illinois, 1874–1885. Fulton County, Ill.: Fulton County Historical and Genealogical Society, 1990.

Marriage Records of DeKalb County, Illinois; Marriage Book D: July 1870. Marriage Book E: May 1874–December 1877. The Genealogical Society of DeKalb County, Ill., 1988.

Muirhead, John W. *A History of African-Americans in McLean County, Illinois, 1835–1975.* Bloomington, Ill.: McLean County Historical Society, 1998.

Norton, Margaret C. *Illinois Census Returns, 1810 and 1818.* Illinois State Historical Library Historical Collections, no. 24. 1935. Reprint. Baltimore: Genealogical Publishing Company, 1969.

_____. *Illinois Census Returns, 1820.* Reprint. Baltimore: Clearfield Company, 1996.
Both this and the above book by Norton are excellent census reproductions, giving listings of free blacks and white slave owners, in addition to the usual information. They can be purchased through the publisher if not available at a local library.

Ogden, Mary Elaine. *The Chicago Negro Community: A Statistical Description.* Chicago: W. P.A., 1939(7).

Pratt, Mildred. *We the People Tell Our Story: Bloomington-Normal Black History Project.* Normal, Ill.: Bloomington-Normal Black History Project, 1987.

Rather, Ernest. *Chicago Negro Almanac and Reference Book.* Chicago: Chicago Negro Almanac Publishing Company, 1972.

Sanders, Walter R. "The Negro in Montgomery County, Illinois," *Illinois State Genealogical Society Quarterly* 10:1 (Spring 1978).

Sapp, Peggy Lathrop. *Madison County Court Records (1813–1818) and Indenture Records 1805–1826, Register of Slaves, Indentured Servants & Free Persons of Color.* Springfield, Ill.: Folkworks, 1993.

Some Chicago Defender Deaths, 1936–1938. Chicago: Patricia Liddell Researchers, 1996. Surname File Index.

The Colored Men's Professional and Business Directory. Chicago: I. C. Harris, 1885.

The History of St. Paul C.M.E. Church: Chicago, Illinois, 1907–1988. Chicago: Margaret U. Ferguson Publication, 1988.

Tingley, Donald E. *The Structuring of a State: The History of Illinois, 1899–1928.* Urbana, Ill., 1980.

Tregillis, Helen Cox. *River Roads to Freedom: Fugitive Slave Notices and Sheriff Notices Found in Illinois Sources.* Bowie, Md.: Heritage Books, 1988.

Washington Intercollegiate Club of Chicago. Frederic H. Robb, editor-in-chief. Chicago: 1927.

Williams, Nola Jones. *Lincoln School Memories: A History of Blacks in Edwardsville, Illinois.* Wheaton, Ill.: Williams, 1986.

Thanks to Thelma Strong Eldridge, President AAHGS/Chicago Chapter for her contribution to this chapter.

Indiana

Important Dates

1746 – Five African-Americans in Indiana were among a group of over forty men at a post on the Wabash River.

1763 – The British took over the region and a cargo of African Americans purchased in Jamaica was brought to the area through Kaskaskia, Illinois on the Mississippi River.

1787 – The Northwest Ordinance of 1787 forbade slavery in Indiana.

1803 – The Vincennes Convention of 1803 petitioned Congress to permit slavery in Indiana.

1810 – Most slaves began arriving with white settlers around 1810, coming mainly from Kentucky, South Carolina, Tennessee, and Virginia. Most settled first in Knox County before moving to other areas. African Americans were required to register with the courts upon emigration to the Northwest Territory after 1831.

1820 – One hundred and ninety African Americans/Native Americans were officially enslaved under laws permitting the transport of slaves into the territory, and several hundred more came as indentured servants.

1820 – The Indiana Supreme Court recognized the 1816 state constitutional abolition of slavery.

1860 – A total of 11,428 African Americans were in the state, with the largest group coming from North Carolina, followed by Virginia, Kentucky, Ohio, and Tennessee. A low total of 329 came from South Carolina, Georgia, Mississippi, Alabama, and Louisiana combined.

1870-1880 – The Emigrant Aid Society, sponsored by the Society of Friends, helped thousands of African Americans migrate from North Carolina to Indianapolis.

1880s – More African Americans migrated from Kentucky and Tennessee, but some Indiana counties barred their entry.

State Archives

Indiana Commission on Public Records
State Archives Division
6440 E. 30th Street
Indianapolis, IN 46219
http://www.in.gov/icpr/archives

The official repository of state governmental records, its extensive database also includes many county and local records, as well as a listing for African-American family history research.

Census Records

Federal Census Records

1820–1880 and 1900–1930 (DNA); 1820–1880, 1900–1920 (InFw, In, and Valparaiso, Rockville, La Porte public libraries). Other libraries in the state have records for a few years.

Mortality Records

1850–1880 (In)

State and County Records

Birth-Marriage-Divorce-Death Records

Vital Records Department
Indiana State Department of Health
2 N. Meridian Street
Indianapolis, IN 46204
http://www.in.gov/isdh/index.htm

The state began keeping vital records in 1900 for deaths, 1907 for births, and 1958 for marriages. Earlier birth and death records are found at the county health departments, while earlier marriage records are located at the Clerk of the Circuit Court. The Vital Records Department's web site provides detailed information about availability of records and where to find them.

Other State and County Records

Many free blacks acquired land upon arrival and their names were, consequently, entered into land records. In most cases there are no racial designations, but knowing the name will then make it possible to trace the ownership of land. These land entries have been copied by Margaret R. Walters and are available at the Indiana State Library.

The Order Book of the General Court of Indiana Territory, the Order Book of the Court of Common Pleas, and the circuit court records of Knox, Harrison, and Clark counties all contain manumission records and other matters pertaining to slaves and free blacks. One example of the kind of record kept is as follows:

Clark County
> Register of Negroes, 1805–10 (In)

Cemetery and Church Records

Cemetery Records

Indiana State Library has some cemetery records specifically related to African Americans and an online searchable cemetery locator index.

Church Records

St. Francis Xavier Parish Records, 1749–1838 (In). Six volumes of records with some baptisms of blacks, from the period beginning in 1753.

Military Records

The Fred J. Reynolds Historical Genealogy Department of the Allen County Indiana Public Library (see "Research Contacts" below) holds an extensive collection of genealogical research material. Military records held include most microfilmed National Archives service and pension records covering every conflict from the Revolutionary War through the Philippine Insurrection. The collection is now expanding into data on 20th-century conflicts, with additions of unit histories for WWI and WWII, and casualty lists for the Korean War, Vietnam War, and Persian Gulf War.

Newspapers

In addition to the collections cited below for the *Freeman*, the Allen County Public Library has a large microfilm collection of African-American newspapers.

Freeman (Indianapolis). 1884–1926? Weekly. Holdings: December 2, 1886, to 1916 (incomplete); CSdS, CSS, CtY, DLC, InNd, MB, MdBJ, MnU, MoSW, NcU, NiP, TNF, TxF, TxFS. July 21, 1888, to 1916 (incomplete); CU, FTaSU, ICU, McP, WHi. February 1892 to November 1, 1924.

Manuscript Sources: Personal Papers, Slave Records, and Diaries

Indiana Historical Society Library (see "Research Contacts" below) has a card file containing references to material on African Americans in Indiana, including fugitive slave cases. See Eric Pumroy's *A Guide to Manuscript Collections of the Indiana Historical Society & Indiana State Library* (Indianapolis: Indiana Historical Society, 1986).

Internet Resources

See the impressive Allen County Public Library (**http://www.acpl.lib.in.us/genealogy/whoweare.html#**) and Indiana State Library and Historical Building (**http://www.statelib.lib.in.us/**) web sites.

Research Contacts

Indiana State Library and Historical Building
140 N. Senate Avenue
Indianapolis, IN 46204
http://www.statelib.lib.in.us/

The Library's impressive list of searchable databases includes a section on African-American genealogy sources in the state and elsewhere.

Allen County Public Library
900 Webster Street
Fort Wayne, IN 46802
http://www.acpl.lib.in.us/genealogy/whoweare.html#

The library, undergoing a major expansion, is already one of the largest public libraries with extensive genealogical resources in the country. The "Genealogy" link on the library's web site is not specific to Indiana, but provides useful links to the world of genealogical research in general.

Bibliography

Gibbs, Wilma L. *Indiana's African-American Heritage: Essays from Black History News & Notes.* Indianapolis: Indiana Historical Society, 1993.
Discusses education, the history of African-American women in Indiana, early African-American rural settlements, art and architecture, and historical societies.

Hine, Darlene Clark. *The Black Women in the Middle West Project: A Comprehensive Resource Guide. Illinois and Indiana.* Indianapolis: Indiana Historical Bureau, 1986.
The book records the historical experiences and the accomplishments of African-American women and their organizations throughout Indiana and Illinois.

Lyda, John W. *The Negro in the History of Indiana.* Terre Haute, Ind.: Author, 1953.

Madison, James H. *Through Tradition and Change: A History of the Hoosier State and Its People. 1920–1945.* Indianapolis, Ind.: Indiana Historical Society, 1982.

Paul, Dorothy, ed., and Jean Spears, comp. *Admission Record, Indianapolis Asylum for Friendless Colored Children, 1871–1900.* Indianapolis: Indiana Historical Society, 1978.
An alphabetical arrangement of children in the orphanage, the book includes the date of admission, dates of transfer, some birth and death dates, and names of parents.

Robbins, Coy D. *Forgotten Hoosiers: African Heritage in Orange County, Indiana.* Bowie, Md.: Heritage Books, 1994.
The founding of the Lick Creek Settlement.

_____. *Reclaiming African-American Heritage at Salem, Indiana.* Bowie, Md.: Heritage Books Incorporated, 1995.
Provides genealogical information—as well as charts, maps, and tables—on African Americans from Kentucky, North Carolina, and Virginia who settled in the area.

_____. *African-American Heritage in Morgan County, Indiana.* Bloomington, Ind.: African-American Historical and Genealogical Society, 1991.

_____. *Indiana Negro Registers, 1852–1865*. Bowie, Md.: Heritage Books, Inc., 1994.
This volume is a compilation of fifteen "Registers of Negroes and Mulattoes" maintained by the Clerk of County Courts between 1852 and 1865.

Rudolph, L. C. *Religion in Indiana: A Guide to Historical Resources*. Ann Arbor, Mich.: Books on Demand, 1986.
The subject index lists over sixty entries for African-American churches.

Sprinkles, Dallas W. *The History of Evansville Blacks*. Evansville, Ind.: Mid-America Enterprises, 1974.

Thornbrough, Emma Lou. *The Negro in Indiana Before 1900*. Bloomington: Indiana University Press, 1993.

_____. *The Negro in Indiana: A Study of a Minority*. Indiana Historical Collections, vol. 37. Indianapolis: Indiana Historical Bureau, 1957.

Witcher, Curt Bryan. *Bibliography of Sources for Black Family History in the Allen County Public Library Genealogy Department*. Fort Wayne, Ind.: The Library, 1989.

Iowa

Important Dates

1839 – Beginning April 1, 1839, no black or mulatto was permitted to settle in Iowa unless he or she could present "a fair certificate of actual freedom under a seal of a judge and give bond of $500 as surety against becoming public charges." This obviously prevented many free blacks from coming to Iowa.

1865 – The African-American population in Iowa tripled. Most of those coming into Iowa came from Missouri and other points down the Mississippi and Ohio rivers.

State Archives

State Historical Society of Iowa
600 East Locust
Des Moines, IA 50319-0290
http://www.iowahistory.org/

The mission of the Society's library and archives is to identify, record, collect, preserve, and share research on Iowa history.

Census Records

Federal Census Records

1840–1930 (DNA) (IQCFr)

Mortality Records

1850–80 (IaHi)

Special Census Records

The state of Iowa has conducted state censuses since 1836. Not all counties/cities are included in these special state and territorial censuses. See **http://iagenweb.org/state/census/iayears.htm** for an explanation of what is covered in each census.

State and County Records

Birth-Marriage-Divorce-Death Records

Iowa Department of Public Health
321 East 12th Street, 4th Floor
Des Moines, IA 50319
http://www.idph.state.ia.us/pa/vr.htm

Iowa began recording vital events on a statewide basis in 1880, although many counties have records that pre-date statewide recording.

Cemetery and Church Records

Iowa Conference Historical Society of the United Methodist Church. Records, 1844–? (IaU). Records of freedmen's organization.

Military Records

Strong, George W. Papers, 1863–1908 (IaU). Collection includes letters, memos, orders, and supplies of Strong as Commander of Company H, 1st Regiment of Tennessee Infantry, African Descent and 59th Colored Infantry, Regiment 16th Corps, 1863-65.

Adjutant-General's Office. *Roster and Register of Iowa Soldiers in the War of Rebellion. 32d-48th Regiments-Infantry, 1st Regiment African Infantry and 1st-4th Batteries Light Artillery.* Vol. 5. Des Moines: E.H. Engist, State Printer, 1908–11 (IaHi). Lists the members of the only black regiment from Iowa in the Civil War.

Newspapers

Iowa Bystander (Des Moines). 1894– . Weekly. Title varies as *Bystander*; *Iowa State Bystander*. Holdings: 1896– ; IaDH. 1896–1900; Csds, CtY, DLC, FTaSU, IaMpl, InNd, MB, MdBJ, MnU, MoSW, NcU, NiP, TNF, WHi.

Manuscript Sources: Personal Papers, Slave Records, and Diaries

Iowa Wesleyan College Archives, Mt. Pleasant (IaMpl). First black students' graduation, 1885; 1887; 1891.

Internet Resources

See the State Historical Society web page at **http://www.iowahistory.org**.

Bibliography

Bergmann, Leola Nelson. *The Negro in Iowa*. Iowa City, Iowa, 1969.

Dykstra, Robert R. *Bright Radical Star: Black Freedom & White Supremacy on the Hawkeye Frontier*. Ames: Iowa State University Press, 1997.

Goudy, Willis, and Rogelio Saenz. *Iowa's Black Residents*. Ames: Cooperative Extension Service, Iowa State University, 1983.

Hill, James L. "Migration of Blacks to Iowa: 1820–1960." *Journal of Negro History, 66* (1981–1982): 289–303.

Schwieder, Dorothy. *Buxton: Work and Racial Equality in a Coal Mining Community*. Ames: Iowa State University, 1987.

Kansas

Important Dates

1861 – Kansas entered the union as a free state.

1865 – Kansas's African-American population increased to 12,527.

1877 – A second great wave of black migration to Kansas began, establishing several all-black communities, the best known of which was Nicodemus in western Kansas.

State Archives

Kansas State Historical Society
Center for Historical Research
Reference Department
6425 S.W. Sixth Avenue
Topeka, KS 66615-1099
http://www.kshs.org/research/collections/documents/govtrecords/ index.htm

Since 1905, the historical society has served as the state's archives, collecting unpublished state documents, as well as county and local official records.

Federal Records

Federal Census Records

*1860–1880, 1900–1930 (DNA); 1860–1880, 1900–1920 (KH, and Wichita and Lawrence Public libraries)

---

*Two slaves are listed in the 1860 census for Anderson County. They are included in the population schedules and are the only slaves reported in the entire state.

Mortality Records

1860–1880 (DNA, DNDAR)

Special State Census Records (KH)

1855 census: lists eligible voters with ages given by decimals. Some entries list names of family members; some give only the number of members.

1865 census: lists all members of the household by name, and gives age, sex, race or color, state or country of birth, marital status, and military records, including company and regiment.

1875 census: same as 1865, with the addition of last place of residence before coming to Kansas.

1885 census: same as 1875; in addition, the following is added to the military records: condition of discharge, state of enlistment, and name of prison, if confined in one.

1895, 1905, and 1915 censuses: same as 1885.

1925 census: same as 1885, with the addition of relationship to head of household, year of immigration to the United States, and year of naturalization, if applicable.

State and County Records

Birth-Marriage-Divorce-Death Records

Kansas State Vital Records Office
Office of Vital Statistics
1000 S.W. Jackson Street, Suite 120
Topeka, KS 66612-2221
http://www.kdhe.state.ks.us/vital/index.html

The state office holds birth and death records from 1911, marriage records from 1913, and divorce records from 1951. Before 1911 the county clerk recorded births and deaths, and the probate court recorded marriages and divorces. County records vary, although generally they begin in the 1880s.

Military Records

In addition to the standard military sources for those who served from Kansas, the Kansas State Historical Society has records of the Buffalo Soldiers (African-American soldiers who remained in the U.S. Army following the Civil War, in the Ninth and Tenth Cavalry regiments).

Newspapers

Kansas is blessed with an exceptional collection of newspapers published by and for African Americans.

Afro-American Advocate (Coffeyville). September 2, 1891, to September 1, 1893. Weekly. Holdings: 1891–93 (incomplete); CSdS, CtY, DLC, InNd, KH, MB, MdBJ, MnU, NcU, NjP, TNF, WHi.

American (Coffeyville). February 19, 1898, to 1899. Weekly. Holdings: April 23, 1898, to April 1, 1899 (incomplete); CSdS, CtY, DLC, InNd, KH, MB, MdBJ, MnU, NcU, NjP, TNF, WHi.

American Citizen (Kansas City). July 26, 1889, to 1909? Weekly. Holdings: 1889 to August 2, 1907 (incomplete); CSdS, CtY, CU, DLC, FTaSU, InNd, KH, MB, MnU, NjP, TNF, WHi.

American Citizen (Topeka). Holdings: February 23, 1888, to July 19, 1889; CSdS, DLC, InNd, KH, MB, MdBJ, NcU, NjP, TNF, WHi.

Atchison Blade. July 23, 1892, to January 20? 1894. Weekly. Holdings: July 23, 1892, to January 20? 1894; CSdS, CtY, DLC, FTaSU, InNd, KH, MdBJ, MnU, NcU, NjP, TNF, WHi.

Benevolent Banner (Topeka). May 21 ? 1887, to ? Weekly. Holdings: May 21 and October 22, 1887; CSdS, CSS, DLC, KH, LU-NO, MdBMC, MiKW, TNF, WHi.

Colored Citizen (Fort Scott). April 19 to July 5, 1878. Weekly. Holdings: April 19 to July 5, 1878; CSdS, CtY, DLC, InNd, KH, MB, MdBJ, MnU, NcU, NjP.

Colored Citizen (Topeka). July 26, 1878, to 1880?; June 17, 1897, to 1900? Weekly. See also the *Topeka Tribune* (below). Holdings: July 26, 1878, to December 27, 1879; June 17, 1897, to November 16, 1900 (incomplete); CSdS, CtY, DLC, InNd, KH, MB, MdBJ, MnU, NcU, NjP, TNF, WHi.

Colored Patriot (Topeka). 1882–? Weekly. Holdings: April 29 to June 22, 1882; CSdS, CSS, CU, DLC, KH, LU-NO, MdBMC, MiKW, TNF, WHi.

Herald of Kansas (Topeka). January 30 to June 11, 1880? Weekly. Holdings: January to June 1880; CSdS, CSS, CU, DLC, KH, LU-NO, MdBMC, MiKW, TNF, WHi.

Kansas State Ledger (Topeka). July 22, 1892, to June 16? 1906. Weekly. Title varies as *State Ledger.* Holdings: 1892–1906 (incomplete); CSdS, CtY, DLC, FTaSU, InNd, KH, MB, MdBJ, MnU, NcU, NjP, TNF, WHi.

Leavenworth Advocate, 1888 to August 22, 1891, Weekly. Continued by *Times Observer*, Topeka. Holdings: August 18, 1888, to 1891; CSdS, CtY, DLC, InNd, KH, MB, MdBJ, MnU, NcU, NjP, TNF, WHi. 1887 to July 19, 1889. Weekly.

Leavenworth Herald. 1894–1899? Weekly. Holdings: 1894–98 (incomplete); CSdS, CtY, DLC, KH, MB, MdBJ, MnU, NcU, NjP, WHi.

Parsons Weekly Blade. August 20? 1892, to December 27, 1901? Weekly. Holdings: September 24, 1892, to 1900 (incomplete); CSdS, CtY, DLC, InNd, KH, MB, MdBJ, MnU, NcU, NjP, TNF, WHi.

Pittsburg Plaindealer. May 20? 1899, to May? 1900. Weekly. Continued by the *Wichita Searchlight.* Holdings: August 1899 to May 12, 1900 (incomplete); CSdS, CtY, DLC, InNd, KH, MB, MdBJ, MnU, NcU, NjP, TNF, WHi.

Topeka Tribune. 1880–18813 Weekly. Continues the *Colored Citizen*, July 26, 1878, to 1803 (cited above). Holdings: June 24 to December 25, 1880; CSdS, CtY, CU, DLC, InNd, KH, MB, MdBJ, MnU, NcU, NjP, TNF, WHi.

Weekly Call (Topeka). May 33 1891, to 1898? Weekly. Title varies as *Topeka Call.* Holdings: June 28, 1891, to October 29, 1898; CSdS, CtY, DLC, InNd, MB, MdBJ, MnU, NjP, TNF, WHi.

Manuscript Sources: Personal Papers, Slave Records, and Diaries

Freedmen's Relief Association Papers, 1879–81 (KH)
    Activities and recipients of organizational help.
Marstella Family Papers, 1810–54 (KXSM)
    Collection containing indenture papers, lists of slaves, circuit court papers on runaway slaves, and records of the value and disposition of slaves.
Slave Papers, 1824–65 (KXSM)
    Eight bills of sale for slaves.

Internet Resources

In addition to the Kansas State Historical Society's web page on African-American history (**http://www.kshs.org/research/collections/ documents/bibliographies/ethnic/african_american.htm**), there's a site currently under development that provides state and worldwide resources for the African-American researcher (**http://www.afrigeneas.com/states/ ks/**). See also a web site devoted to the history of Nicodemus, Kansas maintained by the Nicodemus Historical Society (**http://www.coax.net/ people/lwf/nic_mig.htm**).

Research Contacts

Kansas Collection at Kansas City Public Library
625 Minnesota Avenue
Kansas City, KS 66101
http://www.kckpl.lib.ks.us/kscoll/kscoll2.htm

Located at the Main Branch of the Kansas City Public Library, the special Collections Department (**http://www.kclibrary.org/sc/ethnic/ africanamer/resources.htm**) includes useful information on African Americans in Kansas, particularly on families who settled or lived around Kansas City, Kansas.

Bibliography

Athearn, Robert G. *In Search of Canaan: Black Migration to Kansas, 1879–80*. Lawrence: University Press of Kansas. 1978.

Bruce, Henry Clay. *The New Man: Twenty-Nine Years a Slave, Twenty-Nine Years a Free Man, Recollections of H.C. Bruce*. Lincoln: University of Nebraska Press, 1996.

Chu, Daniel, and Bill Shaw. *Going Home to Nicodemus: The Story of an African-American Frontier Town and the Pioneers Who Settled It*. Parsippany, N.J.: Silver Burden Press. 1995. [A book for young readers.]

Cordley, Richard. *A History of Lawrence, Kansas from the First Settlement to the Close of the Rebellion*. Reprint. Bowie, Md.: Heritage Books Incorporated, 1991.

Cox, Thomas C. *Blacks in Topeka Kansas, 1865–1915*. Baton Rouge, La.: Louisiana State University Press, 1982.

Crockett, Norman L. *The Black Town*. Lawrence, Kan.: Regents Press of Kansas, 1979.

Kansas State Historical Society. *In Search of the American Dream: The Experiences of Blacks in Kansas, A Resource Booklet for Teachers*. Topeka, Kan.: Kansas State Historical Society, 1984.

Kentucky

Important Dates

1751 – An African-American servant in the company of Christopher Gist came into the territory along the Ohio River.

1760 – An African-American slave traveled with Daniel Boone across the Blue Ridge Mountains during the hunting season.

1777 – The African-American population grew rapidly during the pioneer period, comprising about 10 percent of the inhabitants.

1790 – Kentucky was home to 11,830 slaves and 114 free blacks.

1860 – The African-American free population numbered 10,684.

1870 – African Americans won voting rights.

State Archives

Kentucky Department for Library and Archives
300 Coffee Tree Road
P.O. Box 537
Frankfort, KY 40602-0537
http://www.kdla.state.ky.us/

Responsible for the equitable access to public records and information, the Kentucky Department for Library and Archives [KDLA] provides oversight to libraries and public records statewide. Online databases and a guide to African-American research are among its numerous and varied sources.

Federal Records

Federal Census Records

1810–1880, 1900–1930 (DNA), 1810–1920 (KyLoF, KyHi, KyBqW). Also available for some years at other public libraries.

Mortality Records

1850–1880 (DNA, DNDAR)

Slave Schedules

1850, 1860 (DNA)

Special Census

1890: Civil War Union Veterans and Widows (partial)

State and County Records

Birth-Marriage-Divorce-Death Records

Kentucky State Vital Records Office
Office of Vital Statistics
275 East Main Street
Frankfort, KY 40621
http://publichealth.state.ky.us/vital.htm

Kentucky began keeping vital records in 1852, but the law mandating this was repealed in 1862 and not reinstated until 1911. Vital records exist between 1852–1859 and then scattered records until 1911. The Kentucky Department for Libraries and Archives has an excellent description of available records on its web site (**http://www.kdla.state. ky.us/arch/vitastat.htm**), with links to the University of Kentucky online index of vital records (Deaths 1911–1992; Marriages 1973–1993; Divorces 1873–1993).

Other State and County Records

The Kentucky Historical Society in Frankfort (see "Research Contacts" below) has extensive records for every county, including wills, marriages, births, and deaths for 1852–61 and 1874–78; pensions; cemetery records; and tax records. In addition, excellent collections of Kentucky state and county histories are available.

Examples of county records available in other parts of the state are as follows:

Breckenridge County Courthouse
Eighty volumes of deeds, including slave deeds and affidavits of slave ownership filed when entering the state.

Jessamine County Courthouse
   Deed books with slave sale records, dates not noted.
Meade County Courthouse
   Life estate records with affidavits of slave ownership.

Cemetery and Church Records

Cemetery Records

The Kentucky Historical Society (see "Research Contacts" below) maintains an extensive statewide index of cemetery records.

Church Records

Beech Creek Baptist Church, Shelby County, 1825–40 (KyLoF). List of black members.
   Buffalo Lick Baptist Church, 1805–38 (KyLoF). List of black members.
   Christenburg Baptist Church, 1810–75 (KyLoF). Church records, including black members.
   Newburg Christian Church, Newburg, Kentucky (KyLoF). Church records; list of black members.

Military Records

Record Group 109, "War Department Collection of Confederate Records" (DNA). Regiments, battalions, and companies of Kentucky troops, including a list of black cooks.
   Record Group 94, "Records of the Adjutant General's Office, 1780's–1917" (DNA). Slave Claims Commission register of claims for Kentucky, 1864–67.

Newspapers

Lexington Standard. 1892–1912? Weekly. Holdings: March 1900 to February 7, 1903; KyLxT January 27, 1900; CSdS, CSS, CU, DLC FTaSU, KH, LU-NO, MdBMC, MiKW, TNF.

Manuscript Sources: Personal Papers, Slave Records, and Diaries

Bills of Sale, Kentucky Papers, 1787–1883 (NHi)
> Records for Fayette and Lincoln counties. MS 66–1792

Hickman-Bryan. Papers, 1796–1920 (MoU)
> Missouri, Louisiana, and Kentucky families with land and slave records. MS 60–1817

Kentucky Colonization Society Reports and *African Repository*, 1830–74 (KyBqW)
> Includes diaries and letters from Liberia. Library also has an excellent research collection, which needs to be surveyed for black genealogical material.

Strange, Agatha Jane (Rochester). Papers, 1852–89 (KyBgW)
> Includes slave records of families in Bowling Green. MS 70–2088

Another large group of slavery materials can be found at the Kentucky Historical Society in Frankfort (see "Research Contacts" below). Materials include slave compensation papers, emancipations, deeds, bills of sale for slaves, evaluation paper for slaves, and an extensive collection of Kentucky family Bibles.

Hord, William, 1798–1823 (KyLoF)
> Account book with list of black births and the names of their children.

Miller, Howard, 1857–67; 1878–88 (KyLoF)
> Civil War diary of events involving freeing of the slaves.

Taylor, Francis, 1786–92; 1794–99 (KyLoF)
> Midland Plantation business and military pursuits in Orange County, Virginia, and Kentucky.

Internet Resources

See the web sites of the Kentucky Department for Library and Archives (**http://www.kyhistory.org/**) and the Kentucky Historical Society Library (**http://www.kdla.net/links/blackhis.htm**).

Research Contacts

Kentucky Historical Society Library
100 West Broadway
Old Capitol Annex   *Mailing Address:* P.O. Box 1792
Frankfort, KY 40601   Frankfort, KY 40602-1792
http://www.kyhistory.org/

Bibliography

Brown, Richard C. "The Free Blacks of Boyle County, Kentucky, 1850–1860." *The Register of the Kentucky Historical Society.* 87 (1989) 426–438.

Byars, Lauretta. "Lexington's Colored Orphan Industrial Home, 1892–1913." *The Register of the Kentucky Historical Society.* 89 (1991) 147–178.

Craven, Patricia and Richard Pangbum. *From Out of the Dark Past Their Eyes Implore Us: The Black Roots of Nielson County, Kentucky Research.* Bardstown, Ky.: P. Craven, R. Pangburn, 1996.

Dunnigan, Alice Allison. *The Fascinating Story of Black Kentuckians: Their Heritage and Traditions.* Washington, D.C., 1962.
History of blacks and famous blacks in Kentucky.

Howard, Victor. *Black Liberation in Kentucky: Emancipation & Freedom, 1862–1884.* Ann Arbor: Books on Demand, n.d.
History of black participation in the Civil War.

Johnson, William Decker. *Biographical Sketches of Prominent Negro Men and Women of Kentucky.* Manchester: Ayer Company Publishers, 1977.

Lucas, Marion B. *A History of Blacks in Kentucky: From Slavery to Segregation, 1760–1891.* Vol. 1. Frankford, Ky.: Kentucky Historical Society, 1992.

Montell, William Lynwood. *The Saga of Coe Ridge: A Study in Oral History.* Knoxville: University of Tennessee Press, 1970.
This history of a black town in Monroe County, Kentucky is based on interviews with the inhabitants. It includes a short genealogy of both the black and white branches of the Coe family.

Streets, David H. *Slave Genealogy: A Research Guide with Case Studies.* Bowie, Md.: Heritage Books, 1989.
Three case studies that use Wayne County, Kentucky records are included.

Sue, Jacqueline Annette. *Black Seeds in The Blue Grass.* Corte Maderea, Calif.: Khedcanron Publishing, 1983.

Thomas, Herbert A., Jr. "Victims of Circumstance: Negroes in a Southern Town, 1865–1880." *Register of the Kentucky Historical Society,* 71(3):253–271.

Wright, George C. *A History of Blacks in Kentucky in Pursuit of Equality, 1890–1980.* Frankfort, Ky., 1992.
This volume follows up on Marion Lucas's work listed above and is considered a must—read for understanding African-American history in Kentucky.

_____. *Life Behind a Veil: Blacks in Louisville.* Baton Rouge, La., 1985.
A well-researched and documented book of black life in Louisville from the end of the Civil War until 1930.

Louisiana

Important Dates

1709 – The first two blacks came to the French colony of Louisiana as slaves of Governor Jean Baptiste.

1782 – Spain imposed a duty on slave imports in order to encourage trading.

1844 – There were 464 plantations of 200 acres or more.

1860 – There were 400,000 slaves in the state, clustered in the southeast and near the Mississippi and Red rivers.

State Archives

Louisiana State Archives
3851 Essen Lane
Baton Rouge, LA 70809
http://www.sec.state.la.us/archives/archives/archives-index.htm

Louisiana is divided into jurisdictions called "parishes" instead of into counties. The State Archives is the agency responsible for the preservation of state and local governmental documents. The Archives' library maintains a searchable database of over 2 million names connected with the large variety of source materials for family history research.

Census Records

Federal Census Records

1810–1880, 1900–1930 (DNA, LU-Ar); many libraries throughout the state have schedules for some years.

Mortality Records

1850–1880 (DNA, DNDAR)

Slave Schedules

1850, 1860 (DNA)

Special Census

1890: Civil War Veterans and Widows

State Census

Louisiana has a number of census records for the pre-statehood period, some located in France and Spain. See the first edition of *Black Genesis* (1978) for listings, and consult the Louisiana State Archives holdings.

State and County Records

Birth-Marriage-Divorce-Death Records

Louisiana Office of Public Health
Vital Records Registry
P.O. Box 60630
New Orleans, LA 70160
http://oph.dhh.state.la.us/recordsstatistics/vitalrecords/

All marriage records—other than those of Orleans Parish, which are in the Louisiana State Archives—are kept by the parish clerk of the court. Birth, marriage, and death records for Orleans Parish and death records before 1950 for the remainder of the state can be viewed at the State Archives.

Cemetery and Church Records

St. Louis Cathedral Archives, New Orleans. First book of marriages of "Negroes and mulattoes" in the parish of St. Louis in the city of New Orleans, 1777–1830. Marriage register of "Negroes and mulattoes" of St. Louis Cathedral from July 1, 1720, to December 4, 1730. (See also "Internet Resources" below.)

Military Records

McConnell, Roland Calhoun. *Negro Troops of Antebellum Louisiana: A History of the Battalion of Free Men of Color.* Louisiana State University Studies, Social Science Series, no. 13. Baton Rouge: Louisiana State University Press, 1968.

Provides excellent background reading for tracing African-American veterans before the Civil War.

Newspapers

Black Republican (New Orleans). April 14, 1865, to ? Weekly. Holdings: April 15, 22, 29, May 13, 20, 1865; CSdS, CSS, CU, DLC, FTaSU, LU-NO, MdBMC, MiKW, TNF, WHi.

New Orleans Daily Creole. June 16, 1856, to ? Daily. Holdings: July 1856 to January 1857; CSdS, CSS, C+Y, DLC, InNd, LN, LU-NO, MdBJ, MnU, MoSW, McU, TxFS, WHi.

Semi-weekly Louisianian (New Orleans). December 18, 1870, to April 21, 1872. Semiweekly. Title varies as *Louisianian.* Continued by *Weekly Louisianian* (next entry). Holdings: 1870–72; CSS, C+Y, CU, DLC, InNd, LN, LU, LU-NO, MB, MdBJ, MnU, MoSW, NcU, NjP, TNF, TxFS, WHi.

Weekly Louisianian (New Orleans). April 27, 1872, to June 17, 1882. Weekly. Continues: *Semi-weekly Louisianian* (see above). Holdings: 1872–74; CSdS, CSS, Cty. DLC, InND, LN, LU, LU-NO, MB, MdBJ, MnU, MoSW, NcU, NjP, TNF, WHi.

Weekly Pelican (New Orleans). December 4, 1886, to 1889. Weekly. Holdings: December 1886 to November 1889; CSdS, CtY, DLC, InNd, LN, LU, LU-NO, MB, MdBJ, MnU, MoSW, NcU, TNF, WHi.

Manuscript Sources: Personal Papers, Slave Records, and Diaries

Bolton and Dickens Company Slave Trade Records (NHi)
A record of slave purchases and sales to the Memphis and New Orleans areas. Contains about 1,500 names of slaves.

Chelette, Atala. Family Papers, 1819–1919 (LU-Ar)
> Includes personal and business papers of Joseph Perot, free Negro, land and slave owner, and other papers of the family of free Negroes, of Natchitoches Parish, 1840–99. MS 71–241.

Descriptions of Slaves Being Transported (NHi)
> Manifests of "Negroes, Mulattoes, and Persons of Color" taken on board various vessels, particularly from Alexandria, Virginia. The manifests give slave's name, age, sex, height, color, and the owner of the shipper's name and place of residence. Many of the records indicate that the slaves were going to New Orleans.

Houmas Plantation James Amedee Gaudet Collection, #2334, 1785–1927. (NcU)
> Family and business papers of Gaudet, secretary-treasurer of the Miles Planting and Manufacturing Company, which controlled thirteen large sugar plantations; developer of a New Orleans subdivision; and business representative of William Porcher Miles. Series I contains papers relating to the ownership of the Houmas plantations and other Louisiana property, and includes lists of slaves and free blacks (1840s–1850s).

Martin, Charles. Civil War Papers
> Includes poll tax records of "colored people" in Louisiana. MS 62–4285

McCollam, Andrew. Papers, 1795–1935 (NcU)
> Planter of Donaldsonville. Papers include records of slaves. MS 64–1054

Murrell Family Papers, 1704–1886 (ViU)
> Correspondence includes sales of slaves of "Tally Ho" near New Orleans. MS 71–1960

New Orleans Slave Trade. 118 items (NNC)
> Miscellaneous sources and letters dealing with the slave trade to New Orleans, and police reports on blacks sentenced to gangs, 1780–1833.

New Orleans. Mayor. Papers, 1811–43 (NN-Sc)
> Papers, bonds, and reports of the Mayor on the employment of slaves.

Norton Family Papers, 1760–26 (NcU)
> Includes slave records (1820–32) for families in Virginia, Mississippi, and New Orleans. MS 64–594

Phanor Prudhomme Papers, #613, 1804–1940 (NcU)
> Primarily business papers and volumes of Phanor Prudhomme and later of J. Alphonse Prudhomme relating to cotton growing at the family plantation at Ile Breville (later called Bermuda), Natchitoches Parish, Louisiana. The papers include slave lists and items relating to the buying and selling of slaves (1804–

1854); a slave bill of sale from Francois Gacion Metoyer, a freedman, to Phanor Prudhomme (1857); notes on sending slaves to work on town fortifications (1862); and letters requesting safe passage to move slaves (1865). Plantation records include a slave work record (1836) and slave lists (1837, 1839–1842, 1856–1863, 1860–1864). The collection also contains records of accounts with freedmen (1866–1878). Many items in French; microfilm.

Slack Family Papers, #3598, 1805–1891 (NcU)
> Personal and family correspondence and financial, legal, and military papers of the Slack family of Iberville Parish, Louisiana. Originally from Massachusetts, the Slacks were first cotton and then sugar planters with some family members serving in the Confederacy. The collection contains papers relating to slave purchases and sales (1828, 1831), and a list of slave names.

Thompson Family Papers, #1460, 1809–1924 (NcU)
> Chiefly family letters and financial and legal materials of the Thompson family of Alabama, Louisiana, and Mississippi, and the related Malone family of Alabama. An account book belonging to Goodloe W. Malone contains a slave list of about seventy names and ages.

"U.S. Customs Service records, port of New Orleans, LA, inward slave manifests. 1807–1860" IMPRINT (Wilmington, Del.): Scholarly Resources, 1996, 12 microfilm reels.

Diaries

Anonymous, 1835–37 (LU-Ar)
> Plantation life.

Batchelor, Albert A., 1856–1930 (LU-Ar)
> Plantation life.

Bateman, (Mary), 1856 (LU-Ar)
> Her plantation life. Original manuscript is at the University of North Carolina.

Capell, Eli J., 1842–50; 1867 (LU-Ar)
> Pleasant Hill Plantation diary, Amite County, Mississippi.

DeClouet, Paul L., 1866–70; 1880–88 (LU-Ar)
> Plantation operations. MS 75–732

Foster, Robert Watson, 1862–64 (RHi)
> Plantation life near Apolousas, Louisiana.

Hickman-Bryan. Papers, 1796–1920 (MoU)
> Missouri, Louisiana, and Kentucky families with land and slave records. MS 60–1817

Hilliard, Mrs. Isaac H., 1849–50 (LU-Ar)
> Describes plantation life at Vicksburg. Also available at the Shreve Memorial Library in Shreveport.

Jenkins, Dr. John Carmichael, 1841–55 (LU-Ar)
> Includes purchases and health of slaves. MS 70–220

Liddell, St. John R., 1839–44; 1867–68 (LU-Ar)
> Health of slaves.

McCollan, Ellen E., 1842–51 (LU-Ar)
> Plantation and family life.

Magruder, Eliza L., 1846–57 (LU-Ar)
> Treatment of slaves.

Marston, Henry W. 1822–32; 1855–84 (LU-Ar)
> Plantation problems.

Mather, Joseph, 1852–59 (LU-Ar)
> Sugar Plantation, health of slaves.

Monette, James, 1848–63 (LU-Ar)
> Plantation diary.

Moreland, William F., 1834–50 microfilm (LU-Ar)
> Plantation diary.

Palfrey, William T., 1842–68 (LU-Ar)
> Palfrey Plantation, St. Martin and St. Mary parishes, Louisiana.

Pascal, Paul, 1830 (MH)
> New Orleans slave dealer's letters to B. Roux of Norfolk, Virginia, with bills of sale.

Seale, H. M., 1853–57 (LU-Ar)
> Daily accounts of plantation.

Taylor, William, 1838–42 (LU-Ar)
> Sugar and cotton plantation life.

Internet Resources

Although it applies primarily to New Orleans, an excellent web resource can be found at the New Orleans Public Library's Louisiana Division and City Archives (**http://www.nutrias.org/~nopl/guides/black.htm**). Included are cemetery, census, church, land, military, death, marriage, and civil court records.

Research Contacts

Hill Memorial Library, Special Collections
Louisiana State University
Baton Rouge, LA 70803
http://www.lib.lsu.edu/special/

Although one of the finest sources of African-American genealogical materials for Louisiana is located here, no published survey exists of the records found in this collection. The university's archives has a large number of family papers of slave owners; church records (which list slave and free black members); business records of merchants dealing with freedmen and black farmers; slave inventories arranged in family groups, or listing mothers with names and dates of birth of their children. For the Civil War period, there is a large number of papers of free black families, predominantly planters from the Francophone area. A few of the diaries, listed above under "Diaries," are included.

The university's press (P.O. Box 25053, Baton Rouge, LA 70894) publishes a CD-ROM searchable database of more than 100,000 slaves, which was developed by Gwendolyn Midlo Hall, a New Orleans native. See **http://www.lsu.edu/lsupress/index.html**.

New Orleans Public Library
219 Loyola Avenue
New Orleans, LA 70112
http://www.nutrias.org/

Another important group of parish records is located at the New Orleans Public Library. The State of Louisiana ordered that all free blacks who arrived in Louisiana had to register their names with the parish judge. The registers for 1840–57, 1856–59, 1859–61, and 1861–64 are available at the library.

Bibliography

Blassingame, John W. *Black New Orleans, 1860–1880*. Chicago: University of Chicago Press, 1976.

Dill, Harry F. *African-American Inhabitants of Rapides Parish, Louisiana: 1 June–4 September 1870*. Bowie, Md.: Heritage Books, 1998.

Dill, Harry F., and William Simpson. *Some Slaveholders and Their Slaves, Union Parish, Louisiana, 1839–1865*. Bowie, Md.: Heritage Books, 1997.

Hall, Gwendolyn Midlo. *Africans in Colonial Louisiana: The Development of Afro-Creole Culture in the Eighteenth Century*. Baton Rouge: Louisiana State University Press, 1995.

Hardy, Linell L. *Abstract of Account Information of Freedman's Savings and Trust: New Orleans, Louisiana, 1866–1869*. Bowie, Md.: Heritage Books, 1999.
This information can also be found in the newly published Freedman's CD (see Part I).

Perkins, A. E. *Who's Who in Colored Louisiana*. Baton Rouge, La.: Louisiana State University Press, 1930.

Ripley, C. Peter. *Slaves & Freedmen in Civil War Louisiana*. Ann Arbor, Mich.: Books on Demand, 1976.

Maine

Important Dates

1783 – Slavery ended in Maine, which was still part of Massachusetts, when the Massachusetts Supreme Court ruled that the "free and equal" clause of the state constitution made the practice of slavery illegal.

1833 – Reuben Ruby was Portland's most prominent antebellum African-American businessman. Ruby worked as a waiter and coachman, and used his earnings to acquire a considerable amount of land. He served as one of Maine's two delegates to the 1833 National Negro Convention and presided over the convention in Philadelphia in 1835.

1850 – Forty-one percent of African Americans for whom jobs are listed in the 1850 census were seamen. (These seamen could possibly have been from the Cape Verdean Islands.)

State Archives

Maine State Archives
State House Station #84
Augusta, ME 04333-0084
http://www.state.me.us/sos/arc/

The Public Search Room at the Maine State Archives has a wide variety of materials helpful to genealogical research. The web site outlines some of these resources and provides links to searchable databases.

Census Records

Federal Census Records

1790–1880, 1900–1930 (DNA); 1790–1880, 1900–1920 (MeHi)

Mortality Records

1850–1880 (Me-Vs)

Special Census

1890: Civil War Union Veterans and Widows

State and County Records

Birth-Marriage-Divorce-Death Records

Office of Vital Statistics
State House Station #11
Augusta, ME 04333-0011
http://www.state.me.us/dhs/faq.htm#certificates

Statewide recording of vital records began in 1892. Records before this date, if they were kept, can be found in the local town clerk's office. Records of vital events between 1892 and 1922 are located at the Maine State Archives. Records of events from 1923 on are available from the Office of Vital Statistics, above. An index of deaths 1960–1996, and marriages 1892–1966 and 1976–1996, is searchable on the Internet at **http://www.state.me.us/sos/arc/geneology/homepage.html**.

Probate Records

All of Maine's wills entered into probate before 1760 have been published and indexed. See William Marshall Sargent's *Maine Wills, 1640–1760* (1877. Reprint. Baltimore: Genealogical Publishing Company, 1972).

Manuscript Sources: Personal Papers, Slave Records, and Diaries

Howard, Oliver Otis, 1843–1910 (MeB)
This collection contains sixty-two volumes of papers related to the founding of Howard University, and Howard's work with the Freedman's Bureau.

Thurston, Charles Brown, 1843–1920 (GEU)
> Some papers relate to Thurston's service with the 13th Maine Infantry, including information on the lives and activities of the Colored Troops. (MS 73–556)

Internet Resources

The Maine State Archives' web site has useful links to vital, cemetery, and military records and newspaper resources for the state. See **http://www.state.me.us/sos/arc/geneology/homepage.html**.

Research Contacts

African American Archives of Maine Reading Room
223E Bailey Hall, Gorham Campus Library
37 College Avenue
Gorham, Maine 04038-1038
http://library.usm.maine.edu/speccoll/aaarchives.html

The Jean Byers Sampson Center for Diversity in Maine, located at the library, contains books and manuscript materials donated by Gerald E. Talbot and others regarding African Americans in Portland and Maine. Included are materials on the Maine branch of the NAACP, the Talbot family, and other African Americans in local and state government and public affairs in the state.

Bibliography

True North [videorecording]: *African-Americans in Maine*. Maine Public Television; executive producer, Brad Smith; associate producer, Steve Dunn. Publisher Lewiston, Me.: Maine Public Broadcasting, c1999.

Williamson, Joseph, "Slavery in Maine." *Collection of the Maine Historical Society* 7 (1867): 207-16.

Maryland

Important Dates

1690 – Few African Americans were in Maryland until after 1690, when the number of European indentured servants declined and large numbers of Africans were brought to Maryland.

1704 – Only 4,000 blacks, most of them slaves, lived in Maryland.

1755 – Approximately one-half of all Maryland families owned slaves.

1780 – Maryland permitted African Americans to enlist in the militia.

1810 – A new state law prohibited free black men who met the same property qualifications as whites to vote. The state's first constitution had allowed such voting.

1812 – During the war of 1812, some slaves fled to freedom behind British lines.

1860 – Forty-five percent of the state's African Americans were free.

State Archives

Maryland State Archives
350 Rowe Boulevard
Annapolis, MD 21401
www.mdarchives.state.md.us

Known also as the Maryland Hall of Records, this is the official repository for state, legislative, executive, and judicial records. The Archives' web site is developing an extensive online search of a variety of early records in the state. In addition, the Maryland State Archives maintains vital records for the twenty-three counties and Baltimore City. For a general description of these records, see *A Guide to Government Records at the Maryland State Archives: A Comprehensive List by Agency and Records Series*, by Edward C. Papenfuse, Christopher R. Allan, and Patricia V. Melville. See also Phebe R. Jacobsen's *Researching Black Families at the Maryland Hall of Records*.

179

Census Records

Federal Census Records

1790–1880, 1900–1930 (DNA). Also available for some years in a few other libraries in the state.

Mortality Records

1850–1880 (MdPM)

Slave Schedules

1850–1860 (DNA)

Special Census

1890: Civil War Veterans and Widows (DNA, MdAA, MdPM, MdHi)

State and County Records

Birth-Marriage-Divorce-Death Records

Division of Vital Records
Department of Health and Mental Hygiene
6550 Reisterstown Road Plaza   *Mailing Address:* P.O. Box 68760
Baltimore, MD 21215-0020   Baltimore, MD 21215-0020
http://www.dhmh.state.md.us/html/vitalrec.htm

Statewide records begin in 1898, although some earlier records exist on a county level. See **http://www.vitalrec.com/md.html#State** for a detailed explanation of what records are available at the Division of Vital Records, the Maryland State Archives and county vital records offices.

Other State and County Records

The following is a list of records found at the Hall of Records in Annapolis and in county courthouses. It is an updated synopsis of the Works Progress Administration's survey of Maryland, which corresponds to an extensive listing on the Maryland State Archives web site (**www.mdarchives.state.md.us**).

All of the records listed were scanned and found to contain African-American genealogical material. Land records, in many instances, include records of manumissions, bills of sale, and other African-American records. Wills and inventories contain names of African Americans who were left to white family members. In many cases African Americans mentioned in a will were not listed in the inventories, especially if the will freed the slave or if the slave was in a favored position. Naturalization records contain names of African Americans who were considered aliens. Indentures contain records of African Americans who were indentured to the service of a family voluntarily or by force. Guardian Bonds include records of African Americans who were placed under the guardianship of whites, in some cases as a legal guise for slavery. Orphan's Court records contain names of African Americans who came before that court for manumission, indentures, or to be made wards. HR indicates those records at the Hall of Records, CH indicates those records found in the various courthouses.

Allegheny County

Inventories, 1791–1899. HR
Land Records, 1791–1949 (microfilmed). HR
Naturalization Dockets, 1945. CH
Naturalization Petitions, 1906. CH
Orphan's Court Wills, 1790–1955 (indexed). HR

Anne Arundel County

Assessment Books of Negro African-American slaves for the City of Annapolis. CH
Bills of Sale, 1829–62. HR
Certificates of Freedom, 1810–64 (Indexed). HR
Certificates to Free Negroes, 1805–64; 1807–20. HR (in Orders and Petitions)
Guardian Bonds, 1780–1820 (microfilmed). HR (in Administration Books section)
Indentures, 1796–1919. HR (in Orders and Petitions)
Inventories, 1777–1962 (microfilmed). HR
Land Records, 1653–1853 (microfilmed). HR
Manumission Records, 1797–1866 (indexed). HR
Naturalization Records of Declaration and Naturalization. CH

Receipts and Releases, 1826–42. HR
Slave Statistics, 1867 (indexed). HR
Wills, 1777–1961 (microfilmed and indexed). HR

Baltimore City

Certificates of Freedom, 1805–64. CH
Chattel Records, 1750–1814. HR
Guardian Accounts, 1786–1851. HR
Indentures, 1794–1916. HR
Inventories, 1666–1852 (microfilmed). HR
Land Records, 1661–1949 (microfilmed). HR
Lands Records Index, 1659–1849. HR
Naturalization Docket and Naturalization Record of Minors. CH

Baltimore County

Assessments, 1805, 1813, 1818, 1823–24, 1833, 1841. HR
Chattel Records, 1851 (microfilmed). HR
Chattel Records Index. CH
Indentures, 1851–1913. CH
Inventories, 1851. CH
Land Records, 1851–1949 (microfilmed). HR
Land Records Index (microfilmed). HR
Orphan's Court Proceedings, 1851–1954 (microfilmed). HR
Wills, 1851 (microfilmed). HR

Calvert County

Inventories, 1882– . HR
Land Records, 1840–1952 (microfilmed). HR
Wills, 1881–. HR

Caroline County

Administration Bonds, 1679–1851 (microfilmed; also containing certificates of freedom). HR
Certificates of Freedom, 1806–57 (microfilmed.). HR. See also Administration Bonds.
Indentures, 1785–1970. HR

Inventories of Caroline and Dorchester, 1680–1850 (microfilmed). HR
Land Records, 1774–1950 (microfilmed and indexed). HR
List of Orphans Placed under Guardians or as Apprentices, 1760–77.
  HR
Naturalization Records, 1905. CH
Wills, 1688–1853 (microfilmed and indexed). HR (includes Dorchester
  County)

Carroll County

Certificates of Freedom, 1838–64 (indexed by name of slave). CH
Chattel Records, 1837 (includes manumissions). CH
Court Proceedings, 1824–1904 (includes naturalizations). CH
Guardian Accounts, 1837–52 (microfilmed). HR
Inventories, 1837–52 (microfilmed). HR
Land Records, 1837 (microfilmed). HR
Land Records Index. HR (in Liber index)
Manumissions. See Chattel Records above.
Naturalization Records. See Court Proceedings above.
Returns of Luther Walsh Commissioner of Slave Statistics, 1864. CH
  (Basement Room)
Wills, 1837–1910 (microfilmed). HR

Cecil County

Assessment of African-American slaves, 1852–64. CH
Guardian Bonds, 1778–97. HR
Indentures, 1794–1894 (in Guardian Books). CH
Inventories, 1675–1850 (microfilmed). HR
Land Records, 1674–1949 (microfilmed). HR
Land Records Index (Liber index). HR
Naturalization Records, 1860–1903. CH
Orphan's Court Proceedings, 1798–1955 (microfilmed). HR
Wills, 1675–1961 (microfilmed). HR
Wills Index (microfilmed). HR

Charles County

Apprentices (Indentures), 1915–27. CH
Guardian Accounts, 1788–1823 (microfilmed). HR

Guardian Bonds, 1778–1825. HR
Inventories, 1673–1951 (microfilmed). HR
Land and Court Records (includes probate and vital records), 1658–1949 (microfilmed). HR
Land and Court Records Index (Liber Index microfilmed). HR
Manumission Records, 1826–60. CH
Naturalization Records, 1911–29. CH
Orphan's Court Proceedings, 1791–1951 (microfilmed). HR
Wills, 1665–1958 (microfilmed). HR
Wills Index, 1665–1948 (microfilmed). HR

Dorchester County

Inventories, 1857. CH
Land Records, 1669–1875 (microfilmed). HR
Land Records Index, 1669–1875 (microfilmed). HR
Naturalization Certificates, 1898–1926. CH
Orphan's Court Proceedings, 1845–1952 (microfilmed). HR
Slave Statistics (Robert Bell's Book), 1867. CH
Wills. Most Dorchester County wills were destroyed by fire.
Wills Index. HR

Frederick County

Certificates to Free Negroes, 1815–63. HR
Certificates of Free Negroes Record, 1865. HR
Guardian Bonds, 1778–1853 (microfilmed). HR
Guardian Bonds Index. CH
Indentures, 1794–1815 (microfilmed). HR
Inventories, 1749–1851 (microfilmed). HR
Land Records. 1748–1949 (microfilmed). HR
Land Records Index (microfilmed). HR
Naturalization Records, 1799–1906. CH
Orphan's Court Proceedings, 1853 (microfilmed). HR
Orphan's Court Proceedings Index (microfilmed). HR
Wills, 1748–1948 (microfilmed and indexed). HR

Garrett County

Indentures (includes date of contract, names of parents, name of master, race, and sex). CH
Land and Mortgage Records, 1873–present. CH

Harford County

Certificates of Freedom, 1774–1842. HR
Free Negroes List, 1832. HR
Guardian Accounts, 1801–73 (microfilmed). HR
Inventories, 1777–1852 (microfilmed). HR
Land Records, 1773–1949 (microfilmed). HR
Land Records Index, 1773–1949. HR
Orphan's Court Proceedings, 1800–1953 (microfilmed). HR
Wills, 1774–1950 (microfilmed). HR

Howard County

Chattel Records, 1840 (Clerk of Circuit Court, 19 vols.). CH
Chattel Records Index. HR
Civil Commissions Trustees and Officers Bonds, 1840–Twelve volumes
    under Liber of Successive Clerks Commissioners and Negroes. One
    volume, 1840–63, contains "Record of Free Negroes." CH
Guardian Bonds, 1840–1942 (microfilmed). HR
Inventories, 1840–54 (microfilmed). HR
Land Records, 1839–1949 (microfilmed). HR
Manumissions, 1943–63 (Justice of the Peace; records include one vol-
    ume of Records of Release of black slaves). CH
Naturalization Records, 1847–1902. CH
Slave Statistics, 1868. CH
Wills Index (microfilmed). HR

Kent County

Bonds: Bills of Sale, 1751–1851. HR
Bonds: Indentures. HR
Bonds Index, 1750–1845. HR
Certificates of Freedom, 1849–61. HR
Guardian Bonds, 1778–1860 (microfilmed). HR
Inventories, 1709–1850 (microfilmed). HR
Land Records, 1648–1949 (microfilmed). HR
Land Records Index (microfilmed). HR
Naturalization Records, 1822–1908. HR
Orphan's Court Proceedings, 1803–1852 (microfilmed). HR
Slave Records, 1864. HR
Wills, 1674–1950 (microfilmed). HR

Montgomery County

Assessment Books, 1798 (records of African-American slaves). CH
Certificates of Freedom, 1806–63. CH
Deeds. See Guardian Bonds below.
Guardian Bonds, 1777–1858 (from Record Books; contain deeds, mortgages, and indentures of orphaned Negroes). CH
Indentures. See Guardian Bonds above.
Inventories. CH
Land Records, 1777–1949 (microfilmed). HR
Mortgages. See Guardian Bonds above.
Naturalization Certificates, 1905. CH
Naturalization Records, 1906. CH
Orphan's Court Minutes and Proceedings, 1779–1954 (microfilmed). HR
Record Books, 1777–1858 (microfilmed). HR
Slave Statistics, 1864. CH
Wills Index, 1777–1942. HR
Wills in Record Books. HR

Prince George's County

Certificates of Freedom, 1820–52. HR
Guardian Bonds. See Orphan's Court Proceedings below.
Indentures. See Orphan's Court Proceedings below.
Inventories, 1697–1795 (microfilmed). HR
Inventories Index, 1697–1948 (microfilmed). HR
Land Records, 1696–1949 (microfilmed). HR
Land Records Index. HR
Manumission Records, 1806–29. HR
Naturalization Certificates, 1904–26. HR
Orphan's Court Proceedings, 1802–1954 (contains Guardian Bonds and Indentures). HR
Slave Statistics, 1867–69. HR
Wills, 1698–1955 (microfilmed). HR and CH
Wills Index, 1698–1948 (microfilmed). HR

Queen Anne's County

Administration Accounts, 1790–1952 (microfilmed). HR
Assessment of Negroes, 1813, 1817, 1826, 1832, 1840, 1852. HR

Certificates of Freedom, 1807–63. HR
Indentures, 1771–1880. CH; 1815–61. HR
Inventories, 1791–1950 (microfilmed). HR
Land Records, 1707–1949 (microfilmed and indexed). HR
Manumission Records, 1828–64. HR
Orphan's Court Proceedings, 1799–1954 (microfilmed). HR
Wills, 1706–91 and 1791–50 (microfilmed). HR

St. Mary's County

Assessment Books, 1793–1826 (microfilmed). HR
Guardian Bonds, 1779–1862 (microfilmed). HR
Inventories, 1795–1953. HR
Land Records, 1781–1851. HR
Land Records Index, 1781–1851 (microfilmed). HR
Naturalization Certificates, 1908–17. CH
Orphan's Court Proceedings, 1777–1949 (microfilmed). HR
Wills, 1658–1950 (microfilmed). HR

Somerset County

Certificates of Freedom, 1821–64. HR
Indentures, 1864–1909. HR
Inventories, 1726–1850 (microfilmed). HR
Land Records, 1665–1850 (microfilmed). HR
Land Records Index (microfilmed). HR
Orphan's Court Proceedings, 1778–1938. HR
Wills, 1664–1950 (microfilmed). HR

Talbot County

Administration Bonds, 1664–1852. HR
Census of Free Negroes, 1832. HR
Certificates of Freedom, 1807–60. HR
Land Records, 1662–1949 (microfilmed and indexed). HR
Negro Docket (record of Negroes seized in the county), 1855–67. HR
Orphan's Court Proceedings, 1787–1946 (microfilmed). HR
Wills, 1668–1955 (microfilmed). CH and HR

Washington County

Assessments of Land (valuation of African-American slaves), 1803. CH
Certificates of Freedom, 1827–63. CH
Certificates of Freedom, Juvenile Court, 1836–57. CH
Guardian Bonds, 1780. HR
Indentures, 1794–1917. HR
Inventories, 1777–1850 (microfilmed). HR
Judgment Records, 1798 (24 vols.; contains records of litigations between masters and African-American slaves). CH
Land Records, 1777–1949 (microfilmed and indexed). HR
Manumission Records, 1827–63. HR
Naturalization Records, 1798–1906. CH
Orphan's Court Proceedings, 1806–1954 (microfilmed).
Wills, 1749–1955 (microfilmed). HR

Wicomico County

Indentures, 1868–1900. CH
Land Records, 1867. CH
Naturalization Certificates. CH
Orphan's Court Minutes, 1867–1944 (microfilmed). HR

Cemetery and Church Records

The Maryland State Archives' collections include the records of several African-American congregations, which have been preserved through the Archives' Preservation Microfilming Program—Churches. (See "Internet Resources" below.)

Military Records

See the Maryland State Archives web site (**http://www.mdarchives. state.md.us**).

Newspapers

Afro-American (Baltimore). August 1892–present. Weekly.
Holdings: 1892–present; Published, WaU. 1892–98 (incomplete);

CSS, WHi. 1892–1969; WaOE, 1894–present; CFIS.

Single issues of the *Afro-American Ledger* (Baltimore) and the *Negro Appeal* (Baltimore; Annapolis) exist in the Maryland State Archives' collections as well as scattered issues of the *Lancet* (Baltimore) on microfilm for the years 1902–1903. Other newspapers available include:

Afro-American (Baltimore) 1892–1900?
Afro-American (Capital edition) (Baltimore) 1932?–1937?
Afro-American (National edition) (Baltimore) 1915–
American Citizen (Baltimore) 1879–?
Commonwealth (Baltimore) 1915–?
Ledger (Baltimore) 1898–1899
Lyceum Observer (Baltimore) 1863–?
Race Standard (Baltimore) 1894?–1898?

See *Guide to Maryland Newspapers*, edited by Nancy M. Bramucci and Elizabeth Ellis (Annapolis: Maryland State Archives, 1995), for title history and source information for these newspapers.

Manuscript Sources: Personal Papers, Slave Records, and Diaries

Here are a few notable sources in manuscript form. See also the Maryland State Archives web site (**http://www.mdarchives. state.md.us**).

Gittings Family Papers, 1815–96 (MdHi)
> Includes a list of slaves belonging to David S. Gittings (1822–59). MS 71–266

Maryland State Colonization Society Papers, 1827–71 (MdHi)
> Manumission books; registers of births, deaths, and marriages of names of blacks who went to Liberia from Maryland.

Peabody, George Foster, 1830–57 (MSaE)
> Extensive slave-trading records for Massachusetts; Washington, D.C.; and Maryland.

Richardson, Levin. Papers, 1831–61 (MdHi)
> James L. Dorcey of Church Creek, Dorchester County, describes his slaves. MS 67–1661

Internet Resources

Maryland State Archives' web site offers an excellent series of links to sources for African-American research in the state, including books, manumissions, and church and cemetery records. See **http://www. mdarchives.state.md.us/msa/refserv/genealogy/html/ethnic.html# African Americans**.

Paul Heinegg's work *Free African Americans of Virginia, North Carolina, South Carolina, Delaware and Maryland* is available on the web at **http://www.freeafricanamericans.com/**.

Research Contacts

Maryland Museum of African-American Historical & Cultural Commission
Pratt and President Streets
Baltimore, MD (Under construction. Contact executive director: 100 Community Place, Crownsville, MD 21032)
http://www.mdarchives.state.md.us/msa/mdmanual/26excom/de-funct/html/25mus.html

Enoch Pratt Free Library, African American Collection
400 Cathedral Street
Baltimore, MD 21201
http://www.pratt.lib.md.us/slrc/afam/

In addition to the above resources, there are chapters of the Afro-American Genealogical Society in Baltimore, Prince Georges County, and Central Maryland. See **http://www.rootsweb.com/~mdaahgs/** for current presidents and addresses.

Bibliography

Adams, Carolyn Greenfield. *Hunter Sutherland's Slave Manumissions and Sales in Harford County Maryland, 1775–1865*. Bowie, Md.: Heritage Books, 1999.

Brumbaugh, Gaius Marcus. *Maryland Records: Colonial, Revolutionary, County and Church from Original Sources*. 2 vols. 1924. Baltimore: Genealogical Publishing Company, 1993.
There are hundreds of names of blacks listed in the records; in

most cases only the first name is given, although surnames are sometimes recorded. The names of blacks are grouped with the white families they were living with, making the records even more valuable.

Chappelle, Suzanne Ellery Greene. *Baltimore: An Illustrated History.* Sun Valley: American Historical Press, 2000.

Chapelle, Suzanne E., Jean Baker, Dean Essinger, Whitman Ridgeway, Jean Russo, Constance Schulz, and Gregory Steverson. *Maryland: A History of Its People.* Baltimore: Johns Hopkins University Press, 1986.

Clayton, Ralph. *Free Blacks of Anne Arundel Co., Maryland, 1850.* Bowie, Md.: Heritage Books, 1987.

Clayton, Ralph. *Slavery, Slaveholding, and the Free Black Population of Antebellum Baltimore.* Bowie, Md.: Heritage Books, 1993.
An excellent book on slavery in Baltimore.

_____. *Black Baltimore, Eighteen Twenty to Eighteen Seventy.* Bowie, Md.: Heritage Books, 1987.
A collection of articles that include a listing of free black households with slaves, notices of runaway slaves published in newspapers, and the 1870 census listing blacks by name, age, etc., for East Baltimore.

Fields, Barbara Jeanne. *Slavery and Freedom on the Middle Ground: Maryland During the Nineteenth Century.* New Haven, Ct.: Yale University Press, 1985.
Thorough background book on free blacks in Maryland.

Hartdagen, Gerald E. "The Vestry as a Unit of Local Government in Colonial Maryland." *Maryland Historical Magazine* 64 (1972): 363–88.

Pages 363–64 illustrate the practice of bringing slaves before the vestry to have their ages adjudged and certified. The example given in the article includes the names, estimated ages, and names of owners for several slaves.

Hynson, Jerry M. *Maryland Freedom Papers.* Westminster, Md.: Willow Bend Books, 1997.
Certificates of freedom, which give name of slave or "freeborn" African Americans, date of certificate, age, height, physical markings, owner. These certificates begin in 1810 and contain names of slaves, owner, date freed, and date of record.

Meyer, Mary K. *Free Blacks in Harford, Somerset, and Talbot Counties.* Mt. Airy, Md.: Pipe Creek Publishers, 1991.

Pedley, Arvil J. *The Manuscript Collections of the Maryland Historical Society.* Baltimore: Maryland Historical Society, 1968.

This is an excellent guide to family papers containing a wealth of slave records. A survey of records here involving blacks would be an essential contribution to black genealogy.

Wilcox, Shirley L., ed. *Eighteen Twenty-Eight Tax List Prince George's County Maryland.* Bowie, Md.: Prince George's County Genealogical Society, Incorporated, 1985.

Massachusetts

Important Dates

1638 – First African Americans were brought as slaves to Noodles Island (East Boston), Massachusetts.

1641 – The Massachusetts Body of Liberties paved the way for the possible future enslavement not only of Indians but also African Americans.

1720 – There were 2,000 African Americans in the colony, the vast majority were unfree.

1780 – Massachusetts' new state constitution included a declaration of natural rights.

1790 – The state reported 5,369 free African Americans and no slaves in the first federal census.

State Archives

Massachusetts State Archives
220 Morrisey Boulevard
Boston, MA 02125
http://www.state.ma.us/sec/arc/

As the state's repository for official governmental documents, the Massachusetts State Archives makes available for public access a diverse and comprehensive collection, including vital, federal and state census, land, probate, and military records; passenger lists; and naturalizations.

Census Records

Federal Census Records

1790–1880, 1900–1930 (DNA, M-Ar)

Mortality Records

1850–1880 (DNA, M-Ar)

Special Census

1754: Slave census lists only the aggregate number of slaves in each town; occasionally provides name.

1771: Town valuations include free blacks (noted in code under "Status").

1890: Civil War Union Veterans and Widows are listed.

State Census Records

1855: Individuals listed as white/black/mulatto

1865: Individuals listed as white/black/mulatto/Indians of owners

State and County Records

Birth-Marriage-Divorce-Death Records

Registry of Vital Records and Statistics
150 Mount Vernon Street, 1st floor
Dorchester, MA 02125-3105
http://www.state.ma.us/dph/bhsre/rvr/rvr.htm

The Registry of Vital Records and Statistics, a division of the Massachusetts Department of Public Health, holds vital records (official birth, death, and marriage records) for Massachusetts beginning in 1911. However, vital records have been registered in individual towns in Massachusetts since 1635. Statewide collection began in 1841. Records for events that occurred from 1841–1910 are available at the Massachusetts State Archives. Earlier records may be available at the town or city in which the event occurred. Published versions of pre-1850 vital records for many towns are widely available. See also **http://www.mass-doc.com/vitals_research.htm**.

Other State and County Records

Court Records

Pre-1860 records of the Supreme Judicial Court, the Court of General Sessions of the Peace, the Court of Common Pleas, and the Admiralty

Court include test cases against slavery and issues of ownership; references to witchcraft; and cases against and between specific African Americans.

Secretary of State/Archives Records

The Massachusetts State Archives Collection entry under "Negroes" in the card catalog includes general references, followed by citations for individuals:

Passports/Travel permission/Certificates for seamen covers 1815–1860; records related to legislation requiring inclusion of all residents, regardless of color (includes such things as two certificates (1842, 1845) for "free coloreds going south").

Guardians of Indians accounts and expenditures of whites appointed to handle Indian affairs includes 1832 enumeration of Mashpee proprietors and non-proprietors (including African Americans living on Indian lands).

Cemetery and Church Records

See the web sites of Massachusetts State Archives (**http://www.state.ma.us/sec/arc/**) and Massachusetts Historical Society (**http://www.state.ma.us/sec/arc/**).

Military Records

See Massachusetts State Archives web page: **http://www.state.ma.us/sec/arc/arcgen/genidx.htm**.

Newspapers

Boston Advocate. January 1885 to 1888? Weekly. Holdings: 1885–86 (incomplete); MB, MHi.

The Liberator (Boston). January 1, 1831, to December 29, 1865. Weekly. Holdings: January 1831 to December 1865; CFS, CtU, CU, DLC, GEU GStG, IHi, KyMoreU, LU-NO, MB, MiDW, MiYEM, MnU, MWiW, NHi, NN, OC, OKentU, PEsS, PPiD, WaSpC, WaU, WHi.

Manuscript Sources: Personal Papers, Slave Records, and Diaries

America Freedmen's Inquiry Commission, 1862–63 (MH)
> Papers on ex-slaves' conditions.

Anti-Slavery Collection, 1820–1900 (MB)
> Account books, manuscripts, letters related to freedmen's school and fugitive slaves. There are also items involving slavery and the West Indies. This collection includes the Mather family papers, 1632–89.

Collection of Account Books (MWA)
> Includes slave account books. MS 62–3523

Freedmen's Aid Society, 1869–71 (MH)
> Daily journal.

Hammond, Eli Shelby, 1895 (MH)
> A slave's recollections of his life on a pre-Civil War plantation.

Jacobs, Phillip (MwalAJ)
> Bill of sale for slave. MS 68–139

Liberia College Collection, 1842–1927 (Mhi)

Lincoln, William, 1770 (MH)
> Bill of sale for slave.

Massachusetts Anti-Slavery Society Records (NHi)
> List of slaves aided. MS 1801

Massachusetts Colonization Society Papers, 1842–1911 (Mhi)

Moore, Samuel Preston, 1776 (MH)
> Manumission certificate.

New England Freedman's Aid Society Papers (Mhi)

Peabody, George Foster, 1830–57 (MSaE)
> Extensive slave-trading records for Massachusetts, Washington, D.C., and Maryland.

Sheftall, Mordecai, 1761–1873 (MwalAJ)
> Bills of sale for slaves.

Ship Logbooks (MSaP)

Siebert, Wilbur Henry (MH, OHi)
> This material was used to write *The Underground Railroad*. It is indexed by states. MS 68–1705

Slavery Papers (MH)
> Sales, advertisements, apprenticeships, and certificates.

Slave Traders Papers, 1846–64 (MWA); 1759–69 (MMeHi)

Internet Resources

Both the Massachusetts State Archives (**http://www.state.ma.us/sec/ arc/**) and the New England Historic Genealogical Society (**http:// www.newenglandancestors.org**) web sites have searchable databases of catalogs and holdings.

Research Contacts

The Massachusetts Historical Society
1154 Boylston Street
Boston, MA 02215
http://www.masshist.org/

The Massachusetts Historical Society holds thousands of records with notations about slaves and slavery.

New England Historic Genealogical Society
101 Newbury Street
Boston, MA 02116
http://www.newenglandancestors.org

Bibliography

Carvalho, Joseph, Jr. *Black Families in Hampden County, Massachusetts, 1650–1855.* Boston: New England Historic Genealogical Society, 1984.

Dorman, Franklin A. *Twenty Families of Color in Massachusetts, 1742–1998.* Boston: New England Historic Genealogical Society, 1998.

Hayden, Robert C. *African-Americans in Boston: More than 350 Years.* Boston: Boston Public Library, 1992.
An introduction to significant African-American events and people in Massachusetts.

Smith, James Avery. *The History of the Black Population of Amherst, Massachusetts, 1728–1870.* Boston: New England Historic Genealogical Society, 1999.

Michigan

Important Dates

1780 – The trader Jean Baptiste Du Sable, of African descent and founder of Chicago, moved to the Michigan area and allegedly married a Potawatomi woman.

1805 – When the Michigan Territory was established, there were relatively few African-American residents.

1830 – Slavery persisted into the 1830s, leaving its mark on the laws of territory and state.

1837 – Michigan became a state and formally abolished slavery.

1860 – A second Convention of Colored Men was held at Battle Creek.

State Archives

State Archives of Michigan
Michigan Historical Center
702 W. Kalamazoo Street
Lansing, MI 48909-8240
http://www.michigan.gov/hal/0,1607,7-160-17445_19273_19313---,00.html

Documents date back to 1782 and provide a rich source of state and local governmental records of particular relevance to genealogical research.

Census Records

Federal Census Records

1820–80 and 1900–1930 (DNA); 1820–1880, 1900–1920 (MiD, MiMtpT)

Mortality Records

1860–1880 (DNDAR, MiHi)

Special Census

1890: Civil War Veterans and Widows (DNA, MiMtpT, MiD)

State Census

1827, 1830, 1834, 1845, 1850, 1854, 1864, 1870, 1874, 1880, 1884, 1894.

Not all counties have extant census records for each of these years. The 1894 appears to be the most comprehensive. See **http://www.rootsweb.com/~micheboy/statecen.htm** for a complete listing of available state censuses by county and their location.

State and County Records

Birth-Marriage-Divorce-Death Records

Michigan Dept of Community Health
3423 N. Martin Luther King Boulevard
P.O. Box 30721
Lansing, MI 48909
http://www.mdch.state.mi.us/PHA/OSR/vital_records/index.htm

Michigan's birth, marriage, and death records begin in 1867, with divorces indexed beginning in 1897. An online searchable database of early records is available.

Cemetery and Church Records

American Home Missionary Society Records, 1825–1947 (MiU)(?)
Five reels of microfilm dealing with the mission's work. Genealogical material on blacks is probably included.

Military Records

The military records at the state archives relate to several aspects of military service. Records pertain to service in armed conflicts both in the United States and abroad. The conflicts documented include the Civil War, the Spanish-American War, World War I, World War II, and the Korean War. See the Michigan State Archives web page (**http:// www.sos.state.mi.us/history/archive/index.html**) for more information. Examples of the material held there include the following:

First Infantry-Colored Troops, 1861–1865.
List of Colored Army Dead, 1917–1919.

Newspapers

Michigan Liberty Press (Battle Creek). April 13, 1848, to 1849. Weekly. Continues *Signal of Liberty* (see below). Holdings: April to August 1848; mid-b., *Plaindealer* (Detroit). May 16, 1883, to 1895? Weekly. Holdings: September 1889 to May 1893; CSdS, CtY, DLC, InNd, MB, MdBJ, Mi, MnU, NcU, NiP, TNF, WHi.

Signal of Liberty (Ann Arbor). April 26, 1841, to February 5, 1848. Weekly. Continued by *Michigan Liberty Press* (see above). Holdings: 1841–48 (incomplete); MiD-B.

Manuscript Sources: Personal Papers, Slave Records, and Diaries

Gregg, Phineas. Papers, 1849–1925 (MiU)
 Records of the Sounders Colony of freed slaves in Calvin Township in Cass County. MS 65–286
Historical Records Survey, 1936–41 (MiU)
 Material used in compiling the WPA's *Inventory of the County Archives* and *History of Negroes in Michigan* (MiD-B). This collection contains extensive holdings of newspapers, diaries, manuscripts, and papers on the history of African Americans in Michigan and the Old Northwest. Included are the papers of Fred Hart Williams, descendant of an African American who was an early Detroit settler. The papers include the manuscript of *Detroit Heritage: A History of Negroes in Detroit*, Niles Public Library, Niles, 1957, by Hoyt Fuller; includes biographies.

Diaries

Perry, Mr. (MiLl). Undated diary of an African American who escaped and settled in Cass County, Michigan. MS 651355

Also see manuscripts and items concerning slavery in Michigan at **http://www.michigan.gov/documents/mhc_sa_circular29_50003_7 .pdf**. An example of the type of information here includes the "Joseph Anderson Manumission Certificate, 1842."

Internet Resources

The Michigan State Archives web site provides a useful directory of Michigan county clerks. Clerk offices maintain public records of great interest to genealogists. See the web page at **http://www.michigan.gov/ hal/0,1607,7-160-17449_18635_20736-50010--,00.html**.

Research Contacts

Burton Historical Collection
Detroit Public Library
5201 Woodward Avenue
Detroit, MI 48202
http://www.detroit.lib.mi.us/burton/

Their collection of genealogy and local history resources include federal census population schedules; family histories; cemetery inscriptions; church records of baptisms, marriages, and deaths; military records; probate indexes and records; vital records; obituaries; and land records.

The State Archives of Michigan (**http://www.sos.state.mi.us/history/ archive/index.html**) has state, municipal, and county records on microfilm. Records for the French period in Michigan can be found in the Canadian Archives and Paris Archives.

Bibliography

Banner, Melvin E. *The Black Pioneer in Michigan.* Midland, Mich.: Pendell Publishing Co., 1973.

Hesslink, George K. *Black Neighbors: Negroes in a Northern Rural Community.* 2nd edition. Indianapolis, Ind.: Bobbs-Merrill, 1974. Based on extensive sociological studies of Cass County, Michigan, in the 1960s and 1970s. Studies Quaker attempts to settle freedmen and ex-slaves on nearby farmlands, and the way in which both groups have interacted since the arrival of African Americans in the area.

Johnson, Georgia A. *Black Medical Graduates of the University of Michigan (1872–1960 Inclusive) and Elected Black Michigan Physicians.* Lansing, Mich.: G. A. Johnson Pub. Co., 1995.

Moon, Elaine L. *Untold Tales, Unsung Heroes: An Oral History of Detroit's African-American Community, 1918–1967.* Detroit: Wayne State University Press, 1994.

Woodson, June Bober. "A Century with the Negroes of Detroit, 1830–1930" (Master's thesis, Wayne State University, 1949).

Winslow, Benjamin C. *The Rural Black Heritage Between Chicago and Detroit, 1850–1929: A Photograph Album & Random Thoughts.* Third Edition, Reprint, Kalamazoo: Western Michigan University, New Issues Press, 1991.

Minnesota

Important Dates

1787 – Slavery was banned by Northwest Ordinance.

1825 – African-American slaves came to the area and worked as servants. They were stationed at Fort Snelling and as domestics to southern slave owners who vacationed in Minnesota.

1857 – Dred Scott, who was brought to Minnesota in 1836 by his owner, Dr. John Emerson, an army surgeon, sued for his freedom, resulting in the U.S. Supreme Court's decision that African-American slaves had no constitutional rights.

1860 – Some 259 African Americans resided in 22 of the newly designated State of Minnesota's 87 counties.

1868 – African Americans in Minnesota were given the right to vote.

1872 – George Bonga, son of an Ojibwa woman and Pierre Bonga, a free African American, died, leaving behind children who would produce hundreds of descendants.

1900 – The African-American population reached 5,000.

State Archives

Minnesota Historical Society
345 Kellogg Boulevard West
St. Paul, MN 55102-1906
http://www.mnhs.org/

As the world's largest collection of materials on Minnesota, the library of the Minnesota Historical Society preserves a large variety of materials appropriate to genealogical research. The archives collection includes local and state governmental sources from the territorial period to the present.

Census Records

Federal Census Records

1850–1880, 1900–1930 (DNA), 1850–1880, 1900–1920 (Mn-Ar)

Mortality Records

1860–80 (MnHi, DNDAR, DNA); 1870 (DNA)

Special Census

1890: Civil Union Veterans and Widows

State Census Records

1857, 1865, 1875, 1895, 1905 territorial and state censuses (DNA); (MnHi, Mn-Ar)

State and County Records

Birth-Marriage-Divorce-Death Records

Minnesota State Vital Records Office
Minnesota Department of Health
Birth and Death Records
717 Delaware Street
SE Post Office Box 9441
Minneapolis, MN 55440-9441
http://www.health.state.mn.us/index.html

The Department of Health maintains birth and death records for the entire state beginning in 1900 and 1908, respectively. Marriage and divorce records are maintained by the county in which the event occurred. A statewide index for marriages exists from 1958–1998; for divorces from 1970–1998.

Cemetery and Church Records

Pilgrim Baptist Church, St. Paul, Minn. (MnHi). Brief records from this church and a few other churches are available.

St. Mark's African Methodist Episcopal Church, 1893–1957 Microfilm M277 (MnHi)

Note: Access the Minnesota Historical Society web site and search under the category of "African Americans." You will see notations for several African-American churches in Minnesota.

Military Records

Montgomery, Thomas, microfilmed Letters, 1862–67 (MnHi)

Captain of Company 1, 65th Regiment, and Company B, 67th Regiment, of U.S. Colored Infantry. Includes information on a proposed black farming community in St. Peter Land District, Minnesota. MS 60–1360

Manuscript Sources: Personal Papers, Slave Records, and Diaries

Bailey, Everett Hoskins. Family Papers, 1839–1954 (MnHi)
    Letters with data on views on slavery. MS 62–1613
Gilman, Robbins. Family Papers, 1699–1952 (MnHi)
    Small collection of information on blacks in Minneapolis, and N.A.A.C.P., 1920

Internet Resources

The Minnesota Historical Society web site (**http://www.mnhs.org/**) includes a helpful step-by-step guide to research in the state, a series of stories about African Americans in Minnesota, and collections of materials such as church, social group, and civic organization records.

Research Contacts

The web site of the history department at the University of Minnesota offers a number of important links to research sources, not all of which apply solely to Minnesota. See **http://www.hist.umn.edu/~hist20c/ internet/african.htm**.

Bibliography

Taylor, David V. *Blacks in Minnesota: A Preliminary Guide to Historical Sources.* St. Paul: Minnesota Historical Society Press, 1976.

_____. "Pilgrim's Progress, Black St. Paul and the Making of an Urban Ghetto." (Ph.D. dissertation. University of Minnesota, 1977).

Mississippi

Important Dates

1817 – Four in ten residents were African American.

1840 – Free African Americans totaled 1,366, while 195,211 were slaves.

1860 – The number of free African Americans fell to 773.

1865 – The emancipation of slaves was proclaimed.

1910–1960 – Over one million African Americans left the state and migrated north.

State Archives

Mississippi Department of Archives and History
100 South State Street   *Mailing Address*: P.O. Box 571
Jackson, MS 39201   Jackson, MS 39205-0571
www.mdah.state.ms.us/

The Mississippi Department of Archives and History [MDAH] provides assistance to local and state governmental agencies in the preservation of public records related to life in Mississippi.

Census Records

Federal Census Records

1830–1880; 1900–1930 (DNA, Ms-Ar, MsSM, MsU)

Mortality Records

1850–80 (Ms-Ar)

Slave Schedules

1850–1860 (DNA)

Special Census

1805, 1810 and 1816: Territorial Census (Ms-Ar)
1890: Civil War Union Veterans and Widows (DNA, Ms-Ar, MsHaU)

State and County Records

Birth-Marriage-Divorce-Death Records

Mississippi State Department of Health
571 Stadium Drive   *Mailing Address:* P.O. Box 1700
Jackson, MS 39215   Jackson, MS 39215
   http://www.msdh.state.ms.us/

Instructions on obtaining birth, death, and marriage records from the state are readily available on the Department's web site at **http://www. msdh.state.ms.us/phs/index.htm**. Birth and death records are available from 1912 and marriages from 1926. Prior to these years, recording of vital events was not required, but many counties do have some records. In addition, from 1926 to 1938 marriage records were kept only by the county.

Cemetery and Church Records

Greenwood Cemetery, Jackson, 1862–1938 (Ms-Ar)
   List of blacks buried. MS 62–1967

All of the following include lists of African-American and white members:
   Mississippi Baptist Church, 1819–1957 (MsSM) MS 66–888; 183768 (MsSM) MS 72–1569
   Mississippi Church of Christ Records, 1900–1957 (MsSM) MS 66–889
   Mississippi Methodist Church, 1833–1957 (MsSM) MS 66–890; 1843–85 (MsSM) MS 72–1570
   Mississippi Presbyterian Church, 1823–1925 (MsSM) MS 66–1192; 1843–85 (MsSM) MS 72–1571

Mississippi Primitive Baptist Church, 1819–1957 (MsSM) MS 66–891
St. Philips Episcopal Church, Kirkwood, 1848–88. Records include
vestry minutes; parish register; lists of communicants, baptisms, marriages, confirmations, and funerals of blacks and whites. This church
is located near the governor's mansion (see Governor Alcorn's diary,
below).
See also "Bibliography" below.

Newspapers

Free State (Brandon). 1898–1904? Weekly. Holdings: January 20,
1900; CSdS, CSS, CU, DLC, FTaSU, LU-NO, MdMC, MiKW, TNF,
WHi. GOLDEN RULE (Vicksburg). 1898–1902? Weekly. Holdings:
January 27, 1900; CSdS, CSS, CU, DLC, FTaSU, LU-NO, MdBMC,
MiKW, TNF, WHi.
Light (Vicksburg). 1891–1922? Weekly. Holdings: January 18, 1900;
CSdS, CU, DLC, FTaSU, Lu-NO, MdBMC, MiKW, TNF, WHi.

Manuscript Sources: Personal Papers, Slave Records, and Diaries

Alcorn, Governor James L., 1859, 1879 (Nc-Ar)
    Mississippi property and slave records.
Anonymous, 1828–32 (Ms-Ar)
    Plantation account book and diary.
Clark, Charles, 1870–74 (Ms-Ar)
    Lists former slaves and accounts of Doro Plantation in Bolivar
    County. MS 60–2583
Cooper, William, 1862; 1865; 1872; 1886. (NcU)
    The diary of Cooper, homeowner in Tuscumbia, Alabama, and
    plantation owner in Coahoma County, Mississippi. Entries record
    daily incidents in plantation management including his dealings
    with slaves and free black laborers. The diary mentions the sale
    of slaves (1862); supplies given to black workers on credit (1865,
    1872); slave births (1865); and evangelical services held by Mrs.
    Frame, a black minister in Tuscumbia, Ala. (1886).
Capell, Eli J., 1842–50, 1867 (LU-Ar)
    Pleasant Hill Plantation diary for Amite County. MS 71–240

Darden Family, 1835–1944 (MsSM) MS 66–881
Bills of sale and slave receipts.
Dupree, H.T.T., 1878–1900 (Ms-Ar)
Plantation account books, Hinds County. MS 60–747
Eggleston, Dick Hardeway, 1850 (LU-Ar)
Diary of the Learmont Plantation, near Woodville. MS 75–739
Ethelbert, William Ervin Journals: 1839–1856 (NcU)
Plantation diaries of Ervin, cotton planter and owner of Liberty Hall Plantation in Lowndes County, Mississippi. Entries record slave birth and death dates, information on buying and selling slaves, the hire of slaves owned by others, distribution of blankets, hats, and other clothing to slaves, payments made to slaves for their "Christmas work," and occasional accounts of the amount of cotton picked by slaves.
Everard, Green Baker: 1848–1876. (NcU)
Personal diaries and plantation journal of Baker of Jefferson, Panola, and Hinds Counties, Mississippi, containing references to farming, household matters, philosophical ideas, recipes, and rules for plantation living. Diaries record events in the lives of Baker's slaves, including illnesses, holidays, and an attack on an overseer (26 May 1854).
Hairston and Wilson Family Papers: 1751–1928. (NcU)
Correspondence, financial and legal papers, and account books of six generations of the Wilson and Hairston families, planters and merchants of Henry and Pittsylvania counties, Virginia, and Davie, Rockingham, and Stokes counties, North Carolina. The papers include bills of sale for slaves; receipts for hiring out slaves (1789–1813); and slave lists. Several volumes contain information on the sale and purchase of slaves; lists of slaves; and lists of clothes and other items given out to slaves.
Manuscript Collection, 1803–1900 (MsVHi)
Contains bills of sale and slave receipts.
McCall, Duncan G., 1835–51; 1852–54 (NcD)
Mississippi plantation journal and diary.
McGovern, Patrick Francis, and Charles Sauters, 1857 (Ms-Ar)
Records work, treatment, punishment, food, clothing, illnesses, births, and deaths of slaves.
Nannie Herndon Rice Papers, 1824–1963 (MsSM) MS 69–340
Bills of sale and slave receipts.
Plantation Records, 1818–65 (Ms-Ar) MS 61–2343
Adams County: Aventine, Artornish, and Loch Leven plantations
Amite County: Brooksdale Plantation
Claiborne County: Nailer and Belmont plantations

Hinds County: Learned Plantation

Percy, Mississippi: Panter Burn Plantation

Nanechehaw Plantation, owned by Charles B. Allen (county not listed)

Washington, Marshall, and Jackson counties: unnamed plantation

Register of Freedmen's Contracts, 1865 (MsSM)
Located in Bertie Shaw Rollins Collection. MS 66–896

Ross, Isaac, 1845–89 (MsSM)
Estate papers including will with slave manumissions. MS 69–342

Sizer, Henry E., 1844–67 (Ms-Ar)
Personal papers include bills of sale for slaves purchased in New Orleans, Richmond, and Nashville. MS 61–2724

Smith, A.F. Records, 1851–52 (OCIWHi)
Plantation accounts of births and deaths of slaves in Princeton.

Thompson Family Papers: 1809–1924. (NcU)
Chiefly family letters and financial and legal materials of the Thompson family of Alabama, Louisiana, and Mississippi, and the related Malone family of Alabama. An account book belonging to Goodloe W. Malone contains a slave list of about seventy names and ages.

Vick and Phelps Family Papers, 1810–1906 (Ms-Ar)
Includes list of blacks sold or mortgaged to the Bank of the United States, 1834–49. MS 60–1732

Wade, Walter, 1834–54 (Ms-Ar)
Ross Wood Plantation diary from Jefferson County. Lists slaves. MS 60–205

Internet Resources

Among the searchable databases on *Christine's Genealogy Website* (**http://ccharity.com**) is an accounting of the discovery of a book of Certificates of Slaves for Adams County, Mississippi in the 1850s and 1860s.

Research Contacts

Mississippi Historical Society
P.O. Box 571
Jackson, MS 39205-0571
http://www.mdah.state.ms.us/admin/mhistsoc.html

The Mississippi Department of Archives and History and the Mississippi Historical Society jointly publish *The Journal of Mississippi History*, a quarterly featuring articles on the state's history.

Bibliography

Capers, Charlotte, ed. "Census of Franklin County Mississippi Territory, 1810." *Journal of Mississippi History* 13 (1951): 249–55.

_____. "Births, Deaths, and Aged Persons for Wilkinson County, Mississippi, 1822." *Journal of Mississippi History* 16 (1954): 121–50.

_____. "Census of Jefferson County, 1810." *Journal of Mississippi History* 15 (1953): 33–46.

_____. "Census of Wilkinson County, Mississippi Territory, 1805." *Journal of Mississippi History* 11 (1949): 104–10.

Cobb, James A. *The Most Southern Place on Earth: The Mississippi Delta and the Roots of Regional Identity.* New York: Oxford University Press, 1994.

Crouch, Evelyn B., and Christie Genola. *Montgomery County, Mississippi Cemetery Records.* Carrollton, Miss.: Pioneer Publishing Company, 1996.
This book lists 116 cemeteries and more than 20,000 entries from Montgomery County, with a few cemeteries just across the line in surrounding counties. African-American cemeteries are included.

Hendrix, Mary Flowers. "Births, Deaths, and Aged Persons for Claiburne County, 1822." *Journal of Mississippi History* 16 (1954): 37–46.

King, J. Estelle Stewart. *Mississippi Court Records, 1799–1835.* Reprint, Baltimore: Clearfield Company, 1999.
Indicates court records, some of which include African Americans.

Lee, Carol. *Early Records of College Hill Church, Lafayette County, Mississippi with Cemetery Inscriptions.* Carrollton, Miss.: Pioneer Publishing Company, 1997.
Servants (slaves) were members of this church and included in their records. A list of baptisms, births, and deaths are also included here. The cemetery records were copied in November 1996 and include slave cemetery records.

McBee, May Wilson. *Mississippi County Court Records.* Reprint, Baltimore: Clearfield Company, 1999.
Contains court records and wills, with names of slaves included.

McCain, William D., ed. "Census of Baldwin County, Mississippi Territory, 1810." *Journal of Mississippi History* 11 (1949): 207–13.

Moody, Anne. *The Coming of Age in Mississippi.* New York: Dell Publishing, 1992.

Morgan, Model Jacobs, ed. "Census of Claiburne and Warren Counties, Mississippi Territory, 1870." *Journal of Mississippi History* 13 (1951): 5063.

Russ, Williams, E. *Marion County, Miss., Miscellaneous Records: Orphans Ct. Records, Wills and Estates, 1812–1859; Deeds 1812–1840; Territorial & Federal Census Recs. & Mortality Schedules; Old Road Books; 1813 Lawrence County Tax Lists.* Reprint, Greenville, S.C.: Southern Historical Press, 1985.
Orphan's Court records are valuable African-American genealogical sources. This is a fine example of the material that should be available in such court records for every county and state.

Wharton, Vernon Lane. *The Negro in Mississippi, 1865–1890.* Reprint, Westport, Conn.: Greenwood Publishing Group, 1984.
Records on African Americans and slaves are indicated.

Wiltshire, Betty C. *Attala County, Mississippi Pioneers.* Bowie: Heritage Books, 1991.

_____. *Choctaw and Chickasaw Early Census Records.* Carrollton, Miss.: Pioneer Publishing Company, 1997.
These records will be a valuable aid in the difficult research of early Indian ancestors in Mississippi.

_____. *Carroll County, Mississippi Pioneers: With Abstracts of Wills, 1834–1875 & Divorces 1857–1875.* Bowie, Md.: Heritage Books, 1990.
This book includes original land records, probate records for the years 1834–1848, and some tax lists.

_____. *Carroll County, Mississippi Estate Records, 1840–1869 with Freedman Apprenticeships.* Carrollton, Miss.: Pioneer Publishing Company, 1997.
Slaves are frequently listed by name, sometimes giving ages and relationships, as well as value.

_____. *Holmes County Mississippi Pioneers.* Reprint, Carrollton, Miss.: Pioneer Publishing Company, 1997.
This book contains early records: tax lists, the 1850 slave schedule, newspaper abstracts, abstracts of Will Book I 1833–1888, and forty-five brief family genealogies.

_____. *Marshall County, Mississippi Will and Probate Records.* Carrollton, Miss.: Pioneer Publishing Company, 1996.

Inventory records include ownership of slaves, often giving names and occasionally ages and relationships.

_____. *Mississippi Newspaper Obituaries, 1662–1875.* Carrollton, Miss.: Pioneer Publishing Company, 1994.
The newspapers contain reports of deaths of many blacks as well as whites.

_____. *Yalobusha County, Mississippi Will Abstracts and Estates Records Index.* Carrollton, Miss.: Pioneer Publishing Company, 1997.

Missouri

Important Dates

1717 – Slave-owning Jesuit French missionaries came to area.

1720 – Phillip Renault brought 500 African Americans to work in lead mines.

1803 – At the time that the United States acquired the territory of Missouri following the Louisiana Purchase, there were 10,340 people in the area—1,320 of them African American slaves.

1820 – Under the Missouri Compromise, Missouri was admitted as a slave state.

1860 – Half of Missouri's 3,752 free African Americans were located in St. Louis.

1865 – Slavery was banned.

1898 – Missouri African Americans from the 70th Regiment fought in the Spanish-American War.

1917 – More than 10,000 African Americans served in World War I.

State Archives

Missouri State Archives
600 W. Main Street   *Mailing Address:* P.O. Box 1747
Jefferson City, MO 65102   Jefferson City, MO 65102
http://www.sos.state.mo.us/archives/

The archives' extensive collection of African-American research materials is outlined on the Archives' web site. The Archives also houses state and local governmental records pertaining to Missourians throughout the territorial and statehood periods.

Census Records

Federal Census Records

1830–1880; 1900–1930 (DNA), (MoMcPL); 1830–80 (MoHistSoc, MoS)

Mortality Records

1850–80 (MoMcpl)

Special Census

1890: Civil War Veterans and Widows (DNA, MoS, MoHistSoc, MoMcpl)

State and County Records

Birth-Marriage-Divorce-Death Records

Bureau of Vital Records
Missouri Department of Health
930 Wildwood   *Mailing Address:* P.O. Box 570
Jefferson City, MO 65102-0570   Jefferson City, MO 65102
**http://www.health.state.mo.us/BirthAndDeathRecords/
BirthAndDeathRecords.html**

The Bureau of Vital Records holds birth and death records from 1910, and marriage and divorce records from 1948 to the present. Some earlier records may be found at county offices. Marriages are filed with the recorder of deeds, and divorces with the clerk of the circuit court.

Other State and County Records

Clay County, Missouri Marriage Records, Negro & Index, 1865–1891. Missouri State Archives film C-1792
Jackson County, Missouri Black Marriage Records, 1865–1882; Missouri State Archives film C-3145 (also a printed and indexed abstract)

St. Louis City, Index to Marriage Records. Vol. 1 1806–1854; Vol. 2 1854–1871. 1 roll (marriages of slaves and colored persons at end of alphabet for each volume)

Clay County—Freed Negro Registry, 1836–56 (WHMC)

Lists slaves freed between February 8, 1836, and January 7, 1856. There may be similar registers for other counties located elsewhere in the state.

Columbia, Missouri—Social and Economic Census of the Colored Population, 1901 (WHMC)

Consists of family reports listing members with ages, income, and living conditions.

There are some territorial court and Missouri supreme court cases pertaining to African Americans. These are primarily slave freedom cases located at the Missouri State Archives.

Cemetery and Church Records

African Methodist Episcopal Church Records (WHMC)

Baptist Association Records (WHMC)

Christian Church of Missouri, Annual Meetings (WHMC)

All of the above are from the late 19th and early 20th century period. The historical society indicates that the records are of relevance to blacks, but does not specifically state their contents.

Concordia Historical Institute, Concordia, Missouri

Extensive records on the Lutheran Church in Missouri, and its Synod missions in the South and in Africa are held in this institute. The records are restricted.

See "Bibliography" on page 224.

Military Records

Missouri State Archives has some records of African-American Civil War troops in their military collection. The following is an example of what is available:

Bentzoni, Charles, Report (C995, V. 19, #516) 1866 2 pp., typed copy. List of members of the 56th U.S. Colored Infantry who died of cholera, August 1866.

Newspapers

Rising Sun (Kansas City). 1869?-1919? Weekly. Holdings: January 16, 1903, to 1907 (incomplete); CSdS, CSS, DLC, FTaSU, TNF, WHi, MoHistSoc.

Sedalia Times. 1894–1905? Weekly. Holdings: August 31, 1901, to December 19, 1903; January 21 to February 4, 1905; CSdS, CtY, DLC, InNd, MB, MdBJ, MnU, MoHistSoc, MoSW, NcU, NjP, TNF, WHi.

Manuscript Sources: Personal Papers, Slave Records, and Diaries

Applegate, Lisbon. Papers, 1819–99 (WHMC)
> Surveyor and county judge of Chariton County. Includes letters from the Civil War period and records the hiring and selling of slaves. MS 64–26

Botts-Lewis Family Letters (C213) 1837–1877 (SHSM)
> Letters from the Botts and Lewis families in Virginia to the Peyton and James Botts families in Missouri. Farm crops, operations, land conditions, prayer meetings, collection of debts, slave prices, family matters, and other miscellaneous topics.

Bradley, T.T., Letters (C2388) 1859 (SHSM)
> Letter to the parents of a "Negro" slave on behalf of their son; letter to the parents about their son; and letter to Bradley's cousins describing his return trip from Missouri to Texas after purchasing slaves.

Breckenridge Family Papers, 1750–1960 (MoHistSoc)
> Accounts of slave sales are included. MS 68–1310

Brown, James, Papers (C231) 1856–1866 (SHSM)
> Letters from H.C.N. Brown, Front Royal, 1856, concerning the hire of Henry and wife Catherine, probably slaves. Poem: *Death of Virginius Brown in Civil War.* Political conditions, 1866, money, crops, and desertion of slaves.

Buckner, John, Biographical Information (C1878). (SHSM)
> Information concerning John Buckner and his slave, Abe, their service in the Civil War, and settlement in Scotland County, Missouri, in the 1870s.

Burt, Franklin. Papers, 1843–1903 (WHMC)
> Contains Calloway County tax records with an 1858 list of landowners and slaves. MS 60–1979

Conway, Joseph. Papers, 1798–1922 (MoHistSoc)

Conway was a St. Louis County pioneer. Bills of slave sales are included. MS 64–322

Corby Family Papers (C86) 1804–1905 (WHMC)
Papers of a pioneer St. Joseph, Missouri, family: deeds, bills of sale for slaves, tax receipts, legal papers, stock certificates, Pony Express bills, and material on early St. Louis area. Record book of the Mercantile Company, 1856; bank book, 1861–1869; volume of clippings concerning St. Joseph, 1881–1903.

Diamant, Henry A. Collection, 1805–75 (MoHistSoc)
Records emancipations and sale of slaves. MS 64–337

Elliott, Newton G. Papers, 1834–1909 (MoHistSoc)
Contains slave papers of Elliott of Howard County. MS 65–682

Emmons Family Papers, 1796–1938 (MoHistSoc)
Includes land and slavery papers. MS 65–683

Groom, William B., Papers (C321) 1843–1872 (SHSM)
Papers of a California, Missouri, resident. Two notices of the sale of "Negro" children; promissory notes.

Hamilton, Frederick A., Papers (C2026) 1837–1844 (SHSM)
Declaration of trust given by Hamilton, pledging three slaves as security for notes. Bill of sale for slaves.

Hempstead, Stephen. Papers, 1754–1927 (MoHistSoc)
Includes four letters from Manuel Lisa. Farm tasks, occupation of Hempstead's slaves, and vital records are recorded. MS 68–1287

Herndon, Archelaus, Record Book (C876) 1830–1859 (SHSM)
List of African Americans belonging to James Herndon. Archelaus Herndon lived in Carrollton, Missouri.

Hickman-Bryon. Papers, 1796–1920 (WHMC)
Missouri, Louisiana, and Kentucky families with land and slave records. MS 60–1817

Hunter, David and Nancy, Papers (C1962) 1832–1842 (SHSM)
Two deeds of sale of "Negro" slaves to David Hunter, 1832. Will deeding slaves to Nancy Hunter from her mother, Elizabeth Phillips, 1842.

Jacobs, George R. (1802–1877), Account Book (C2218) 1853–1877 (SHSM)
Accounts due, personal notes, inventories of land held in Boone and contiguous counties, rents received for slaves hired out, salaries paid out, lists of production of tobacco of slaves for two years, and personal letters to family and friends.

Kibby, George, Emancipation Contract (C995, V. 3, #81) 1853 (SHSM)

Contract between Henry C. Hart, St. Louis, and George Kibby, a free "Negro," guaranteeing the emancipation of Susan upon payment of $1,800 within a specified time.

Machir, John, Papers (C1589) 1852–1866 (SHSM)
Bills of sale for "Negro" slaves to Machir by Michael Fisher, 1852, and Henry F. Garey, 1855.

Manumission documents from St. Louis, Missouri, 1836–1854 (SHSM)

Marshall Family Papers (C204) 1852–1909 (SHSM)
Land deeds and family letters of Joseph Marshall family and Lynch family, Saline County, Missouri, from Fayette, Fulton, Glasgow, Pettis County, Howard County, and Blue Lick, and from Lynch sisters at Oxford Female College, Cooper Female Seminary, and Minnesota with mention of schools, slaves, and California crops.

McCanse, William A. Papers, 1856–68 (WHMC)
Contains a letter and an agreement regarding ownership of slaves.

McKenzie, Kenneth. Papers, 1796–1918 (MoHistSoc)
Bills of sale for slaves, 1828–57. MS 65–695

Missouri, Howard County, Freed "Negroes" Register (C1123) 1836–1861 (SHSM)
Lists "Negroes" set free during the period 26 January 1836–1 April 1861 in Howard County, Missouri Powers Museum, Carthage, Missouri, Collection, 1836–1916

Smith, Thomas Adams (1858–1919), Papers (C166) 1852–1919 (SHSM)
Sales of "Negroes" belonging to the estate of Thomas A. Smith, and accounts of the estate of C.E. Smith.

Smith, Thomas Adams. Papers, 1777–1919 (WHMC)
Saline County landowners' and doctors' records of births, deaths, and sales of 180 slaves from 1777 to 1864, MS 62–4788

Snoddy, Daniel F., Family Papers (C434) 1817–1861 (WHMC)
Bills of sale; county, state, and asylum tax receipts; school tuition receipts; bill of sale for slaves; notice of public sale after death of Daniel F. Snoddy. Letter from Snoddy giving brief description of towns, crops, and trade in Missouri. Letters from relatives in the southern states.

Spradlin, William, Slave Records (C2641) 1849 (SHSM)
Valuation of slaves and their disposition to various heirs.

Sublette Family Papers, 1848–54 (MoHistSoc)
Contains documents on runaway slaves and accounts with B.M. Lauch, slave dealer.

Tiffany, P. Dexter. Pardon Papers (MoHistSoc)
Many St. Louis County documents, including bonds of free blacks, fines on unlicensed free blacks, and an 1841–59 list of licensed free blacks in St. Louis.

Tucker, D.M., and Tucker, J.H. Records, 1833–1902 (WHMC)
Fulton, Missouri slave sale records. MS 60–2476

U.S. Census, Cooper County, Missouri (C1281) 1850 (SHSM)
Vol. 1 (Schedule 1) is the enumeration of free inhabitants giving the age, sex, and place of birth. Vol. 2 (Schedules 2–6) lists slave inhabitants.

White, John R., Slave Record Book (C1292) 1846–1860 (WHMC)
Record of purchase and sale of black slaves. Gives name, age, cost, name of person to whom sold, sale price, and usually the address of purchaser. In some cases the slaves were owned by White and partners.

Internet Resources

The Missouri State Archives web site (**http://www.sos.state.mo.us/ archives/**) maintains a *Guide to African-American History*, with a detailed listing of holdings. The collection includes census, court, military, penitentiary, civil rights, and various county records.

The University of Missouri at St. Louis (**http://www.umsl.edu/ ~libweb/blackstudies/afmoindx.htm**) provides links, information, and articles on African-American life in Missouri.

Research Contacts

The Western Historical Manuscript Collection (WHMC) is held jointly by the University of Missouri system and the State Historical Society of Missouri (SHSM), Columbia. The University of Missouri campuses at Columbia, Kansas City, Rolla, and St. Louis each hold a part of the collection that can be accessed at every campus. The SHSM has a large collection of local history and genealogy books, especially for Missouri.

Annette W. Curtis, Reference Librarian
Genealogy & Local History Branch
Mid-Continent Public Library
317 West 24 Highway
Independence, Missouri 64050

Annette Curtis has put together an outstanding African-American genealogical bibliography with extensive references for Missouri. See: Curtis, Annette W., compiler. *African-American Genealogy Resources in the Genealogy & Local History Branch*. Mid-Continent Public Library. April 2000.

Bibliography

Blassingame, John W. "The Recruitment of Negro Troops in Missouri during the Civil War." *Missouri Historical Review.* 58 (1964): 326–38.

Blattner, Teresa. *People of Color: Black Genealogical Records and Abstracts from MO Sources, Volume 1.* Bowie, Md.: Heritage Books, 1993.
This volume contains the roster of the 56th Regiment U.S.C.T. Infantry; slave schedules of Dunklin, Chariton, and Reynolds counties; church and school records; burial records; plantation records; and other pertinent information.

Blattner, Teresa. *People of Color: Black Genealogical Records and Abstracts from Missouri Sources, Volume 2.* Bowie, Md.: Heritage Books, 1998.
This second volume is a follow-up to the first and compiles information from many sources.

Bowen, Elbert R. "Negro Minstrels in Early Rural Missouri." *Missouri Historical Review.* 47 (1953): 103–9.

DeArmond, Fred. "Reconstruction in Missouri." *Missouri Historical Review.* 61 (1967): 364–77.

Foley, William E. *The Genesis of Missouri: From Wilderness Outpost to Statehood.* Columbia: University of Missouri Press, 1989.

Kot, Elizabeth G., and Shirley P. Thompson. *Missouri Cemetery Inscription Sources.* Walnut Creek, Calif.: Indices Publishing Co., 1995.

Kremer, Gary R., and Antonio F. Holland. *Missouri's Black Heritage.* Lorenzo J. Greene, contributor. Revised, Columbia: University of Missouri Press, 1993.

Morris, Ann, and Henrietta Ambrose. *North Webster: A Photographic History of a Black Community.* John Nagel, photographer. Bloomington, Ind.: Indiana University Press, 1993.

Nelson, Earl J. "Missouri Slavery, 1861–1865." *Missouri Historical Review.* 28 (1934): 260–74.

Sampson, F.A., and W.C Breckenridge. "Bibliography of Slavery and Civil War in Missouri." *Missouri Historical Review* 2 (1908): 320–32.

Slavens, George Everett. "The Missouri Negro Press, 1875–1920." *Missouri Historical Review.* 65 (1971): 505–26.

"The Underground Railroad and the Missouri Borders." *Missouri Historical Review.* 37 (1943): 271–85.

Trexler, Harrison A. "Slavery in Missouri Territory." *Missouri Historical Review*. 3 (1909): 179–98.

Wamble, Gaston Hugh. "Negroes and Missouri Protestant Churches before and after the Civil War." *Missouri Historical Review* 61 (1967): 321–47.

Montana

Important Dates

1870 – The census reported seventy-one African Americans in Helena.

1879 – A group of African Americans in Helena established the Pioneer Social Club and the Lodge of the Good Templars.

1910 – Montana had a population of 1,834 African Americans.

State Archives

Montana Historical Society
Division of Library and Archives
225 N. Roberts Street
Helena, MT 59620
http://www.his.state.mt.us

The archives unit of the Montana Historical Society houses state legislative, judicial, and executive branch records, along with county marriage records, court records, and any other local records in need of preservation. The library's holdings include an extensive collection of books, newspapers, and maps on Montana throughout its territorial history and statehood.

Census Records

Federal Census Records

1860–1880; 1900–1930 (DNA, MtHi)

Mortality Records

1870–1880 (DNA, MtHi)

Special Census

1890: Civil War Union Veterans and Widows (DNA)

State and County Records

Birth-Marriage-Divorce-Death Records

Department of Public Health and Human Services
Vital Records
111 North Sanders
P.O. Box 4210
Helena, MT 59604-4210
http://vhsp.dphhs.state.mt.us/dph_12.htm

Birth and death records from 1907 and marriages from 1943 are available from this department. Earlier records are kept in the county in which the event took place.

Newspapers

Colored Citizen (Helena): 1874; DNA.
Montana Plaindealer (Helena): 1906–1911; DNA.

Bibliography

Lang, William L. "The Nearly Forgotten Negroes on the Last Chance Gulch." *Pacific Northwest Quarterly* 70 (1979): 50–57.

Mills, Angie Arnold. *Montana Federation of Colored Women's Clubs.* Butte, Mont., 1921.

Taylor, Quintard. "A History of Blacks in the Pacific Northwest: 1788–1970." (Ph.D. dissertation University of Minnesota, 1977).

Thompson, Lucille Smith, and Alma Smith Jacobs. *The Negro in Montana, 1800–1945: A Selective Bibliography.* Helena: Montana State Library, 1970.
One of a very few sources that has information on African Americans in Montana.

Nebraska

Important Dates

1854 – Kansas-Nebraska Act opened territory to settlement.
1860 – Eighty-two free African Americans and fifteen slaves are listed in the census.
1861 – Territorial legislation abolished slavery.

State Archives

Nebraska State Historical Society
1500 R Street   *Mailing Address:* Box 82554
Lincoln, NE 68501   Lincoln, NE 68501
http://www.nebraskahistory.org/lib-arch/index.htm

The Library/Archives Division collection not only contains government records but also a wide variety of books and printed materials. While counties are responsible for their own records, many have been microfilmed or otherwise preserved, and are available at the State Historical Society. For more information see the Nebraska State Historical Society's *A Guide to the Archives and Manuscripts of the Nebraska State Historical Society,* compiled by Douglas A. Bakken, Duane J. Reed, and Harold E. Kemble (Historical Society Bulletin, no. 3. Lincoln, 1967). In addition, the following reference leaflets are available free of charge from the Historical Society:

Genealogical Societies in Nebraska
A Guide to Genealogical Research at the Nebraska State Historical Society
Historical Organizations in Nebraska
Index to Naturalizations in Nebraska and Some Iowa Counties, 1906 and Prior

List of Basic Sources on Nebraska History
Nebraska Census Records at the Nebraska State Historical Society.
Nebraska Church Records at the Nebraska State Historical Society
Nebraska County Courthouses
Nebraska Court Records
U.S. Government Land Laws in Nebraska, 1854–1904

Census Records

Federal Census Records

*1860–1880; 1900–1930 (DNA, NbHi)

Mortality Records

1860–1880, 1885 (DNA): 1860–80 (NbHi)

Special Census

1890: Civil War Union Veterans and Widows (DNA)

State and County Records

Birth-Marriage-Divorce-Death Records

Nebraska Health & Human Services System
Vital Records
301 Centennial Mall   *Mailing Address*: P.O. Box 95065
Lincoln, NE 68509   Lincoln, NE 68509
http://www.hhs.state.ne.us/ced/cedindex.htm

Birth and death records beginning in 1904, and marriage records beginning in 1909, are available from the state office. Earlier records, where they exist, may be located at the county level.

---

*The 1860 census for Kerney County names five slaves; the census for Atlas County lists ten slaves, but they are not named.

Cemetery and Church Records

The Nebraska Historical Society has records on microfilm from a number of Nebraska churches. Research has not yet been undertaken to determine whether African Americans are present in these records.

Military Records

African-American soldiers of the Ninth and Tenth Cavalry Regiments (called "Buffalo Soldiers" by the Plains Indians) were garrisoned at Fort Robinson for eighteen years and played an important role in northwestern Nebraska's history. Organized in 1866, the regiments first served in the Southwest. In 1885 the Ninth Cavalry arrived at Fort Robinson, which was regimental headquarters from 1887 to 1898. In 1902 the men of the "Fighting Tenth" Cavalry, veterans of the Battle of San Juan Hill, made their headquarters at Fort Robinson. See the Nebraska State Historical Society web site (**http://www.nebraskahistory.org/lib-arch/index.htm**) for more information.

Newspapers

The Nebraska Historical Society has more than 30,000 rolls of Nebraska newspapers dating from the territorial period to the present on microfilm. African-American newspapers include the following:

Afro-American Sentinel (Omaha). October 1896 to March? 1899. Weekly. Holdings: February 1896 to March 1899 (incomplete); CSdS, CtY, DLC, InNd, MB, MdBJ, MnU, MoSW, NcU, TNF, WHi. NbHi.

Enterprise (Omaha). January 1893 to 1911. Weekly. Holdings: August 1895 to July 1897 (incomplete); January 12, 1900; DLC, TNF, WHi August 1895–February 1911; August 1895 to July 1897 (incomplete); CSdS, CSS, CtY, InNd, MB, MdBJ, MnU, MoSW, NcU, NjP. NbHi.

Monitor. July 3, 1915–suspended January 1929; film 326 has 1915–1929 complete file, few missing issues. NbHi.

The Omaha Guide. February 12, 1927–apparently discontinued May 1, 1949. NSHS has July 16, 1932–August 3, 1956. NbHi.

Omaha Progress. 1889. (This is on film at the Library of Congress.) NSHS has 3 issues, Nov. 20, 1890; March 22, 1890 and March 7, 1891. NbHi.

The Omaha Star. June 10, 1933–still being published 1978. NbHi.
Lincoln, Nebraska African-American Newspapers. NbHi.
The Voice. Oct 11, 1946—suspended May 14, 1953 (Nebraska Historical Society has complete file).
Weekly Review. January 5, 1933; Nebraska Historical Society has 1933, January 5, 12, 26; February (all); March 2, 30.
The Western Post. August 1876, Nebraska Historical Society has no coverage (editor Horace G. Newsom, first African-American editor in Nebraska); paper was published in Hastings.

Manuscript Sources: Personal Papers, Slave Records, and Diaries

Day, Mrs. Lee. Letters: (NbHi)
　　Experiences of early black homesteaders in Nebraska.
Delta Sigma Theta Collection of Negro History and Culture (NbHi)
　　Fine collection of life and history of blacks; mostly books.
Nebraska State Farmers Alliance Records, 1874–1920 (NbHi)
　　Includes mailing lists, petitions, letters, and biographical sketches of members.

Internet Resources

The W.P.A. Federal Writers Project for Nebraska published *The Negroes in Nebraska*, which has been made available on the Internet at **http://www.livgenmi.com/1940NEnwptitle.htm** through the USGenWeb project. Other materials are also linked to this site.

Access the Nebraska Historical Society web site (**http://www. nebraskahistory.org**) and search under category "slaves" for pictures of homesteaders and former slaves by Solomon Butcher (see Bibliography below for Butcher's book).

Bibliography

Anderson, Robert. *From Slavery to Affluence: Memoirs of Robert Anderson, Ex-Slave* Hemingford, Nebr.: The Hemingford Ledger, 1927. Recalls his life as a successful African-American Nebraska homesteader-rancher.

Anthony-Welch, Lilian. "Black People: the Nation-Building Vision." *In Broken Hoops and Plains People.* Lincoln, Nebr.: Nebraska Curriculum Development Center, 1976.

Bish, James D. "The Black Experience in Selected Nebraska Counties, 1854–1920." (Master's thesis, University of Nebraska at Omaha, 1989).
Two memoirs and two autobiographical novels provide accounts of life on the high plains.

Butcher, Solomon D. *Photographing the American Dream.* Lincoln, Nebr.: University of Nebraska Press, 1985.

Calloway, Bertha W., and Alonzo Smith. *Visions of Freedom on the Great Plains: An Illustrated History of African-Americans in Nebraska.* Virginia Beach, Va.: Donning Company Publishers, 1999.

Nebraska Writers Project. *The Negroes of Nebraska.* Lincoln, Nebr.: Woodruff Printing Co., 1940.

Nevada

Important Dates

1850s – African Americans enter Nevada territory.

1868 – African Americans became citizens by constitutional amendment.

1900–1940 – A large African-American community resided in Reno, where the Bethel African-American Methodist Episcopal Church, the oldest African-American church in the state, was established.

State Archives

Nevada State Library and Archives
100 North Stewart Street
Carson City, NV 89710
http://dmla.clan.lib.nv.us/docs/NSLA/archives/

The Nevada State Library and Archives preserves and makes available to the public all of the state's governmental records from the territorial period to the present, including the records of the executive, legislative, and judicial branches. In addition, some county records are available there for genealogical research purposes.

Census Records

Federal Census Records

1870–1880; 1900–1930 (DNA, NvL)

Mortality Records

1860–1880, 1885 (DNA); 1860–1880 (NbHi)

Special Census

1890: Civil War Union Veterans and Widows (DNA, NvL, NvU)

State and County Records

Birth-Marriage-Divorce-Death Records

Office of Vital Records
Nevada State Health Division
505 East King Street, Rm #102
Carson City, NV 89710
http://health2k.state.nv.us/vital/

Birth and death records from 1887 to the present are recorded in each county, either in the office of the county recorder or county health officer. The Nevada State Office of Vital Statistics has birth and death records from 1911 and marriage and divorce records from 1968 to the present for all counties. Marriage certificates are filed with the county recorder in the county where the marriage license was issued, not where the marriage took place. Divorces are civil court actions, and divorce records from 1862 to the present are kept in the office of the county clerk for each county. Civil court cases are filed by case number and indexed by plaintiff and defendant.

The Archives has some records for marriages and divorces for Carson County, Utah and Nevada territories, 1856–1862; marriage records for Douglas, Lyon, Ormsby, Storey, and Washoe counties for 1862–1900.

Other State and County Records

Territorial Records: For Carson County Utah and Nevada Territory, 1855–1862.

The records include those of the county recorder, clerk of the probate court, and clerk of the county court. Divorces were handled in the probate court.

Manuscript Sources: Personal Papers, Slave Records, and Diaries

The Nevada Historical Society's manuscript collection has not been surveyed for material related to African-American genealogical sources.

Internet Resources

Clark County makes available an online searchable database for the county's marriage records: **http://www.co.clark.nv.us/RECORDER/ mar_srch.htm**.

See also **http://dmla.clan.lib.nv.us/docs/dca/thiswas/thiswas43.htm** *(Slavery in Nevada)* and **http://dmla.clan.lib.nv.us/docs/shpo/ projects.htm** *(Virginia City's African American Community)*.

Research Contacts

Nevada Historical Society
1650 N. Virginia Street
Reno, NV 89503
http://dmla.clan.lib.nv.us/docs/museums/reno/his-soc.htm

Bibliography

Coray, Michael S. "African-Americans in Nevada," *Nevada Historical Society Quarterly*, XXXV (Winter 1992), 239–257.

Glasrud, Bruce., comp. African Americans in the West: A Bibliography of Secondary Sources, with contributions by Laurie Champion, William H. Leckie, Tasha B. Stewart., and edited by Sheron Smith Savage. Alpine, Tex.: Sulross State University Center for Big Bend Studies, 1998. **http://www.coax.net/people/lwf/ ns_west.htm**

Nevada Black History Project. *Nevada Black History: Yesterday and Today*. Reno, Nev., 1992.

Rusco, Elmer. *Good Time Coming: Black Nevadans in the Nineteenth Century*. Westport, Conn.: Greenwood Press, 1976.

_____. "The Evolution of a Black Community in Las Vegas: 1905–1940." *Nevada Public Affairs Review* (1987, no. 2): 23–28.

New Hampshire

Important Dates

1645 – The first slave arrived in Portsmouth.

1664–1666 – The Dutch were encouraged by the colony's allocation of additional land for every slave imported.

1707 – Seventy slaves were reported in census records.

1775 – Six hundred and fifty-six slaves were reported in census records.

1776 – Prince Whipple served with distinction in the Revolutionary War.

1801 – Several free African Americans and their families settled in New Hampshire.

1896 – The first African-American church in the state was founded in Portsmouth.

1900 – Most African Americans in New Hampshire lived in Portsmouth.

1920 – African-American laborers came to Nashua from the south to work in the wood-treating plants that manufactured railway ties.

1950 – A new wave of African-American migrant workers, including professionals, arrived in New Hampshire.

State Archives

Division of Records Management and Archives
71 S. Fruit Street
Concord, NH 03301-2410
http://www.state.nh.us/state/index.html

The Archives holds all pre-1771 colonial records, state governmental records to the present, and some county and local records. A web site guide is available.

Census Records

Federal Census Records

1790–1880; 1900–1930 (DNA, Nh)

Mortality Records

1850–1880 (Nh); 1850–70 (USIGD)

Special Census

1890: Civil War Union Veterans and Widows (DNA, Nh)

State and County Records

Birth-Marriage-Divorce-Death Records

New Hampshire Bureau of Vital Records
6 Hazen Drive
Concord, NH 03301
http://www.dhhs.state.nh.us/

While vital records were recorded in New Hampshire towns before 1883, it was not mandatory to do so and all records before 1901 are not as complete as those after that date. A card index of those records available throughout the state is located at the Bureau of Vital Records.

Military Records

Nell, W.C. *New Hampshire's Colored Patriots of the Revolution.* See
http://www.seacoastnh.com/blackhistory/patriots.html

Newspapers

Granite Freeman (Concord). June 20, 1844, to April 23, 1847. Weekly. Holdings: 1844–47; NhHi. 1847 (incomplete); MiU-C, MWA, NhD.

Herald of Freedom (Concord). January 24, 1835, to October 23, 1846. Weekly, semimonthly, Title varies as *Abolitionism.* Suspended publication, June 14, to July 5, 1844; December 6, 1844, to March 14, 1845. Holdings: 1835–46 (incomplete); MiDW, PHC, PU.

Manuscript Sources: Personal Papers, Slave Records, and Diaries

Hooper, William. Memorandum Book, 1780–83 (NN)
Contains sales and purchases of blacks in New Hampshire. New Hampshire Historical Society has a handwritten copy of a census of each town in 1777, with the names of male and female slaves (compiled by Aaron H. Cragin).

Internet Resources

Richard Haynes and Valerie Cunningham have created in-depth web pages that provide a solid foundation for African-American family history research in New Hampshire; see **http://www.seacoastnh.com/ blackhistory/**.

Research Contacts

African American Resource Center
P.O. Box 5094
Portsmouth, NH 03801-5094

New Hampshire Historical Society
The Tuck Library
30 Park Street
Concord, NH 03301-6384
http://www.nhhistory.org

Bibliography

Cunningham, Valerie. "The First Blacks of Portsmouth." *Historical New Hampshire* (Winter 1989): 180–201.

Lambert, Peter. *Amos Fortune the Man and His Legacy.* Jaffrey, N.H.: Amos Fortune Forum, 2000.

Sammons, Mark, and Valerie Cunningham. *Black Heritage Trail Resource Book.* Portsmouth, N.H.: Strawbery Banke Museum, 1998.

Schmidt, Elizabeth W. *Minority Military Service, New Hampshire, Vermont 1775–1783*. Washington, D.C.: National Society Daughters of the American Revolution, 1991.

White, William L. *Lost Boundaries*. New York: Harcourt Brace and Co., c1947.

New Jersey

Important Dates

1618 – The Dutch founded the Village of Bergen (Jersey City).

1680 – New Jersey's first slaves were bought for a plantation in Shrewsbury.

1726 – The slave population numbered 2,600.

1790 – The slave population numbered 12,000.

1800 – Free African Americans outnumber slaves in Quaker-dominated South Jersey.

1804 – The Emancipation Act of all slaves in New Jersey was enacted.

State Archives

New Jersey State Archives
225 West State Street-Level 2   *Mailing Address:* P.O. Box 307
Trenton, NJ 08625-0307   Trenton, NJ 08625-0307
http://www.state.nj.us/state/darm/

The New Jersey State Archives collects and preserves all the colonial, state, county, and local governmental records for the state. The public research collections include early birth, marriage, and death records.

Census Records

Federal Census Records

1830–1880; 1900–1930 (DNA, Nj-Ar); several other public libraries and historical societies have schedules available for some years.

Mortality Records

1850–1880 (DNA, DNDAR, Nj)

State Census

1855, 1875, 1885, 1915

Special Census

1890: Civil War Union Veterans and Widows (DNA, Nj-Ar, NjRuF);

State and County Records

Birth-Marriage-Divorce-Death Records

New Jersey State Department of Health and Senior Services
State Registrar Search Unit
P.O. Box 370
Trenton, NJ 08625-0370
http://www.state.nj.us/health/vital/vital.htm

This state office has vital records from 1878 to the present. Divorce records are located at the county clerk of the superior court.

The New Jersey State Archives also has the following:

• Colonial Marriage Bonds, 1711–1797 (8 reels) and its Index (2 reels). Records the names of the bride and groom, county of residence, and the date of the marriage bond
  • New Jersey Colonial Marriage Bonds: 1711–1795
  • New Jersey State Vital Records: May 1848–May 1878
  • New Jersey State Vital Records: births, June 1878–1923; marriages, June 1878–1940; deaths, June 1878–1940.

Other State and County Records

In 1942 the Works Progress Administration conducted a survey of New Jersey counties and discovered some slave birth records. Today many of those records have been published in book form and some, such as those for Monmouth County, can be found on the Internet. See "Internet Resources" below. Also available are the following:

Middlesex County

New Brunswick Register of Black Children, 1804–44 (NjR)

Piscataway Township

Certificates of Abandoned Black Children, 1805–7 (NjR)

Residential Directories

List of Blacks compiled and in the information held by New Jersey Historical Society in Newark (Nj-HS)

South Jersey Towns

List of Blacks, 1798–99. Compiled by New Jersey Abolition Society (NjGbS)

The information below was provided by the New Jersey State Archives:

New Jersey Wills and Inventories: 1670–1900 (Nj-Ar)
New Jersey Wills, 1670–1900 (Nj-Ar)
County Clerk's records on microfilm (Nj-Ar)
  mortgages: 1765–1850
  deeds: 1785–1900 (usually do not mention race)

County Clerk's Records

New Jersey passed a gradual abolition of slavery law in 1804. As a result, each county clerk's office began to record slave births and manumissions. Most of these records are still held by each county clerk's office. The New Jersey State Archives has the following records:

Bergen Co. 1804–1846 slave births; 1804–1841 manumissions
Burlington Co. 1804–1826 slave births; 1820–1853 manumissions
Essex Co. 1804–1843 slave births; 1805–1817—manumissions;
    1805–1853—manumissions
Hunterdon. 1804–1835 slave births; 1788–1836 manumissions
Middlesex. 1800–1825 manumissions
Monmouth. pub. book—1804–1848 slave births
    pub. book 1791–1844 manumissions

Morris. pub. book—1756–1841 slave records; 1804–1841 slave births
Salem. 1600–1841 manumissions
Somerset. 1804–1830 slave births; 1823–1862 manumissions
Sussex. 1801–1835 slave births; 1802–1838 manumissions

Cemetery and Church Records

Quaker Collection (NjGbS)
    This collection contains Salem County manumissions, 1777.

Military Records

New Jersey Military Records (Nj-Ar)
    Index to Revolutionary War Manuscripts (9 reels): alphabetical
    index to New Jersey men who served on the American side of
    conflict. Abstracts information and cites references to the State
    Archives' manuscript records.
Sherman, Adelbert C. Papers, 1864–1908 (NjR)
    Includes reports, rolls, and returns of personnel and equipment
    of Company G, 28th U.S. Infantry (Colored), 1864–66. MS 66–
    145

Newspapers

    The Sentinel (Trenton). January 26? 1880, to November 13? 1882.
Weekly.
    Holdings: 1880–82 (incomplete); CSdS, CtY, CU, DLC, InNd, MB,
MdBJ, MnU, MoSW, NcU, Njp, NjT, TNF, WHi.

    See also the New Jersey State Archives web site (**http://www.state.
nj.us/state/darm/**) for a list of New Jersey newspapers on microfilm.

Manuscript Sources: Personal Papers, Slave Records, and Diaries

African Association of New Brunswick Records, 1817–24 (NjR)
    Information on black and white members, including owner's
    certificate permitting slave to join.

New Brunswick Colonization Society Records, 1838–54 (NjR)
Members listed.
McKeag Family Papers, 1827–1939 (NjR)
Includes slave bonds, releases, and indentures. MS 65–1679
Smith, Miles C. Papers, 1826–1930 (NjR)
Includes slave certificates, 1821–25. MS 66–149
Still, Peter. Papers, 1798–1875 (NjR)
Letters attempting to buy his wife and children, who were
Alabama slaves; genealogy included.
Van Liew-Voorhees. Papers, 1777–1859 (NjR)
Includes bills of sale for slaves. MS 66–178

Internet Resources

Excellent resources can be found at **http://www.blacktowns.org/**,
which tells the story of several African-American towns in New Jersey.
Another town, Dunderhook, a purported slave community connected
to Paramus, New Jersey, is described at **http://www.lutins.org/
dunkerh.html**.

Research Contacts

James Brown African Room
Newark Public Library
5 Washington Street
Newark, NJ 07102
http://www.npl.org/Pages/Collections/afroam.html

Bibliography

Epstein, Bette, Daniel P. Jones, and Joseph R. Klett, eds. *Guide to Family History Sources in the New Jersey State Archives.* (3rd edition). Trenton: New Jersey State Archives, 1994.
Revised for the second time in 1994, this guide describes the family history and genealogical holdings of the New Jersey State Archives. The state archives holds the most extensive holdings of primary research materials relating to New Jersey family history and genealogy. Among these records are wills prior to 1900; vital records, 1848–1878; decennial state censuses, 1855–1915; revolutionary war tax ratables; colonial deeds; and over

10,000 microfilm reels of county records. The *Guide* describes these and many other records and explains their usefulness for genealogical research. It also cites indexes to and transcriptions of the Archives' genealogical records.

Price, Clement Alexander. *Freedom Not Far Distant: A Documentary History of Afro-Americans in New Jersey.* Newark, N.J., 1980.

Steward, William, and Theophilus Gould Steward. *Gouldtown, A Very Remarkable Settlement of Ancient Date.* Philadelphia: J.B. Lippincott Co., 1913.
This is an unusual look at an early African-American family. The book deals specifically with the descendants of Elizabeth Fenwick, daughter of John Fenwick, one of New Jersey's founders. Elizabeth married an African man named Adam, whose descendants—the Goulds, Pierces, and Murrays—founded Gouldtown. Gouldtown exists today in the vicinity of Bridgetown (now Bridgeton), New Jersey. The area should be studied for the results of extensive intermarriages.

Walling, Richard S. *Men of Color at the Battle of Monmouth, June 28, 1778: The Role of African Americans and Native Americans at Monmouth.* Hightstown, N.J.: Longstreet House, 1994.
Contains a brief history of these men of color and a presentation of nearly two hundred names and identifications.

Wright, Giles R. *Afro-Americans in New Jersey: A Short History.* Trenton, N.J., 1988.

New Mexico

Important Dates

1528 – Steven Dorantes (also known as Black Steven, Little Steven, and Estevan), the slave of explorer Andres Dorantes, crossed the Southwest as one of the survivors of the Cabeza de Vaca expedition.

1903 – "Blackdom," an African-American community was established.

State Archives

New Mexico Commission of Public Records
State Records Center and Archives
1205 Camino Carlos Roy
Santa Fe, NM 87505
http://www.nmcpr.state.nm.us/

The permanent and historical records at the New Mexico State Records Center and Archives, as listed on the web site, include the official records of the Spanish government in New Mexico, 1598–1821 (the earliest surviving document is dated 1621) [Spanish]; Mexican government records, 1821–1846 [Spanish]; territorial government records, 1846–1912 [Spanish and English]; state government records, 1912 to the present [English]; county records, 1850–1912 [Spanish and English]; and private papers, including letters, diaries, wills, maps, and photographs pertaining to New Mexico or the Southwest [Spanish and English].

Census Records

Federal Census Records

1850–80, 1885, 1900–1930 (DNA); 1850–1930 (NmU, NMCPR)

Mortality Records

1885 (DNA, NmU)

Special Census

1890: Civil War Union Veterans and Widows (DNA, NmU)

State and County Records

Birth-Marriage-Divorce-Death Records

New Mexico Vital Records and Health Statistics
1105 St. Francis Drive   *Mailing Address:* P.O. Box 26110
Santa Fe, NM 87502   Santa Fe, NM 87502
http://dohewbs2.health.state.nm.us/VitalRec/

Birth and death records from 1920 are available from the state office vital records office. Marriage and divorce records are located at the county clerk's office and magistrate court, respectively.

Other State and County Records

The following historical files are located at the State Records Center and Archives in Santa Fe:

Land Grant Records of New Mexico
Spanish Archives of New Mexico, 1621–1821
Mexican Archives of New Mexico, 1821–1846
Territorial Archives of New Mexico, 1846–1912
State Corporation Commission—Documents pertaining to Blackdom, New Mexico

Research Contacts

For further information on African Americans in New Mexico, contact the African-American Studies Department at the University of New Mexico (Mesa Vista Hall Room 4021 Albuquerque, New Mexico 87131; **http://www.unm.edu/~afamstds/piopic.htm**)

The New Mexico State University Library catalog online (**http://libcat.nmsu.edu/**) provides additional resources on African Americans in New Mexico.

Bibliography

Bandelier, A.D.F. ed., *The Journey of Alvar Nunez Cabeza de Vaca*. New York: A.S. Barnes and Company, 1905.

Beltran, Aguirre Gonzalo. "The Integration of the Negro into the National Society of Mexico," in Magnus Morner, ed., *Race and Class in Latin America*. New York: Columbia University Press, 1970. 11–27.

Billington, Monroe Lee. *New Mexico's Buffalo Soldiers, 1866–1900*. Niwot, Colo.: University Press of Colorado, 1991.

Forbes, Jack D. "Black Pioneers: The Spanish-Speaking Afro-Americans of the Southwest," *Phylon* 27:3 (Fall 1966): 233–246.

Hallenbeck, Cleve, ed. *The Journal of Fray Marcos de Niza*. Dallas, Tex.: University Press, 1949.

Hammond, George P. and Agapito Rey, eds. *Don Juan de Onate: Colonizer of New Mexico, 1595–1628*. Albuquerque, N.Mex.: University of New Mexico Press, 1953.

Journal of the New Mexico Genealogical Society Vol. 37.
Nos. 2, 3, 4 include a three-part article by David Snow, which lists individuals of African descent in colonial New Mexico.

Katz, William Loren. *Black People Who Made the Old West*. Trenton, N.J.: Africa World Press, Inc., 1992.

_____. *The Black West*. Seattle, Wash.: Open Hand Publishing, Inc., 1987.

Miller, Darlis A. "Cross-Cultural Marriages in the Southwest: The New Mexico Experience, 1846–1900." *New Mexico Historical Review* (October 1982): 335–360.

Mock, Charlotte K. *Bridges: New Mexican Black Women, 1900–1950*. Albuquerque, N.Mex.: 1976.

Palmer, Colin. *Slaves of the White God: Blacks in Mexico*. 1570–1650. Cambridge, Mass.: Harvard University Press, 1976.

Richardson, Barbara J. *Black Directory of New Mexico*. Rio Rancho, N.Mex.: 1976.

_____. *Black Pioneers of New Mexico: A Documentary and Pictorial History*. Rio Rancho, N.Mex.: Panorama Press, 1976.

Schubert, Frank N. *Buffalo Soldiers, Braves and the Brass*. Shippensburg, Pa.: White Mane Publishing Company, 1993.

Sunseri, Alvin R. *Seeds of Discord: New Mexico in the Aftermath of the American Conquest, 1846–1861*. Chicago: Nelson Hall, 1979.

Weber, David J. *The Mexican Frontier, 1821–1846: The American Southwest Under Mexico.* Albuquerque, N.Mex.: University of New Mexico Press, 1982.
An example of a successful integration of African-American western history into a larger narrative.

New York

Important Dates

1790 – The total African slave population as counted in the census amounted to 21,324.

1827 – The Emancipation Act of 1827 prohibited slavery in the state.

1821 – The African Methodist Episcopal Zion denomination was formed in New York City and established congregations across the state and, eventually, in other states.

1900–1930 – The Great Migration, mostly from southern states, created a large increase in black population.

State Archives

New York State Archives
State Education Department, Eleventh Floor
Albany, NY 12230
http://www.archives.nysed.gov/

The extensive records at the New York State Archives cover primarily state governmental records from the state's earliest history to the present. Some county and local records are available, but most are still located in the counties. The Archives has an excellent search engine and research leaflets available on its web site. See *Records Relating to African Americans* at **http://www.archives.nysed.gov/a/researchroom/ rr_pgc_afri_amer.shtml**.

Census Records

Federal Census Records

1790–1880; 1900–1930 (DNA); 1800–1880; 1900–1920 (NNGB, NN-Sc, N). Also available at some public libraries and colleges throughout the state.

Mortality Records

1850–1880 (N)

State Census

1825, 1835, 1845, 1855, 1865, 1875, 1885, 1905, 1915, 1925—available for many counties (see **http://www.nysl.nysed.gov/genealogy/nyscens.htm** for further information and a complete listing of availability)

Special Census

1890: Civil War Union Veterans and Widows (DNA, NN, and a few other libraries).

State and County Records

Birth-Marriage-Divorce-Death Records

Vital Records Section
New York State Department of Health
Empire State Plaza
Albany, NY 12237-0023
http://www.health.state.ny.us/nysdoh/consumer/vr.htm

New York State vital records for 1881 are available from the state office for all locations except New York City.

New York City Department of Health
125 Worth Street
New York, NY 10013
http://www.nyc.gov/html/doh/html/vr/vr.html

New York City records (for all boroughs)— including records before 1881, where available—are available from Worth Street office of the Department of Health. See also "Internet Resources."

Other State and County Records

A large variety of records related to African-American genealogy are available for New York. The following records, along with those mentioned on the New York State Library web site, are only a small sampling of the total resources:

Albany County (Courthouse)
    Miscellaneous Certificates (1810–90)
    Slaves, Register of Manumitted (1800–1828)

Albany County (Secretary of State's Office)
Extensive collection of bills of sale for slaves and other records on blacks.
Albany County (Institute of History and Art)
Records of slave ownership, bills of sale, and inventories related to blacks, including a county census.
Albany County (NYHS)
Ledger of Mrs. Robert Sanders' sales of merchandise to blacks living in Albany.
Columbia County (Historical Society, Kinderhook)
Slave Sale Records, 1686–1836
Erie County (Grosvenor Library, Buffalo)
Anti-Slavery Society Records of West Aurora
Bills of sale
Certificates of Freedom of the Negro, 1804–11
Greene County (Historical Society, Coxsackie)
Blacks Born in Coxsackie: Gives name of owner, mother of child, name, age, and sex of child, date of birth.
Free Children Born to Slaves, 1800–1823
Kings County (St. Francis College, Brooklyn)
Slave Births and Manumissions (extensive)
Montgomery County (Department of History and Archives, Fonda)
Town and Village Records, 1783–1934; includes assessment rolls and slave births.
Nassau County (Historical and Genealogical Society, Adelphi College)
Register of Black Residents.
Nassau County (Westbury Children's Library)
Manumission of Slaves, 1776–77, carried out by John Hicks, Esther Seaman, and Richard and Samuel Willis.
Nassau County (NYHS)
Oyster Bay, L.I. Negro Ledger, 1761–62
Records of sales of merchandise to blacks, probably kept by William Townsend.
New York County (NHi)
Association for the Benefit of Colored Orphans, 1836–present Indenture records, admissions, discharges, visitors, births, deaths, and marriages. There are more than 10,000 names of black children, and in some cases names of their parents. The records from 1900 to the present are restricted until 2000.
New York City 1741 Riot Records
List of volunteers and aides.
New York Manumission Society Records, 1785–1845
Lists name of owner, manumitted black, county, and date of manumission.

New York Public School Society
> Records include "colored" schools.
> Slave Births, 1800–1818
> More than 200 certificates of slave births, giving names of child, mother, and owner.

Richmond County—Town of Castleton (NHi)
> New York Town Book, 1800–1927. Includes all children born to slaves after July 1, 1799.

Schoharie County (Historical Society)
> Slave Sales.

Steubin County (NIC)
> Slave Sales, 1808.

Tompkins County (NIC)
> "Early Settlers and Freemen of Tompkins County," written in 1862. Found in the Sydney Hollingsworth Galloway Collections.
> Certificates of Manumission, 1722–1835, town of Beekman.
> New Born Slaves, 1722–1835, town of Beekman *Old Town Book*, 1773–1816. Found in the Brackett Collection. Gives names of slave owners.

Westchester County (Thomas Paine Memorial House)
> White Plains Certificates of Birth and Manumission of Slaves, dates not given.

Westchester County (Historical Society, White Plains)
> Business records of Westchester
> Manumissions
> Tax List, public records, and original wills
> Yonkers Tax List, 1822–30

Cemetery and Church Records

See "Internet Resources" below.

Military Records

See "Internet Resources" below.

Newspapers

The Schomburg Center for Research in Black Culture (See "Research Contacts" below) has a collection of more than 400 black newspapers. Some of these have been microfilmed and are available in other libraries outside the state. See the web site at **http://www.nypl. org/research/sc/sc.html**. Examples of newspapers in the collection include the following:

Frederick Douglass' Paper (Rochester). June? 1851 to February 17, 1860? Weekly. Continues the *North Star* (see below). Holdings: 1851–59 (incomplete); CtU, CtY, CU, DLC. 1851–55 (incomplete); KyMoreU, MnU, MoJcL, NRU. February 1, 1856; September 17, 1858; July 8, 1859; February 17, 1860; CSdS, CSS, FTaSU, LU-NO, MdBMC, MiKW, TNF.

National Anti-slavery Standard (New York). June 11, 1840, to December 1872. Weekly, monthly. Holdings:1840–71; CSdS, HU, LU-NO, MB, OKentU, TxHTSU, WaBeW, WHi.

New York Age. October 15, 1887, to 1953. Weekly. Continues *New York Freeman* (see directly below). Continued by *New York Age-defender.* Holdings: 1887–1900; CSdS, CSS, CtY, CU, DLC, InIB, InNd, MB, MdBJ, MoSW, NjP, TNF, TxU.

New York Freeman. November 22, 1884, to October 8, 1887. Weekly. The title was *Freeman* from November 22 to December 6, 1884. Continues *New York Globe* (see directly below). Continued by *New York Age* (see directly above). Holdings:1884–87; CSdS, CSS, CtY, CU, DLC, ICU, InIB, InNd, MB, MdBJ, MnU, MoSW, NcU, NiP, TNF, TxU.

New York Globe. 1880 to November 8, 1884. Weekly. Continued by *New York Freeman* (see directly above). Holdings: 1883–84; CSdS, CtY, CU, DLC, InIB, MB, MdBJ, MnU, MoSW, NcU, NiP, TNF, TxU.

New York Gazette. February 16, 1759, to December 28, 1767. Weekly. Title varies—sometimes known as *Weyman's New York Gazette.* Holdings: 1759–67; CFS, CNoS, CSdS, InNd, LU-NO, MB, MBAt, MdBJ, MeU, NcGrE, NHi, NNC, OKentU, OU, PesS, RPB, Readex, ScU.

New York Gazette and Weekly Mercury. February 1, 1768, to November 10, 1783. Weekly. Continues *New York Mercury* (see below). Holdings: 1768–83; CFS, CNoS, CSdS, Cst, CLI, DeU, InNd, LNT, MB, MBAt, MdBJ, MeU, MWA, NbOU, NcD, NcGrE, MdU, NN, OKentU, OU, PEsS, RPB, Readex, ScU, TNJ, ViWi, WaBeW, WvU.

New York Gazette or Weekly Post-boy. January 1, 1753, to March 12, 1759. Weekly. Continues *New York Gazette Revived in the Weekly Postboy* (see below). Continued by *Parker's New York Gazette or Weekly Post-boy* (see below). Holdings: 1753–59; CSt, CU, CU-Riv, IU, MBAt, MdBJ, NhD, NHi, OKentU, RPB, TNJ, WaBeW.

New York Gazette or Weekly Post-boy. May 6, 1762, to August ? 1773. Weekly. Continues *Parker's New York Gazette or Weekly Post-boy* (see below). Holdings: 1762–73; CSt, CU, CU-Riv, IU, MBAt, MdBJ, NhD, NHi, OKentU, RPB, TNJ, WaBeW, WaU.

New York Gazette Revived in the Weekly Post-boy. January 19, 1747, to December 1752. Weekly. Continues *New York Weekly Post-boy* (see below). Continued by *New York Gazette or Weekly Post-boy* (1753–59, see above). Holdings: 1747–52; CSt, CU, CU-Riv, IU, MBAt, MdBJ, MWA, NhD, NHi, OKentU, PPT, RP, TNJ, ViWi, WoBeW, WaLl.

New York Journal or General Advertiser. May 29, 1766, to August 29, 1776. Weekly. Continues the volume numbering of *New York Gazette or Weekly Post-boy* (see above). Holdings: 1766–76; CSmH, CoFS, CoU, CLI, DeU, FU, InU, MBAt, MWA, NHi, NvU, PHarH, PHi, PSt, RP, ViWI, WoBeW, WHi.

New York Mercury. August 3, 1752, to January 25, 1768. Weekly. Continued by *New York Gazette and Weekly Mercury* (see above). Holdings: 1752–66; CFS, CLS, CNoS, CSdS, CSt, CU, CLI-Riv, DeLl, DeWint, GStG, InMuB, InNd, LNT, LU-NO, MB, MBAt, MdBJ, MeLl, MWA, NbOU, NcD, NcGrE, NdU, NN, NSyL1, OKentU, OU, PBL, PEsS, PPAmP, Readex, ScU, TNJ, ViU, ViWi, WaBeW, WoU, WVU, WVU-J.

New York Weekly Post-boy. January 3, 1743, to January 12, 1747. Weekly. Continued by *New York Gazette Revived in the Weekly Post-boy* (see above). Holdings: 1743–47; CU, IU, MBAt, MdBJ, MWA, NhD, NM, OKentU, PBL, PPT, RPB, TNJ, ViWi, WoBeW. *Parker's New York Gazette or Weekly Post-boy.* March 19, 1759, April 29, 1762. Weekly. Continues *New York Gazette or Weekly Post-boy.* Continued by *New York Gazette or Weekly Post-boy* (1762–73, see above). Holdings: 1759–62; CSt, CU, CU-Riv, ICU, IU, MBAt, MdBJ, NhD, NHi, OKenfU, RPB, TNJ, WoBeW, WaU.

North Star (Rochester). November 1, 1847, to 1851. Weekly. Continued by *Frederick Douglass' Paper* (see above). Holdings: 1847–51 (incomplete); CtU, CtY, CU, DLC, KyMoreU, MnU.

Manuscript Sources: Personal Papers, Slave Records, and Diaries

There are extensive collections at the Schomburg Center, the New-York Historical Society, and the New York State Library, all far too numerous to site here.

Internet Resources

The New York State Library web site for genealogy research topics (**http://www.nysl.nysed.gov/genealogy/gentopic.htm**) provides a well-organized, extensive number of links to sources on the Internet. Topics include Library Catalogs, Handbooks and Guides; New York City Vital Records Indexes; Passenger Lists and Indexes; Census Records; U.S. Military Sources; Newspapers and Indexes; City and Telephone Directories; Family Histories, Periodicals and Genealogical Sources of the LDS Church; a list of addresses related to New York Genealogy Sources for Churches and Cemeteries; County and Local historians; a list of Underground Railroad Operators in New York; and more.

See also the web page **http://www.archives.nysed.gov/a/ researchroom/rr_pgc_afri_amer.shtml** (*Records Relating to African Americans in the New York State Archives*). Examples of material related to the topic, "Slavery," include the following:

> Early Dutch settlers brought slaves from Angola and Brazil to work their new farms in the Hudson Valley. Slavery continued in New Netherland and in the succeeding British colony and State of New York over the next two centuries. At the end of the 18th century, New York had the largest number of slaves of any northern state. The institution of slavery is documented in the Dutch and British colonial council minutes and papers, which document official government actions pertaining to slavery [A1809, A1894, A1895]. Ship manifest records document the importation of slaves during the mid-18th century [A3196]. Extensive records of colonial probate courts, particularly wills and estate inventories, document slave ownership [J0038, J0043, J0301]. In 1785 New York State began the gradual process of eliminating slavery by prohibiting the importation of slaves for sale. In 1799 the State ensured the eventual freedom of children born to slaves, and by 1827 all slaves owned by New York

residents were freed. Unique documentation of slave owners and children of slaves is contained in records of the State Treasurer and State Comptroller for the period 1797–1820 [A0827, A3211].

Research Contacts

Schomburg Center for Research in Black Culture
515 Malcolm X Boulevard
New York, NY 10037-1801
http://www.nypl.org/research/sc/sc.html

Perhaps one of the largest collections of research material related to the history of African Americans is part of the New York City Public Library system. While the collection is not specifically geared toward genealogical research, the wealth of rare, unique, and primary materials holds many details about the history and culture of people of African descent in the Americas and Caribbean.

New York State has an extensive system of county and local historians who collect and maintain materials within their jurisdiction. Addresses can be found at **http://www.nysm.nysed.gov/hishistorians.html**.

Bibliography

Eichholz, Alice and James M. Rose. *Free Black Heads of Households in the New York State Federal Census 1790–1830*. Detroit: Gale Research, 1981.

_____. "New York State Manumissions." *The New York Genealogical and Biographical Record* 108 (Oct 1977): 221–225; 109 (1978): 22–24, 71–4, 145–9, 229–33; 110 (1979): 39–42, 66.

_____. "Slave Births in Castleton, Richmond County." *The New York Genealogical and Biographical Record* 110 (Oct 1979): 196–7.

_____. "Slave Births in New York City." *The New York Genealogical and Biographical Record* 111 (Jan 1980): 13–17.

Fordham, Monroe, ed. *The African-American Presence in New York State History: Four Regional History Surveys*. Albany, N.Y., 1989.

Freeman, Rhonda. *The African-American Presence in New York State History*. Albany, N.Y., 1989.

Joslyn, Roger D. "New York," *Ancestry's Red Book: American State, County & Town Sources,* rev. ed., edited by Alice Eichholz (Salt Lake City: 1992), pp. 521–40.
Contains numerous references to published genealogical sources and guides, as well as to records containing genealogical data.

Kobrin, David. *The Black Minority in Early New York.* Albany, N.Y., 1971.

McManus, Edgar J. *A History of Negro Slavery in New York.* Syracuse: Syracuse University Press, 2001.
See footnotes for sources.

Schweitzer, George K. *New York Genealogical Research.* Knoxville, Tenn.: Genealogical Sources Unlimited, 1995.

Yoshpe, Harry B. "Record of Slave Manumissions in Albany, 1800–1828." *Journal of Negro History.* 26 (1941): 499–522.
Gives former slave's name, owner's name, place of residence, and date of manumission.

_____. "Record of Slave Manumissions in New York." *Journal of Negro History.* 26 (1941): 78–107.

North Carolina

Important Dates

1712 – The African-American population numbered around 800.

1790 – The slave population numbered 100,572 by this date, and there was a small free group of African Americans.

1864 – As many as 5,000 African Americans from North Carolina served in the Union Army.

State Archives

North Carolina State Archives
Public Services Branch
109 E. Jones Street   *Mailing Address:* 4614 Mail Service Center
Raleigh, NC 2760   Raleigh, NC 27699-4614
http://www.ah.dcr.state.nc.us/

Census Records

Federal Census Records

1790–1880; 1900–1930 (DNA, NcAr); schedules for some years are available at libraries throughout the state.

Mortality Records

1850–1880 (DNA, Nc-Ar)

Special Census

1890: Civil War Union Veterans and Widows (DNA and several public libraries).

State and County Records

Birth-Marriage-Divorce-Death Records

North Carolina Vital Records
1903 Mail Service Center
Raleigh, NC 27699-1903
http://www.schs.state.nc.us/SCHS/certificates/

Birth and death records were not officially kept statewide in North Carolina before October 1913. Only births from 1913, deaths from 1930, marriages from 1962, and divorces from 1958 are available at the state office. Deaths records between 1913 and 1955 can be obtained from the North Carolina State Archives. Marriage records from about 1868 until the state recording began can be located at the county in which the marriage took place.

State and County Records

County records are especially useful for genealogical research. Almost all of North Carolina's 100 counties have transferred their pre-1868 original records, except deed and will books, to the state archives. At the state archives, each county's records are sorted into nine categories to facilitate research. Descriptive cards in a catalog in the Search Room report precisely what records exist in the state archives for each county (for example: Perquimans County, Apprentice Bonds, 1737–1892).

Sample county records are as follows:

Craven County

Civil Actions Concerning Slaves and Free Persons of Color, 1788, 1806–60, 1885
Criminal Actions Concerning Slaves and Free Persons of Color, 1781–1868
Slaves and Free Negroes, 1775–1861

Duplin County

Marriages of Freed People, 1860
Marriage Certificates, 1866–1868

Durham County

Marriage Licenses, Colored, 1898–1968

Edgecombe County

Slave Papers, 1780–1857

Granville County

Certificates of Marriage, 1851–68
Marriages of Freed People, 1866–67
Records of Slaves and Free Persons of Color, 1755–1874

Greene County

Marriage Register (Negro), 1875–1958

Guilford County

Marriage Licenses (Colored), 1872–1961
Marriage Register (Colored), 1867–1937

Lincoln County

Record of Freedmen: Marriages, 1866

Mecklenburg County

Marriage Record (Colored), 1850–67

Nash County

Division of Slaves, 1829–64
Marriages of Colored People and Division of Slaves, 1862–66
Slave Records, 1781–1864

New Hanover County

Slave Records, 1795–1864

Northhampton County

Slave Records, 1785–1867

Orange County

Negro Cohabitation, 1866–68
Slave Records, 1783–1865

Pasquotank County

Apprentice Bonds for Negroes, 1842–61

Perquimans County

Slave Records, 1759–1864

Randolph County

Records of Slaves and Free Persons of Color, 1788–1887

Rockingham County

Slave Records, 1803–60

Stokes County

Slave Records, 1806–60

Washington County

Freedmen's Marriage Records, 1866–72

Wayne County

Records of Slaves and Free Persons of Color, 1798–1869

Wilson County

Slave Records, 1855–64

Cemetery and Church Records

Advent Episcopal Parish Register (white and black), Williamston, N.C.
    Records of 1850–1917. (Nc-Ar)
First Christian Church (white and black), Williamston, N.C.
    Records of 1939–62. (Nc-Ar)
    Grave inscriptions for many people buried in North Carolina cemeteries prior to 1914 are available, arranged by name of decedent, in a card file index in the North Carolina State Archives Search Room.

Military Records

U.S. Colored Troops in North Carolina web site (**http://www.rootsweb.com/~ncusct/usct.htm**) is under development.
    See extensive military information on the North Carolina State archives web site: **http://www.ah.dcr.state.nc.us/sections/archives/arch/military.htm**.

Newspapers

Gazette (Raleigh). 1883–1900? Biweekly, weekly. Holdings: January 16, 1893; 1896–1898 (incomplete); January 13, 1900; CSdS, CSS, CU, DLC, FTaSU, KI-Ii, LU-NO, MdBMC, MiKW, TNF, WHi.

Manuscript Sources: Personal Papers, Slave Records, and Diaries

Arrington, Archibald Hunter, Papers, 1744–1909 (NcU).
    Nash County, plantation records contain slave lists, slave bills of sale, hiring agreements, and birth dates; records of provisions given to, and contracts made with, freedmen.
Bailey, John Lancaster, Papers, 1785–1874 (NcU)
    Primarily family correspondence and papers of Bailey of Pasquotank County, Hillsborough, and Asheville, North Carolina, superior court judge, 1837–1863. The collection contains deeds of gift and sale of slaves in the 1840s and 1850s; papers concerning lands and slaves (1821–1829).

Burwell, Papers, 1750–1943 (NcU)
    This collection consists of personal, financial, and legal papers
    of the Burwell family of Warren, Vance, and Granville counties,
    North Carolina, and Mecklenburg County, Virginia, and the
    Williams family of Warren County, North Carolina. Included
    are letters that concern slave sales (1736–1799, 1832–1835);
    the hiring of slaves (1820–1835); the division of slaves according
    to an estate settlement (1850s); records of slaves hired and
    purchased (1830–1845, 1845–1860); letters of agreement
    between free blacks and William Henry Burwell of Virginia
    (1866–1873); account books and farm journals that record the
    birth dates of slaves and horses belonging to the Burwell family
    and slave purchases and sales (1805–1860); lists of both black
    and white members of the Tabernacle Society of the Tabernacle
    Methodist Episcopal Church in N.C. (1832–1850); and a school
    register for a black school in Vance County, N.C. (1881–1887).
De Rosset Family Papers, 1581–1940 (NcU)
    Some of the papers contain records of births of slaves in
    Wilmington, North Carolina. MS 64–995
Foy, Robert Lee. Collection, 1762–1875 (NcGrE)
    Includes slave records for Popular Grove Plantation, Scotts Hill,
    New Hanover County. MS 73–505
Galloway, James Clarence. Collection, 1756–1868 (NcGrE)
    Slave sold and rental records included. MS 73–499
Hubard Family Papers, 1741–1907 (NcU)
    Papers of the family in Virginia, Washington, D.C., North
    Carolina, Tennessee, and Florida, including slave lists. MS 64-
    1031
Rowell, James. Papers, 1809–1928 (NcGrE)
    Includes his slave records, Brunswick County. MS 73–517
Smith, Ephram H. Collection, 1795–1919 (NcGrE)
    Includes slave records of a family in Chicod, Pitt County. MS
    73–519
Smith, Peter Evans. Papers, 1738–1944 (NcU)
    A Halifax county family. The papers include a list of Negroes,
    1858–66. MS 64–649
Stark, Armistead. Papers, 1716–1832 (NcU)
    The Armistead family of Windsor and Plymouth, North Carolina.
    The bulk of the collection relates to Armistead's purchases of
    property and slaves in Bertie, Washington, and Chowan counties.
Young, Allen, (NcU)
    Correspondence, deeds, estate records, and other financial and
    legal items of Allen, farmer and slave owner in Wake County,
    North Carolina, and of members of his family. Legal and
    financial items include records of slave sales. (NcU)

See also the North Carolina University, Wilson Library web page (**http:/ /www.lib.unc.edu/mss/shcabout.html#shc**) for further North Carolina slave papers.

Diaries

Ardrey, William E., 1862–1907 (NcD)
  Discusses farming during Reconstruction and use of blacks.
Bateman (Mary), 1856 (NcU, original at LU-Ar)
  Plantation life.
Beale, Edward, 1817–18 (NcD)
  Includes an account of Beale's personal servant Horace. Records treatment of blacks.
Burgwyn, Capt. William Hyslop Sumner, 1858–64 (NcHiC)
  Plantation in Welden, North Carolina. MS 66–1852
Crudup, E.A., 1857–72 (NcD)
  Plantation diary.
Erwin, William, 1846–56 (NcU)
  Plantation records.
Gwyn, James, 1852–84 (NcU)
  Personal and plantation diary. MS 64–512
Harden, Edward, 1834–49 (NcD)
  Plantation records. MS 61–2449
Hill, Col. John, 1830 (NcU)
  Plantation diary.
Justis, Horace Howard, 1857–59 (NcD)
  Notes on slaves by law student and country schoolmaster.
King, Richard Hugg, 1819–23 (Nc-Ar)
  Records of slave deaths.
Lawton, Alexander James, 1810–40 (NcU)
  Comments on crops, slaves, and wealth. MS 64–544
Lovell, William S. (NcU)
  Plantation diary.
Pringle, Elizabeth W., 1868–1915 (NcU)
  Rice planter's diary.
Shaffer, J.J., 1876–79 (NcU)
  Sugar plantation diary.
Simpson, Samuel, 1795 (Nc-Ar)
  Plantation affairs.
Skinner, Tristin Lowther, 1820–62 (NcU)
  Plantation diary.

Wormoth, Henry Clay, Papers, IB42–1931 (NcU)
> Plantation journals including the Magnolia Plantation.
> Reports conditions of blacks after the Civil War.

Internet Resources

Paul Heinegg's compilation of free African Americans in North Carolina can be accessed on the Internet at **http://www.freeafricanamericans. com/**.

Also consult the *Guide to African-American Documentary Resources in North Carolina*, edited by Timothy D. Pyatt, at **http://www.upress. virginia.edu/epub/pyatt/PyaAfro2.html**.

Research Contacts

Special Collections, Perkins Library
Duke University
Durham, NC 27708
http://scriptorium.lib.duke.edu/slavery/

Southern Historical Collection
University of North Carolina at Chapel Hill
Wilson Library, Campus Box 3926
Chapel Hill, NC 27514-8890
http://www.lib.unc.edu/mss/shcgl.html

Bibliography

Byrd, William L. *In Full Force and Virtue: North Carolina Emancipation Records 1713–1860*. Bowie, Md.: Heritage Books, 1999.

Franklin, John Hope. *The Free Negro in North Carolina, 1790–1860*. Chapel Hill: University of North Carolina Press, 1995.

Heinegg, Paul. *Free African-Americans of North Carolina, Virginia, and South Carolina from the Colonial Period to About 1820*. 4th ed. Baltimore: Clearfield Co., 2001.
> This book consists of detailed genealogies of about 350 free black families. This edition traces many families further back to their seventeenth and eighteenth century roots. Researchers will find the names of more than 10,000 African Americans. Utilize the book to note sources for your own search.

Jackson, Ronald Vern, ed. *Federal Census Index, North Carolina 1850 Slave Schedules.* West Jordan, Utah.: Genealogical Services, 1976.

McBride, Ransom "Searching for the Past of the North Carolina Black Family." *North Carolina Genealogical Society Journal* 32 (May 1983).
A must-read in starting your research in North Carolina.

Rackley, Timothy W., ed. *Nash County, North Carolina, Division of Estate Slaves, 1829–1861.* Kernersville, N.C.: Author, 1995.

White, Barnetta McGee. *Somebody Knows My Name: Marriages of Freed People in North Carolina, County by County.* 3 vols. Athens, Ga.: Iberian, 1995.
This book is a godsend for genealogists working on African-American North Carolina ancestors. The records made in North Carolina by local officials have such great validity because the couples were talking with people whom they knew, and who knew them. In North Carolina the General Assembly in 1866 passed An Act Concerning Negroes and Persons of Color or of Mixed Blood. There are records for over 22,400 couples. The following North Carolina counties are covered in this three-volume set: Alexander, Alleghany, Beaufort, Bertie, Brunswick, Caldwell, Camden, Carteret, Caswell, Catawba, Chowan, Columbus, Craven, Cumberland, Currituck, Davidson, Davie, Duplin, Edgecombe, Forsyth, Franklin, Gates, Granville, Guilford, Halifax, Hyde, Iredell, Johnston, Lincoln, Macon, Mitchell, Nash, New Hanover, Northampton, Orange, Pasquotank, Perquimans, Person, Pitt, Randolph, Richmond, Robeson, Rowan, Rutherford, Sampson, Stokes, Surry, Union, Wake, Warren, Washington, Wayne, Wilkes, and Wilson.

White, Barnetta McGhee. *Enslaved Ancestors Abstracted from Granville County, North Carolina Deed Books A-Z 1–2, 1746–1864.* Durham, N. C.: B.M. White, 1993.

Wynne, Frances Holloway. *Marriage Register, Durham County, North Carolina 1881–1906.* Baton Rouge, La.: Oracle Press, 1983.

North Dakota

Important Dates

1832–1880 – Early photos show African-American crew members on almost every steamer moored around Bismarck's waterfront.

1870 – "A colored section" was located in Grand Forks, Devils Lake, Bismarck, and particularly in Minot. They were mainly railroad employees, many with wives and children.

1880 – African Americans were trail riders, cooks, and cowboys and could be found in the Badlands and river breaks of western Dakota.

1884 – William Thornton Montgomery had over 1,000 acres in the Red River Valley. He was a former slave of Benjamin Montgomery of Davis Bend, Mississippi.

1900 – A seasonal type of worker began to arrive during the early planting time.

1915 – At least ninety-five African Americans are known to have acquired homestead land.

State Archives

North Dakota State Archives and Historical Research Library
612 East Boulevard Avene
Bismarck, ND 58505-0830
http://www.state.nd.us/hist/sal.htm

The North Dakota State Archives doubles as the state's historical library. Official state governmental materials, books, newpapers, maps, and periodicals are among its collections.

Census Records

Federal Census Records

1860–1880, 1885 (all as Dakota Territory), 1900–1930 (DNA, NdHi)

Mortality Records

1880 (USlGD); 1885 (NdHi)

State Census

1915, 1925 (NdHi)

Special Census

Civil War Union Veterans and Widows: 1890
Fort Totten Reservation Indian census: 1885–1905, 1910–1939
Fort Berthold Reservation Indian census: 1889–1893, 1895–1939
Standing Rock Reservation Indian census: 1885–1913, 1915–1939
Turtle Mountain Reservation Indian census: 1885–1905 (with Fort Totten Reservation), 1910–1939
Digger Indians census: 1899–1904, 1915–1920. (NdHi)

State and County Records

Birth-Marriage-Divorce-Death Records

Division of Vital Records
600 East Boulevard Avene
Bismarck, ND 58505
http://www.vitalnd.com/

While some birth and death records date back to 1870, most were not recorded until 1920. Marriage records are available on a statewide level from 1925, while earlier ones can be found at the county level.

Internet Resources

See *Black Towns of North Dakota* at **http://www.soulofamerica.com/ towns/ndtowns.html**.

Research Contacts

North Dakota State University Archives
604 East Boulevard Avenue
Fargo, ND 58505
http://www.lib.ndsu.nodak.edu/archives/

Bibliography

Newgard, Thomas P., and William C. Sherman. *African-Americans in North Dakota: Sources and Assessments. Personal Accounts and Background Information as Found in Newspapers, Land Records, Interviews and Miscellaneous Documents.* Bismarck, N.Dak.: University of Mary Press, 1994.
Contains census information concerning Dakota and North Dakota black residents as found in the United States census reports of 1870, 1880, 1885, 1900, 1910, and 1920.

Roper, Stephanie Abbot. "African Americans in North Dakota, 1800–1940." (Master's thesis, University of North Dakota, 1993. [microform]

Sherman, William C., and Playford V. Thorson, eds. *Plains Folk: North Dakota's Ethnic History.* Fargo, N.Dak.: Institute for Regional Studies, 1988.

Ohio

Important Dates

1807 – African Americans had to register and post $500.00 bond when they entered the state.

1841 – The Ohio Supreme Court declared the state to be a safe haven for runaway slaves. Throughout its early history, the state played a crucial role in the Underground Railroad.

1850s – Mt. Union College in Alliance and Antioch College in Yellow Springs began accepting African-American students.

1856 – The Cincinnati Conference of the Methodist Episcopal Church opened Wilberforce University near Tawawa Springs.

1863–65 – Approximately 5,000 African Americans from Ohio served on the Union side in the Civil War.

State Archives

Ohio Historical Society
Archives/Library Division
1982 Velma Avenue
Columbus, OH 43211-2497
http://www.ohiohistory.org/

The state historical society's Archives/Library Division is the official repository for state records, and for the preservation of state and local records.

Census Records

Federal Census Records

1820–1880; 1900–1930 (DNA, OHi, OCIWHi; many other public and college libraries throughout the state have some census records)

Mortality Records

1850–1860 and 1880 (DNA)

Special Census

1890: Civil War Union Veterans and Widows (DNA, OU, OCIWHi, OOxM)

The State of Ohio never took its own census. However, it did conduct "Quadrennial Enumerations" taken every four years between 1803–1811. These show males over twenty-one years of age in each county, with address, race, occupation, and whether a freeholder of land. Prior to 1863 enumerations recorded only white males.

State and County Records

Birth-Marriage-Divorce-Death Records

Ohio Department of Health
Vital Statistics
P.O. Box 15098
Columbus, OH 43216-0118
http://www.odh.state.oh.us/

Birth records from 1908, death records from 1945, and marriage records from 1949 are available at the state office. Death and marriage records going back to 1908, when mandatory recording began, are located at the Ohio Historical Society, as are any available records before that year.

Other State and County Records

City Directories (OHi)
Most major Ohio cities, from approximately 1850
Columbus State Hospital Admissions Registers, 1838–1923; not indexed (OHi)
County History Collection (OHi)
> Published county histories and some transcripts of cemeteries and other Ohio county records. The Surname Index covers many of the published histories, while other books have their own indexes.

Cemetery and Church Records

Cemetery Records

Grave Registration File (OHi)
Compiled by the Adjutant General's office—includes all veterans, regardless of state of service, buried in Ohio.
See also "Internet Resources" and "Bibliography."

Church Records

African Methodist Episcopal Church Records (OWibfU)
Records of the following former bishops have been retained:
Arnett, Benjamin William. Papers, 1860–1900. MS 60–886
Coppin, Levi Jenkins. Papers, 1888–1920. MS 60–884
Payne, Daniel Alexander. Collection of Negro Life and History, 1811–93
Ransom, Reverend Cassius. Papers, 1893–1951. MS 60–885
Allen's Chapel African Methodist Episcopal Church, 1854 (OCHP)
Williams, Samuel Wesley. Papers. MS 63–202. Contains a memorial of members.
Free Will Baptist Church. Records, 1819–1916 (OHi). MS 68–1384
Society of Friends Papers, 1688–1937 (OHi). Mostly topical material, but may include some African-American genealogical sources.
See also "Internet Resources" and "Bibliography."

Military Records

The Ohio Historical Society has excellent resources on Ohio military records, some available by database search or guides. In addition, the following are available:
Curry, William Leontes. Papers, 1832–1926 (OHi)
Extensive microfilm collection of the Civil War in Ohio, including Ohio U.S. Colored Troops. MS 75–966
Lyman, Carlos Parsons. Papers, 1795–1915 (OCIWHi)
Letters and diaries of officers of 100th U.S. Colored Infantry, 1861–65. MS 75–1608
Ohio Militia Records, 1807–67 (OHi). Very fragile records arranged by numerical designation of units; not indexed and not complete. MS 75–1660

Palmer, William Pendleton. Collection, 1861–1927 (OCIWHi). Letters on plantation life and the Underground Railroad. The collection contains military records, including casualty lists and lists of black regiments in the South. MS 62–438

Regimental Papers of Civil War, 1861–65. Extensive material on Ohio regiments. Contains papers of H.G. Crickmore and J.W. Poine of the 4th U.S. Colored Cavalry.

Risdon, Orlando Charles. Papers, 1861–72 (OcIWHi). Organizer of the 53rd U.S. Colored Infantry. MS 75–1698

Service Records (OCIWHi, OHi). Ohio adjutant general's records of servicemen for the War of 1812, Mexican War, Civil War, Spanish-American War, and World War I. Indexed. MS 75–1858

Service Records (Soldiers Claims Division, Office of Adjutant General, Statehouse, Columbus)

Service records of all Ohio men who enlisted after World War I, and National Guardsmen since 1902

Newspapers

Family Visitor (Cleveland & Hudson), January 3, 1850, to 1858? Weekly, biweekly. Holdings: 1850 to May 10, 1853; McP.

Gazette (Cleveland). August 25, 1883, to May 20, 1945. Weekly. Holdings: 1883–1945; CtY, CU, DLC, InNd, MB, MdBJ, MnU, NcU, NjP, OCIWHi, TNF, TxFS, WHi.

Dabney, Wendell Phillips. Papers, 1905–64; OCHP.

This collection contains material related to the fifty-year publication of the *Union*, a Cincinnati African-American newspaper. Some issues from 1918–52 are included in Dabney's papers. MS 71–1532

In addition, there is an extensive collection of African-American newspapers at Kent State University (**http://www.kent.edu**). The Ohio Historical Society web site (**http://www.ohiohistory.org/**) has additional information on the following African-American newspapers: *The Advocate, The Afro-American, The Colored Citizen, The Forum, The Gazette, The Informer, The Journal, The Ohio State Monitor, The Palladium of Liberty, The Tattler, The Union.*

Manuscript Sources:
Personal Papers, Slave Records, and Diaries

Ashtabula County Female Anti-Slavery Society Records, 1835–37 (OCIWHi)
> List of members and memorialists for 1836. MS 75–1880

Barnett, William J. Manumission Papers, 1843–1856 (Ohio Historical Society)
> Legal documents granting freedom to former slaves and their children

Bowen, George Washington. Notebook, 1851–62 (OCIWHi)
> Written at the Cleveland Institute of Homeopathy. Bowen served in the 5th U.S. Colored Cavalry, 1864. MS 75–1861

Gholson, William Yates. Papers, 1795–1870 (OCHP)
> Includes letters from Frances Wright (1795–1852), founder of the Nashoba Colony of freedmen. MS 71–1538

Ladies Aid Society, Brocton, Ohio (OcIWHi)
> Records for January 14 to February 15, 1866. The society was an auxiliary of the New York National Freedmen's Relief Association. MS 75–1880

Miscellaneous Legal Documents Collection, 1800–1860 (OHi)
> Includes slave receipts and manumission papers. MS 75–1104

Peyton, Polly. Papers, 1850–61 (OHi)
> Legal papers and letters concerning the kidnapping of Polly's eight children from Lawrence County, Ohio. She was a free African American.

Pitkin, Perley Peabody. Papers, 1861–68 (OCIWHi)
> Records wages of "contraband" slaves.

Rankin, John, 1798–1886 (OHi)
> Recollections by members of Rankin's family of fugitive slaves who stayed at their home on the Underground Railroad in Ripley, Ohio.

Siebert, Wilbur Henry. Papers, 1866–1961 (OHi)
> Notes and official documents relative to his book on the Underground Railroad. MS 68–1705

Walker, Timothy. Papers, 1806–56 (OCHP)
> Information on African Education and Civilization Society and participants. MS 63–198

WPA. Ex-Slave Narratives, 1937–1938.
> When the Federal Writer's Project interviewed former slaves in 1937–1938, depositing the life histories in The Library of Congress, twenty-seven of those Ohio interviews did not get to the Library of Congress and are only available at the Ohio Historical Society.

Internet Resources

For Internet resources in Ohio in general, see **http://www.ohiohistory. org/resource/index.html**. See also *African Americans in Southeastern Ohio* at **http://www.seorf.ohiou.edu/~xx057/** and the Ohio Historical Society's *The African-American Experience in Ohio* at **http://dbs. ohiohistory.org/africanam/**. The following are examples of the material available from these two Internet sources:

The Story of Rendville, Ohio: An Interracial Quest for Community in the Post Civil War Era

A Black History of Athens County and Ohio University

Ross County, Ohio Records of African Americans

United States Colored Troops—Searchable Database—National Parks Service

Ohio Regional Newspapers Collections—Ohio University Libraries

Index to Ohio Newspapers/Ohio Historical Society

Funeral Homes and Cemeteries in Ohio

Research Contacts

The National Afro-American Museum
1350 Brush Row Road   *Mailing Address:* P.O. Box 578
Wilberforce, OH 45384   Wilberforce, OH 45384
http://www.ohiohistory.org/textonly/places/afroam/

Bibliography

Bigglestone, William E. *They Stopped in Ohio: Black Residents and Visitors of the Nineteenth Century.* Oberlin, Ohio: Author, 1981.

Dooks, Eleanor, and Mary H. Remler, ed. *Hamilton County, Ohio Burial Records: Union Baptist African-American Cemetery.* Bowie, Md.: Heritage Books, 1997.

Hickok, Charles Thomas. *The Negro in Ohio, 1802–1870*. 1896. Reprint, New York: AMS Press, 1975.

Nitchman, Paul E., ed. *Blacks in Ohio, 1880*. Vol. 1. Mansfield, Ohio: Ohio Genealogical Society, 1996.

Pih, Richard W. *The Negro in Cincinnati, 1802–1841*. Oxford, Ohio: Miami University Press, 1968.
Available at the Cincinnati Historical Society.

Wilson, C.J. "The Negro in Early Ohio." *Ohio State Archaeological and Historical Quarterly*. 39 (1930): 717–68.
Descriptive article; good background reading.

Oklahoma

Important Dates

1830s – The Trail of Tears: Native Americans expelled from lands in Georgia, Alabama, and other areas of the Southeast brought thousands of African Americans, both slave and free, with them.

1889 – Oklahoma had a thriving African-American farming class.

1890 – Three thousand African-American homesteads were located in the territory.

1910 – The Oklahoma census listed 113,000 African Americans.

State Archives

Oklahoma Historical Society
2100 North Lincoln Boulevard
Oklahoma City, OK 73105-4997
http://www.ok-history.mus.ok.us/arch/archindex.htm

The Oklahoma Historical Society is the central repository of territorial, state, and local records and has several divisions, including the library and archives.

Census Records

Federal Census Records

1900–1930 (DNA, OkHi)

Mortality Records

None available

Special Census

   1860, 1890: Territorial (OkHi, DNA)
   1890: Civil War Union Veterans and Widows

State and County Records

Birth-Marriage-Divorce-Death Records

Oklahoma State Department of Health
1000 Northeast Tenth, Room 117
Oklahoma City, OK 73117
http://www.health.state.ok.us/program/vital/brec.html

   Birth and death records after 1908 are located at this office. Where available, earlier records are at the Oklahoma Historical Society. Marriages and divorces are kept by the clerk of the court in the county where the event occurred.

Other State Records

   The Oklahoma Historical Society has on microfilm seventy-two volumes of Oklahoma Federal Land Tract Books, which are limited to homesteaders in Oklahoma Territory.

Cemetery and Church Records

   See *Oklahoma Cemeteries: A Bibliography*, compiled by Barbara Pierce and Brian Basore (Oklahoma City: Oklahoma Historical Society, 1993), which deals with materials in the Oklahoma Historical Society Research Library.

Military Records

   The Oklahoma Historical Society has the index of Civil War Confederate pension applications and pensioners for the War of 1812, Revolutionary War, and the Roll of 1883.

Newspapers

Langston City Herald. May 27 1891, to 1902? Weekly. Holdings: 1891–93; January 27, 1900; CSdS, CSS, CtY, DLC, InNd, MB, MdBJ, MnU, NcU, NjP, OkHi, OkS, WHi.

Oklahoma Guide (Oklahoma City). 1898 to August 1903. Weekly, monthly. Title varies as *Guide.* Holdings: 1898–1903; CSdS, CtY, DLC, InNd, MB, MdBJ, MnU, NjP, TNF, WHi.

Manuscript Sources: Personal Papers, Slave Records, and Diaries

Chickasaw Nation Records, 1866–1904 (OkU)
> Papers relating to freed men. MS 62–693

Chicote, Samuel. Papers, 1867–68 (OkU)
> Reports of problems with slaves freed by the Creek Nation.

Five Civilized Tribes. Papers, 1698–1904 (OkTG)
> Includes papers of Cherokee, Chickasaw, Choctaw, Creek, and Seminole nations, ownership of slaves. MS 67–125

Internet Resources

In 1942 former slaves, including those from Oklahoma, were interviewed in the WPA project, including those from Oklahoma, illustrating the relationships between Native-American and African-Americans. See *The African-Native American History & Genealogy Webpage* at **http://www.african-nativeamerican.com/** for excellent resources to help track African-Native Americans, and **http://xroads.virginia.edu/~HYPER/wpa/wpahome.html** for the WPA slave narratives.

Bibliography

Clark, Robert L., Jr., ed. *Guide to Oklahoma Manuscripts, Maps, and Newspapers on Microfilm in the Oklahoma Department of Libraries.* Oklahoma City: Department of Libraries, 1970.

Ellsworth, Carole, and Sue Emler, eds. *Sequoyah County Oklahoma Marriages.* 3 vols. Wyandotte, Okla.: Gregath Publishing Co., 1983.
> Contains records of African-American and Native American marriages.

Franklin, Jimmie Lewis. *Journey Towards Freedom: A History of Blacks in Oklahoma.* Norman, Okla.: University of Oklahoma Press, 1982.

Knight, Thomas. "Towns in Oklahoma: Their Development and Survival." (Ph.D. dissertation, Oklahoma State University, 1975).

Leckie, William L. *The Buffalo Soldiers: A Narrative of the Negro Cavalry in the West.* Norman, Okla.: University of Oklahoma Press, 1975.

Littlefield, Daniel F., and Lonnie E. Underhill. "Black Dreams and 'Free' Homes: The Oklahoma Territory, 1891–1894," *Phylon* 34:4 (December 1973): 342–357.

Rader, Brian P. *The Political Outsiders: Blacks and Indians in a Rural Oklahoma County.* San Francisco, Ca., 1978.

Tolson, Arthur L. *The Black Oklahomans, A History: 1541–1972.* New Orleans: Edwards Printing Co., 1974.

Wright, Muriel H. *A Guide to the Indian Tribes of Oklahoma.* Civilization of the American Indian Series, no. 33. 1951. Reprint, Norman, Okla.: University of Oklahoma Press, 1987.
Many African Americans in Oklahoma have Native American ancestry. For those people, this book is a good place to begin genealogical research. County records are still held by the individual county courthouses.

Oregon

Important Dates

1579 – The area was visited by Sir Francis Drake and his multiethnic crew.

1843–1859 – Slavery was banned. Few African-American pioneers were allowed to stay in Oregon.

1850 – The census listed 207 African Americans.

1859 – The State Constitution forbade African-American residence, employment, property holding, and voting.

1890 – One thousand one hundred and eighty-six African Americans were listed in the state census.

1940 – African Americans arrived in Portland to work in the large ship-building industry.

State Archives

Oregon Secretary of State
Archives Division
800 Summer Street, N.E.
Salem, OR 97310
http://arcweb.sos.state.or.us/

In addition to being the state's repository for state and local governmental records, the Archives Division maintains a well-organized web site that provides important sources and links for genealogy research. For a guide to county records, see **http://arcweb.sos.state.or.us/county/cphome.html**.

Census Records

Federal Census Records

1850–1880, 1900–1930 (DNA, Or-Ar, OrHi)

Mortality Records

1850–1880 (Or-Ar)

Special Census

1890: Civil War Union Veterans and Widows (DNA, Or-Ar, OrHi)

State and County Records

Birth-Marriage-Divorce-Death Records

Oregon Center for Health Statistics
800 NE Oregon Street, Suite 205 *Mailing Address:* P.O. Box 14050
Portland, OR 97232   Portland, OR 97293
http://www.ohd.hr.state.or.us/chs/certif/certfaqs.htm

Although Oregon began requiring the recording of birth and death records in 1903, access to the records (even indexes) is restricted to the immediate family for birth records recorded less than 100 years ago and death records less than 50 years ago. Death records earlier than 50 years ago are located at the Oregon State Archives. Marriage and divorce records beginning in 1906 and 1925, respectively, are at the state office; earlier ones are located in the county in which the event occurred.

Cemetery and Church Records

For an online county-by-county, on-going grave transcription project, see **http://www.rootsweb.com/~orpionpr/Cemeteries.html**.

Military Records

The records of the Military Department at the Oregon State Archives Division (see **http://arcweb.sos.state.or.us/milit.html**) include a variety of materials dating back to 1847.

Newspapers

Portland New Age. 1896–1907. Weekly Holdings: November 25, 1899, to May 4, 1907; OrU. January 27, 1900 to April 20, 1907 (incomplete); CSdS, CSS, CtY, DLC, MB, MdBJ, MnU, MoSW, NcU, NjP, TNF, WHi.

Manuscript Sources: Personal Papers, Slave Records, and Diaries

Shannon, Wesley. Correspondence, 1850–84 (OrHi)
    Some letters relating to free blacks. MS 72–1676

Internet Resources

The Oregon State Archives has a number of searchable databases for materials in its collection, including the city of Portland vital records; a number of early county vital records; and a genealogical surname database and genealogical information locator search. See **http://arcweb.sos. state.or.us/banners/genealogy.htm**.

Research Contacts

Oregon Historical Society
1200 S.W. Park Avenue
Portland, OR 97205
http://www.ohs.org/

The Oregon Historical Society has been collecting, preserving, and making available to the public a vast array of research materials for over 125 years. Its catalog is available for research online at **http://www.ohs. org/homepage.html**.

Oregon Genealogical Society Library
955 Oak Alley
Eugene, OR 97403

University of Oregon Library, Oregon Collection
Eugene, OR 97403
http://libweb.uoregon.edu/speccoll/orc/orc.html

Bibliography

Brownell, Jean B. "Negroes in Oregon before the Civil War." Unpublished manuscript. Oregon Historical Society Library, n.d.

Davenport, T. W. "Slavery Question in Oregon," *Oregon Historical Quarterly* 9:3 (September 1908): 189–253.

Davis, Lenwood G. *Blacks in the State of Oregon, 1788–1971: A Bibliography of Published Works and Unpublished Source Materials on the Life and Achievements of Black People in the Beaver State. 2d ed.* Council of Planning Librarians, Exchange Bibliography, no. 616. Monticello, Ill.: 1974.

Douglass, Jessie. "Origins of Population in Oregon in 1950." *Pacific Northwest Quarterly* 41 (April 1950): 100–101.

McLagan, Elizabeth. *A Peculiar Paradise: A History of Blacks in Oregon, 1788–1940.* Portland: The Georgian Press, 1980.

Taylor, Quintard. "Slaves and Free Men: Blacks in the Oregon Country, 1840–1860," *Oregon Historical Quarterly*, 83:2 (Summer 1982): 153–170.

Pennsylvania

Important Dates

1639 – African people were recorded as being in servitude to Swedish settlers in the Delaware Valley region of southeast Pennsylvania.

1684 – The ship *Isabella* arrived in Philadelphia with the first documented slaves in Pennsylvania.

1826 – Pennsylvania passed a "personal liberty," anti-kidnapping law.

1915–1916 – The Great Migration triggered by the start of World War I transformed many Pennsylvania black communities.

State Archives

Pennsylvania State Archives
350 North Street
Harrisburg, PA 17120
http://www.phmc.state.pa.us/bah/dam/overview.htm

The *Guide to African-American Resources at the Pennsylvania Archives*, edited by Ruth E. Hodge (Harrisburg, Pa.: Pennsylvania Historical and Museum Commission, 2000), is a comprehensive reference to the African-American records, manuscripts, photographs, and microfilm holdings in the Pennsylvania State Archives. On the web site, under the "Holdings" tab, there is a listing of the various record sources available at the archives.

Census Records

Federal Census Records

1790–1880; 1900–1930 (DNA, P, PPiU; several other libraries in the state have schedules for a few of the years)

Mortality Records

1850–1880 (P)

Special Census

1779–1863: State Septennial Census (not true census, incomplete) (P)

1890: Civil War Union Veterans and Widows

State and County Records

Birth-Marriage-Divorce-Death Records

Vital Records, State Department of Health
101 South Mercer Street   *Mailing Address:* P.O. Box 1528
New Castle, PA 16101   New Castle, PA 16101
http://webserver.health.state.pa.us/health/

Mandatory recording of birth and death records in Pennsylvania began in 1906. These records are available at the state office. Some birth and death records before this are available for Philadelphia, Pittsburgh, and Allegheny City. Marriage records are not collected statewide and need to be obtained from marriage license clerks in the county in which the marriage occurred. Divorce records are available from the prothonotary court in the appropriate county.

Other State and County Records

The prothonotary or chief notary is the officer responsible for maintaining the records of the civil division of the court of common pleas in each judicial district. These records relate to civil proceedings, divorce, and equity and also include various types of reports filed by the county, municipal governments, and school districts. Included within these records are a number of county records related to slaves. Following are examples of these records, as listed in the "County Records" section of the Pennsylvania State Archives web site (**http://www.phmc.state.pa.us/ bah/dam/usecorec.htm**):

Adams County
    Register of Negro & Mulatto Slaves, 1800–1820 (Film #P-72)
Bedford County
    Register of Negro & Mulatto Slaves, 1780–1834 (Film #P-96)

Bucks County
  Register of Negro & Mulatto Slaves, 1783–1830 (Film #P-76)
Centre County
  Register of Negro & Mulatto Slaves, 1803–1820 (Film #P-91)
Chester County (CtY)
  Register of Slaves, 1780–1815
Cumberland County
  Register of Negro & Mulatto Slaves, 1780–1814 (Film #P-74)
Cumberland County
  Register of Negro & Mulatto Slaves, 1780–1823 (Film #P-77)
Dauphin County (MiU)
  Slave Records, 1788–1825; records date of freedom
Delaware County
  Release of Slaves, dates unknown
Fayette County
  Register of Negro & Mulatto Slaves, 1788–1826 (Film #P-75),
  with name of slave owner, date of birth, names of children and
  parents
Lancaster City
  Register of Negro & Mulatto Slaves, 1820–1849 (Film #P-88)
Lancaster County
  Register of Negro & Mulatto Slaves, 1780–1834 (Film #P-89);
  shows dates, names and addresses of owners, names of slave
  mothers and children, dates of birth, sex, age, and date of
  manumission. Indexed.

Cemetery and Church Records

In addition to sources listed on the Pennsylvania State Archives web
site and the manuscript sources below, many county historical societies
have transcriptions of the gravestones in that county.

Military Records

Bates, Samuel Penniman. *History of Pennsylvania Volunteers, 1861–
5*. 5 vols. Harrisburg: B. Singerly, State Printer, 1869–71. Black volunteers are listed on the following pages for the designated units: 6th Infantry V, 943–64; 8th Infantry V, 965–90; 22d Infantry V, 991–1010;
24th Infantry V, 1011–25; 25th Infantry V,1026–46; 32d Infantry V,
1047–65; 41st Infantry V, 106–80; 45th Infantry V, 1106–24; 127th
Infantry V, 1125–37

Johnson, Thomas S. Papers, 1839–69 (WHi)
Includes a handbook for 1864–65 of the 127th Regiment of U.S. Colored Troops.
Militia and National Guard records, 1775–1940 (P-Ar)
State Pensions for Revolutionary War and War of 1812 (P-Ar)
Records of Pennsylvania Soldiers in all wars from French and Indian War to World War II (P-Ar)

Newspapers

State Journal (Harrisburg). August 18, 1883, to 1885. Weekly. Continues *Home Journal*. Holdings: December 15, 1883, to January 24, 1883; January 24, 1885; CSdS, CSS, CU, DLC, LU-NO, MdBMC, MiKW, TNF, WHi.

Manuscript Sources: Personal Papers, Slave Records, and Diaries

African Colonization Society. Papers, 1832–72 (PHi)
Biographical sketches of members.
American Negro Historical Society, 1790–1901 (PHi)
Roll books, lists of black organizations participating, including black colleges and churches. MS 60–2033
Chew, Benjamin, 1770 (ICHi)
Lists Chew's slaves in Whitehall, Pennsylvania.
Dutilh and Wachsmuth, Philadelphia, Pa., 1704–1W (PHi, WM)
Slave trade papers with bills of exchange, cargoes, and trade with West Indies. MS 60–1791; MS 62–2064
Haverford College Library. Papers Related to Blacks, 1676–1937 (PHC)
Over 200 items, including records of Friends Freedmen's Association of Philadelphia, 1864–65; considerable collection of Quaker and Anti-Slavery records. MS 62–4731
Historical Society of Pennsylvania. Miscellaneous Papers (PHi)
Sixteenth- to nineteenth-century personal accounts of slaves' lives, and letters and diaries related to or written by blacks.
Jenks, Michael Hutchinson. Papers, 1695–1909 (PDoBHi)
County papers, some related to blacks.
Pennsylvania Society for Promoting the Abolition of Slavery, Papers (PHi)

Over 6,000 manumission documents. The papers are of unusual value because they reveal information on the African background of black slaves in Pennsylvania. These papers are another important prospective editing and publishing project.

Pennsylvania Colonization Society, 1838–1913 (PLuL)
Rosters of lifelong members, register of emigrants, 1834–64; Liberian applications, 1835–38.

Records of Clubs and Societies. Papers, 1775–1825 (PHi)
Membership lists of diverse organizations, including burial societies, colonization societies, lodges, and churches.

Steinmetz, Mary Owen. Papers (PHi)
Includes Berks County cemeteries.

Tallcott, Joseph. Family Papers, 1724–1857 (PHC)
Letters related to the Wilberforce Colony of blacks.

Tilghman, William. Letters, 1772–1827 (PHi)
Account of purchase and sale of slaves.

Wood, Anna Wharton. Collection of Quaker Papers, 1741–1853 (PHC)
Letters related to transporting freed blacks to Haiti, 1826.

Internet Resources

Temple University's web site (**http://www.library.temple.edu/blockson/**) offers a listing of the Blockson Afro-American Collection, as well as other sources for cultural, historical, and genealogical research.

The University of Pennsylvania Library has an online bibliography of sources for African Americans in Philadelphia (**http://www.library.upenn.edu/vanpelt/guides/afamphil.html**).

Several counties have excellent web sites with both general and specific information. One such site is that of Lancaster County (**http://www.lanclio.org/highlights/afamresources.htm**), which includes a large number of records related to the enumeration of slaves. See also "Other State and County Records," above.

Research Contacts

State Library of Pennsylvania
Forum Building
333 Market Street
Harrisburg, PA 17126-1745
http://www.statelibrary.state.pa.us/

Bibliography

Adleman, Debra. *Waiting for the Lord: Nineteenth Century Black Communities in Susquehanna County, Pennsylvania.* Rockport, Maine: Picton Press, 1997.

Barksdale-Hall, Roland C. *People in Search of Opportunity: the African-American Experience in Mercer County, Pennsylvania—A History and Guide.* Shenango: Pennsylvania State University Press, 1998.

Blockson, Charles L. *African-Americans in Philadelphia: A History and Guide.* Charleston, S.Ca.: Arcadia Publishing Company, 2000.

_____. *Pennsylvania's Black History.* Edited by Louise D. Stone. Philadelphia: Flame International, Incorporated, 1981. Bibliography and index are included in this background reading.

_____. *African-Americans in Pennsylvania: Above Ground and Underground, An Illustrated Guide.* Harrisburg, Pa.: R. B. Books, 2001.

Gottlieb, Peter. *Making Their Own Way: Southern Black Migration to Pittsburgh, 1916–1930.* Urbana, Ill.: University of Illinois Press, 1987.

Harris, Richard E. *Politics and Prejudice: A History of Chester, Pennsylvania Negroes.* Junction, Ariz.: Apache, 1991.

Hopkins, Leroy, and Eric Leddell Smith. *The African-American in Pennsylvania.* Harrisburg, Pa.: Pennsylvania Historical and Museum Commission, 1994.

Oblinger, Carl D. *Freedoms Foundations: Black Communities in South Eastern Pennsylvania Towns, 1780–1860.* Northwest Missouri State University Studies, Vol. 33, no. 4. Maryville: Northwest Missouri State University, 1972. A fine article with good bibliographical references.

Pennsylvania Magazine of History and Biography, Vol. 1–. 1877–. Philadelphia: Historical Society of Pennsylvania.
Has a number of articles in its various publications which are relevant to African-American genealogical research. An index is available for vols. 1–77, 1877–1951.

"Philadelphia African-American-Color, Class & Style 1840–1940," An Exhibition in the Museum of The Balch Institute for Ethnic Studies, April 4–July 9,1988, Library of Congress cit# 88-070545, Balch Institute for Ethnic Studies, 1988.

Switala, William. *Underground Railroad in Pennsylvania.* Mechanicsburg, Pa.: Stackpole, 2001.

Rhode Island

Important Dates

17th–19th centuries – Although Rhode Island is the smallest state, it holds a genealogical importance to African Americans out of proportion to its size. The impact of African-American Rhode Islanders migrating during the colonial period was felt particularly in New York, Vermont, and Pennsylvania during the 19th century. See the Bibliography below for more information.

1773 – Beginning in 1773, Newport Quakers began to free, or manumit, their slaves en masse. Former slaves were provided with a certificate attesting to their freedom, in case they should ever be questioned. Slaves younger than eighteen years of age were promised their freedom upon reaching adulthood.

1822 – A Rhode Island law disenfranchised African-American males.

1826 – Thirty-two African Americans, sponsored by the American Colonization Movement, sailed for Liberia.

State Archives

Rhode Island State Archives
337 Westminister Street
Providence, RI 02903–3302
http://www.state.ri.us/archives/

Census Records

Federal Census Records

1790–1880; 1900–1930 (DNA, R, RPPC)

Mortality Records

1850–1880 (R); 1860–1880 (DNDAR)

Special Census

1708, 1730, 1748, 1755, 1774, 1776, 1777 (Military Census), and 1782

The special census records above are found at the Rhode Island Historical Society, and are of excellent quality and very extensive.

1890: Civil War Union Veterans and Widows (DNA)

State and County Records

Birth-Marriage-Divorce-Death Records

Rhode Island Department of Health
Office of Vital Records
3 Capitol Hill, Rm. 101
Providence, RI 02908–5097
http://www.healthri.org/management/vital/home.htm

The Office of Vital Records maintains copies of birth and marriage records from 1899 and deaths from 1849 for all of the state's thirty-nine towns. Mandatory recording began in 1853; however, some vital records for the state begin in the colonial period and can be found in the town in which the event occurred. Copies of these earlier records and a statewide index for births and marriages 1852–1900 and deaths 1853–1945 are available at the Rhode Island State Archives.

Other State and County Records

In Rhode Island the town is the center of governmental life. Because of this, the town clerk's office is the repository for the original town, land, court, probate, and vital records. There is no central repository for original documents, although early material has been microfilmed and is available at the Rhode Island Historical Society in Providence, the Newport Historical Society, and the Westerly Public Library. Rhode Island town and county records are, however, not centralized as is the case in Connecticut and Massachusetts. Records before 1850 have been gathered and published. Below is information on where records are located in each county:

Bristol County

Barrington—Records are at the town office.
Bristol—Records are at town hall.
Warren—Records are at the town office.

Kent County

Coventry—Records are in the village of Anthony.
East Greenwich—Records are at the Kent County Courthouse and in East Greenwich.
Warwick—Records are at Apponouq.
West Greenwich—Probate, town council, and some land records are in the state archives in Providence.

Newport County

Jamestown—Records are at the town hall.
Little Compton—Records are at city hall.
Middletown—Records are at city hall. Abstracts of four volumes of wills are printed in the July and October 1968 issues of *The New England Historical and Genealogical Register*. It is best to use these only as an index and then go back to the originals.
Newport—Saltwater damaged most of the early records before 1779, making some of them unreadable. The Newport Historical Society organized them in 1853 and has some 15,000 books and 1,700 manuscripts of log books, custom house papers, and mercantile records. The Newport County Courthouse has records of births, deaths, and marriages.
Portsmouth—Records are at the town hall, and the earliest records of the town have been printed in book form.
Tiverton—Records are at the town office and are in excellent condition.

301

Providence County

Cranston—Records are at city hall.

Cumberland—Records are at the town office in Lincoln.

Foster—Records are in the village of Foster Center.

Gloucester—Records are at Chepachet.

Johnston—Records are at the town clerk's office. Early town council, town meeting, and probate records are at the Providence City Hall Probate Office.

North Providence—Records for the colonial period are at the clerk's office at Pawtucket City Hall.

Scituate—Records are at North Scituate.

Smithfield—Records are at Central Falls city clerk's office.

Washington County

Charleston—Records are at the town office.

Hopkinson—Records are at the town office.

New Shoreham—Part of Newport County until 1963. Records are at the town office.

North Kingston—Fire damaged all of the town books. They have since been repaired and a great deal of information is still available, although vital records suffered serious damage. What remains is located in Wickford.

Richmond—Records are at the town office.

South Kingston—Records are well kept and organized, and are located in the village of Wakefield.

Westerly—Town records are complete; the Westerly Public Library is the best place to start here.

Cemetery and Church Records

Both the Newport Historical Society and the Rhode Island Historical Society Library have important collections of cemetery and church records. For example, in addition to published sources of town records, The Rhode Island Historical Society Library (121 Hope Street, Providence) has a statewide index to gravestone transcriptions.

The Newport Historical Society has records of the African Methodist Episcopal Church and a fine "Quaker Collection." See "Internet Resources" below.

Military Records

Excellent biographical information can be found at the Rhode Island Historical Society Library, which has lists of African Americans who fought in the Revolution, providing full name, place of enlistment, and sometimes date of birth. Also located at the Rhode Island Historical Society Library is the Providence directory of 1841, which includes a list of "Colored Inhabitants."

Newspapers

No known African-American newspapers are available in the state.

Manuscript Sources: Personal Papers, Slave Records, and Diaries

The Rhode Island Historical Society has a tremendous collection of indexed family papers. A check of the material located there reveals log books, bills of sale, and records of the Providence Shelter for Colored Children. The Newport Historical Society (**http://www.newporthistorical.com/**) has an extensive collection that includes "a unique collection of diaries and journals, ranging in date from the early 18th century to the beginning of the 20th century. The Society's collection of personal diaries includes those of Sarah Osborn, an activist in Newport's Congregational Church and an educator of African Americans, covering the years 1753 to 1784."

The following records are located outside the state:

DeWolf, James, 1764–1837 (MH-B)
Extensive personal papers of slave traders of Bristol.
Lopez, Aaron, 1752–93 (MWalAJ) MS 68–150; 1731–82 (MH-B)
MS 60–1748; 1764–67 (MsaE) MS 73–563
Extensive papers of a Newport slave trader.

Internet Resources

Rhode Island African Americans have made an enormous contribution to the history of America. Newport was the nucleus of thousands of African-American families. The Newport Historical Society has made great strides in documenting records pertaining to African-American history genealogy, including Quaker manumissions, 1775; and records of the African Union Society and its offshoots—the African Humane Society, the African Benevolent Society, the Female African Benevolent Society, and the Union Congregational Church, founded in 1824. See "African-American History Collection" under "Library Special Collections" at **http://www.newporthistorical.com/library1.htm**.

Research Contacts

Rhode Island Genealogical Society
P.O. Box 433
Greenville, RI 02828

Rhode Island Historical Society Library
121 Hope Street
Providence, RI 02906
See its publication, *Selected Resources for African-American Genealogical Research*

Newport Historical Society
82 Touro Street
Newport, RI 02840
http://www.newporthistorical.com/

Bibliography

Bartlett, Irving H. *From Slave to Citizen: The Story of the Negro in Rhode Island*. Providence: Urban League of Greater Providence, 1954.

Chapin, Howard M. *Rhode Island in the Colonial Wars: A list of Rhode Island Soldiers and Sailors in Old French and Indian War, 1755–1762*. Providence: Rhode Island Historical Society, 1918. Lists African Americans from Rhode Island who fought in the war.

Chenery, William H. *The Fourteenth Regiment Rhode Island Heavy Artillery (Colored) in the War to Preserve the Union, 1861–1865*. Providence: Snow & Farnham, 1898.

Conrad, Mark. *A Guide to Census Materials in the Rhode Island State Archives*. Providence: Rhode Island State Archives, 1990.

Cottrol, Robert J. *The Afro-Yankees: Providence's African-American Community in the Antebellum Era.* Westport, Conn.: Greenwood Press, 1982.

Coughtry, Jay. *Creative Survival: The Providence African-American Community in the Nineteenth Century.* Providence, 1984.

Jeters, Henry N. *Twenty-Five Years Experience with the Shiloh Baptist Church and Her History.* Providence: Remington Printing Co., 1901.
Old manuscript available at Brown University, Rockefeller Library, recording the history of the first African-American church in Newport, Rhode Island. Has extremely valuable biographical accounts.

Jones, Rhett S. "Plantation Slavery in the Narragansett Country of Rhode Island: 1690–1790." *Plantation Society in the Americas 2* (1986): 157–170.

Lamar, Christine, ed. *A Guide to City Directories, House Directories, Business Directories in the Rhode Island State Archives.* Providence: Rhode Island State Archives, 1990.

Lamar, Christine, ed. *Rhode Island State Archives, Genealogical Sources in the Rhode Island State Archives.* Providence: Rhode Island State Archives, 1991.

Pierson, William D. *Black Yankees: The Development of an Afro-American Subculture in Eighteenth Century New England.* Amherst, Mass.: University of Massachusetts, 1988.

Stewart, Rowena. *A Heritage Discovered: African-Americans in Rhode Island.* Illustration design by Lawrence Sykes. Providence: Rhode Island African-American Heritage Society, 1975.

Youngken, Richard C. *African Americans in Newport, 1700–1945.* Providence: Rhode Island Historical Preservation & Heritage Commission and the Rhode Island African-American Heritage Society, 1998.

South Carolina

Important Dates

1526 – African-Spanish slaves rebelled and were left behind by Spain when they abandoned their settlement in early South Carolina.

1700s – Many slaves came from Barbados.

1790 – There were 107,094 slaves in the population.

1830 – There were 315,401 slaves and 7,921 free African Americans in the population.

1860 – There were 402,406 slaves and 10,002 free African Americans in the population.

1896 – African Americans were totally disenfranchised by the state constitution.

1910–1920 – Two hundred and forty thousand African Americans headed north during the Great Migration.

State Archives

South Carolina Department of Archives and History
8301 Parkland Road
Columbia, SC 29223
http://www.state.sc.us/scdah

See Paul R. Begley, Alexia J. Helsley, and Stephen D. Tuttle's *African-American Genealogical Research* (Columbia: South Carolina Department of Archives and History, 1997).

Census Records

Federal Census Records

1790–1880; 1900–1930 (DNA, Sc-Ar; several other county, college, and historical society libraries have population schedules for some years)

Mortality Records

1850–1880 (DNA, DNDAR, Sc-Ar)

Special Census

1890: Civil War Union Veterans and Widows (DNA, Sc-Ar, ScRhW)

State and County Records

Birth-Marriage-Divorce-Death Records

Division of Vital Records
South Carolina Department of Health and Environmental Control
2600 Bull Street
Columbia, SC 29201
http://www.scdhec.net/vr/

Statewide records for birth and death started in 1915, for marriages in 1950, and for divorces in 1949. Prior to those years, some birth and death records for the cities of Charleston, Florence, and Newberry are available at the respective county clerk's office. Earlier marriage records are at the county probate clerk's office, while earlier divorce records are held by the county clerk.

Other State and County Records

Allendale County

Old Records Negro Census, 1833

Anderson County

Judge of Probate Office Slave Records, 1812–60
Record of Magistrates and Freeholders, 1842–46, 1789–1811, 1814–18, 1861–68

Dillion County

Official Roster of South Carolina Soldiers in World War I, Vol. 2

Jasper County

Pension Records, years not stated

Oconee County

Judge of Probate, Pension Applications of Negroes Who Served the Confederacy, 1919–32
Clerk of Court, Military Records Official Roster of South Carolina Soldiers in World War II, Vol. 2, Colored

Pickens County

Board of Education Census, years not stated
Court of Magistrates and Freeholders (all African-American cases were held under jurisdiction of this court)
Negro Convictions, 1828–65
Trials of Vagrants, 1829–56
Guardians for Free Person of Color, 1844–63
Index, Circuit Court of Common Pleas (appearance and file books)

Richland County

Board of Education, Annual Report, Register of Negro Pupils, 1914–28
Census Reports, 1917–20
Pension Records, Confederate (Negro)

Saluda County

Pension Record of Confederate Veterans and Negroes, Vol. I

Parish Records

St. Helene's Parish, 1800–1821 (ScHi)
Plantation records
St. John's Parish, 1760–1853, Berkeley County (ScHi)
Property owners lists and records of dealings with runaway or owned slaves. MS 65–851
St. Stephen's Parish, 1833–40
Same as above

South Carolina State Records

Comptroller General Free Negro Roll Books, 1821–46 (ScAr)
Names and addresses of free African Americans in Charleston.
Low Country Land Records, 1696–1854 (ScHi)
Wills, deeds, indentures, and bills of sale involving slaves. MS 63–312
Secretary of the Province and Secretary of State, 1671–1903 (ScAr)
Extensive collection of bills of sale, manumissions, guardianship papers, certificates of freedom, and free birth records.

Cemetery and Church Records

South Carolina Episcopal Church Records, 1694–1962 (ScHi)
Church registers with some references to African Americans.
There are a growing number of gravestone transcriptions, mostly on the Internet. For example, see **http://www.prairiebluff.com/aacemetery/sc.htm** for a listing by county of online gravestone transcriptions for some known African-American cemeteries in the state.

Military Records

104th Infantry Regiment, USCT Colored Civil War Soldiers from South Carolina by J. Raymond Gourdin. 1997. xvii
Confederate States of America, 1861–65 (ScU)
Work and payroll records of African Americans.

Newspapers

South Carolina Leader (Charleston). October 7, 1865, to 1867?
Weekly. Holdings: 1865 to May 12, 1866 (incomplete); CSdS, CSS, CU, DLC, lHi, LU-NO, MBAt, MdBMC, MiKW, TNF, WHi.

Manuscript Sources: Personal Papers, Slave Records, and Diaries

Bacot Family Papers, 1767–1887 (NcU)
>   Correspondence, financial and legal papers, and other items of the Bacot family, cotton planters of the Mars Bluff Plantation near Florence in Darlington District, South Carolina. Included are slave lists (1853)

Ball, William J., Papers, 1804–1890 (NcU)
>   Records of three generations of the Ball family and a group of Cooper River plantations, Charleston District (later Berkeley County) South Carolina. Included are records of slave births, the names of slave mothers, and slave deaths (1808–1835, 1838–1879); an account of blankets and cloth distributed to slaves (1821–1833, 1840–1860); and a hog killing record that details the distribution of meat to slaves (1819–1834). See the extensive collection listed on the University of North Carolina, Wilson Library web site for further information on the slave papers listed above.

Ball, John and Keating Simmons Ball Books, 1779–1911 (NcU)
>   Records of Comingtee, a Cooper River, South Carolina, plantation in Charleston District (later Berkeley County), and of other rice plantations of the Ball family, including Stoke, Kensington, and Bridway. Volumes contain slave records listing supplies issued, births and deaths, names, and other data.

Ball, John, Sr., 1802–13 (ScHi)
>   Account books.

Bratton Family Papers, 1779, 1859–1953 (ScU)
>   Land and slave holdings are included. The family is from York County. MS 72–1261

Brinckerhoff, Isaac W., 1862–63 (NjR)
>   *Port Royal Gazette* experiences of Freedmen's Bureau superintendent on a plantation at Beaufort.

Broughton Family Papers, 1703–1854 (ScHi)
>   Relates to Mulberry Plantation on Cooper River and St. George Plantation at Dorchester County.

Chestnut-Miller-Manning Papers, 1744–1900 (ScHi)
>   Indenture, leases, etc.

Cheves Family Papers, 1777–1938 (ScHi)
>   Advice on plantation managements, plot records, and indentures.

Coker [W.C.] and Co., Society Hill, S.C. Records, 1842–1932 (ScU)
 Papers of a planter and merchant's company. Papers include
 William Coker's plantation book, 1868–69.

Council Journals, Saluda County, 1671–80, 1692, 1721–76 (Sc-Ar)
 These journals contain information on runaway slaves going to
 St. Augustine, records of the Stono slave revolt, and information
 on the 1749 slave revolt alarm.

Cox Family Papers, 1787–1875 (ScU)
 Records of slave sales are among the papers of this Marlboro
 District, Columbia, and Charleston family.

Cross, Paul. Papers, 1768–1803 (ScU)
 Slave traders' bills and receipts.

Jefferies Family Papers, 1771–1936 (ScU)
 Contracts made with freedmen are included in the papers of this
 Union District and Cherokee County family.

Hinson, Joseph Benjamin, 1801–22 (ScHi)
 Account books of Hinson, from Stiles Point, James Island.

Grimball, John Berkely, 1832–84 (ScCC, NcU)
 Plantation records.

Laurens, Henry. Papers, 1747–96 (ScHi)
 Some materials related to slaves.

Law, Thomas Cassels. Papers, 1770–1899 (ScU)
 Contains some slave records of Law, a resident of Darlington
 District.

Lee, Huston. Papers, 1858–65 (ScHi)
 Records slave auctions.

Manigault Family Papers, 1685–1873 (ScHi)
 This collection includes Silk Hope Plantation records and
 memorandum book, 1861–73.

McIver, Sarah Witherspoon Ervin, 1854–89 (ScU)
 Family and plantation life.

Middleton, Nathaniel Russell. Papers, 1761–1919 (NcU)
 Includes plantation account book and slave list (1785–1812) of
 Thomas Middleton of Charleston.

Mulberry Plantation Journal, 1853–89 (ScU)

Oakes, Ziba B., 1854–48 (MB)
 Papers of a Charleston broker dealing in slaves.

Perrin Family Papers, 1790–1918 (NcU)
 Includes slave records, chiefly 1830–62, relating to the Thomas
 County plantations of James M. and Lewis W. Perrin of
 Abbeville District.

Plantation Papers, 1748–1914 (ScHi)
 Includes tax returns, lists of African Americans, indentures for
 cotton and rice plantations on the Ashley, Cooper, Cumbabee,

and Peedee rivers, and for plantations in Georgetown County, St. John's Parish, Berkeley County, St. Mark's Parish, and Orangeburg County.

Porcher-Ford Family Papers, 1797–1925 (ScU)
Almanacs with notes on slave births and deaths.

Ravenel Family Papers, 1790–1918 (NcU)
Includes slave lists of the Ravenel and related families in Charleston and Berkeley counties.

Richardson-Nelson Families Papers, 1765–1935 (ScU)
Some papers concerning slaveholding for firms in Charleston and Sumter.

Sams Family Papers, 1826–1934 (ScU)
Births of family and black members of plantation, 1837–70.

Singleton Family Papers, 1759–1905.(NcU)
Correspondence, financial, legal, and other papers of the Singleton family, planters near Sumter, South Carolina. Correspondence covers various topics including purchase and sale of slaves and runaway slaves. Also included in the collection are bills of William Ellison, a free African-American craftsman (1820–1831)

Smith, Daniel Elliot Huger, 1846–1932 (ScHi)
A Charleston historian's notebook with will abstracts, records of Charleston houses, and records of a low-country plantation.

Smyth, Thomas, 1850–99 (ScHi)
Account books.

Stapleton, John. Papers, 1790–1839 (ScU)
A London lawyer's papers with plantation journals and lists of African Americans, chiefly from the Bull family estate of St. Helena Island, Beauford.

Stoney and Porcher Family Papers, 1799–1862.(NcU)
Records of Charleston District, South Carolina, plantations, including the daily plantation journal of Thomas Porcher; the plantation and slave records of Peter Gaillard Stoney; and the personal diary and notes of Isaac DuBose Porcher. Stoney's papers include the names and records of slaves held at Back River in 1835, 1844, 1854, and 1858–1860.

Trapier, Paul (ScHi)
Autobiography of an Episcopal minister's work with African Americans during the Confederacy and postbellum period.

Webb, Daniel Cannon, 1817–50 (ScHi)
Plantation journal and personal diary.

Weston Family Papers, 1786–1869 (ScHi)
Peedee River, Georgetown District, family with lists of African Americans and estate settlements for the Plowden Weston Plantation.

313

Withers, Francis, Account book, 1833–1840.(NcU)
> The account book of Withers, a rice planter of the Georgetown District, South Carolina. The book contains records of sales and purchases of sales.

Internet Resources

Search for "African-American Records and Genealogies in Allendale County, South Carolina" on a search engine on the Internet for a good example of what can be found online, including African-American cemetery, church, and slave records.

Other good web sites include *African-Americans in South Carolina: Slavery and the Civil War, 1525–1865* at **http://www.sciway.net/afam/slavery/indexs.html**, which provides history, definitions, records, and related sources; and Paul Heinegg's *Free African Americans of Virginia North Carolina, South Carolina, Maryland and Delaware* at **http://www.freeafricanamericans.com/**, which is also available in print in two volumes (Baltimore: Genealogical Publishing Co.).

The SCGenWeb site for Darlington County, South Carolina (**http://www.geocities.com/Heartland/Acres/5641/new/african.html**) provides updated genealogical research pertaining to a group of interconnected African-American families from the county. These families were descended from several groups of African-American slaves living in the eastern part of Darlington County in the late 18th century.

Research Contacts

South Carolina State Library
Senate and Bull Streets   *Mailing Address:* P.O. Box 11469
Columbia, SC 29211   Columbia, SC 29211

The State Library's catalog, which primarily lists books, is available online at **http://www.state.sc.us/scsl/**.

Bibliography

Begley, Paul R., Alexia J. Helsley, and Stephen D. Tuttle. *African-American Genealogical Research*. Columbia: South Carolina Department of Archives and History, 1997.

Bleser, Carol K. *The Promised Land: The History of the South Carolina Land Commission, 1869–1890*. Tricentennial Studies, no. 1. Columbia: University of South Carolina Press, 1969. Reports on land given to whites and free African Americans.

Koger, Larry. *Black Slaveowners: Free African-American Slave Masters in South Carolina, 1790–1860*. Columbia, 1995.

Mackintosh, Robert H., Jr. *Selected Bibliography of County, City & Town History & Related Published Records in the South Carolina Archives Reference Library*. Columbia: South Carolina Department of Archives and History, 1994.

McCawley, Patrick J. *Guide to Civil War Records in the South Carolina Department of Archives and History*. Edited by Judith J. Andrews. Columbia: South Carolina Department of Archives and History, 1994.

Malone, Samuel L., comp., and Ola Copeland, ed. *African-American Families in Cherokee County, South Carolina as Taken from the 1910–1920 Federal Census*. Spartanburg, S.C.: Reprint Co., 1993. This volume contains a list of the descendants of African-American families of Cherokee County, S.C.

McCuen, Anne K. *Abstracts of Some Greenville County, South Carolina, Records Concerning Black People, Free and Slave, 1791–1865*. Spartanburg, S.C.: Reprint Co., 1991.

Sandel, Edward, ed. *African-American Soldiers in the Colonial Militia: Documents from 1639 to 1780*. Roseland, La.: Tabor-Lucas Publications, 1994.

Schweninger, Loren. *African-American Property Owners in the South, 1790–1915*. Urbana, Ill.: University of Illinois Press, 1997.

South Carolina Department of History and Archives Staff. *A Guide to the Local Government Records in the South Carolina Archives*. Columbia.: University of South Carolina Press, 1988.

Tindall, George Brown. *South Carolina Negroes, 1877–1900*. Baton Rouge, La.: Louisiana State University, 1966. Reprint, Columbia: University of South Carolina Press, 1970. Short history of prominent African Americans, with bibliography.

Author Brent Holcomb and *The South Carolina Magazine of Ancestral Research* make available a wide variety of material pertaining to South Carolina at **http://www.scmar.com/**.

South Dakota

Important Dates

1804–1806 – York, a slave owned by William Clark, accompanied Clark on the Lewis and Clark expedition.

1870 – Ninety-four African Americans were listed in census.

1874 – Some African Americans were operating dance halls, gambling houses, and saloons.

1890 – Yanktown was home to sixty-two African-American families, many coming from Alabama.

1920 – Sully County Colored Colony, near Oneida, had a population of fifty-eight African Americans.

State Archives

South Dakota State Archives
South Dakota State Historical Society
Cultural Heritage Center
900 Governors Drive
Pierre, SD 57501–2217
http://www.sdhistory.org/archives.htm

The South Dakota State Archives are part of the South Dakota State Historical Society. The wide variety of material for the state and the territory before statehood includes governmental records and sources for genealogical research. There are online guides to the collection on a variety of topics, including genealogy. The staff will respond to research requests online from the web site.

Census Records

Federal Census Records

1860–1880; 1900–1930 (DNA, SdHi)

Mortality Records

1880 (USIGD); 1885 (SdHi)

Special Census

1890: Federal Civil War Union Veterans and Widows
(See below under "State Census.")

State Census

1885 (Special Census for some counties), 1895 (limited), 1905, 1915, 1925, 1935, 1945

State and County Records

Birth-Marriage-Divorce-Death Records

South Dakota Department of Health
Office of Vital Records
600 E. Capitol
Pierre, SD 57501
http://www.state.sd.us/doh/VitalRec/Vital.htm

Although the state didn't start collecting birth and death records until 1905, some pre-1905 records are included in the statewide index. Otherwise, some earlier birth records and any available marriage records can be found at the appropriate county register of deeds. Divorce records are at the office of the county clerk of courts.

Cemetery and Church Records

WPA Graves Registration: From beginning of the 20th century through 1941 (on microfilm and available through interlibrary loan). Some counties do not list burials, and some cemeteries are updated (updates not on microfilm).

Military Records

See the South Dakota State Archives web site (**http://www.sdhistory. org/archives.htm**) for the availability of military records.

Newspapers

The South Dakota State Archives has all known newspapers in the state from 1861. The staff will search all South Dakota newspapers for obituaries, if the date of death is known. See **http://www.sdhistory.org/ arc_npap.htm**.

Internet Research

See the South Dakota State Archives web site (**http://www.sdhistory. org/archives.htm**) for genealogical sources.

Research Contacts

South Dakota State Library
Mercedes MacKay Building
800 Governor's Drive
Pierre, SD 57501
http://www.sdstatelibrary.com/

Bibliography

Bernson, Sara L,. and Robert J. Eggers. "African-American People in South Dakota History" in *South Dakota History*. 7 (1977): 241–270.

Tennessee

Important Dates

1790 – The Territory of Tennessee was organized. Most settlers lived in East Tennessee, as yeoman farmers, owning one slave or two at most, or relying on free labor.

1800 – By this date over 2,000 slaves had entered the state.

1814 – The Manumission Society of Tennessee was founded.

1826 – Interstate slave trading was banned and repealed in 1855.

1834 – Five thousand free African Americans were disenfranchised by Tennessee constitution.

1840 – Fifty-six thousand slaves were counted in the population.

1862 – Nearly 4,000 African Americans enlisted in the Union Army.

1865 – Tennessee accepted the Thirteenth Amendment.

State Archives

Tennessee State Library And Archives
403 Seventh Avenue North
Nashville, TN 37243-0312
http://www.state.tn.us/sos/statelib/tslahome.htm

A comprehensive research facility and repository for Tennessee history and genealogy, the Tennessee State Library and Archives has several divisions, including the Tennessee History and Genealogy division, which provides access to vital records, census records, maps, military records, and county records.

Census Records
Federal Census Records

1820–1880; 1900–1930 (DNA, T; some years also available at the Knoxville, Fayetteville, Chattanooga, and Memphis public libraries)

Mortality Records

1850–1880 (DNA, DNDAR)

Special Census

1890: Civil War Union Veterans and Widows (DNA, T, TjoS)

State and County Records

Birth-Marriage-Divorce-Death Records

Tennessee Vital Records
Central Services Building
421 5th Avenue North
Nashville, TN 37247–0460
http://www2.state.tn.us/health/vr/

Although statewide birth and death records officially began in 1908, it wasn't until 1914 that the registration of births and deaths was universally carried out. Some earlier birth records for some major cities are also included in the index. All births and deaths recorded between 1908 and 1914 are available in an online index at the Tennessee State Library and Archives web site (**http://www.state.tn.us/sos/statelib/pubsvs/vital3.htm**). Death records between 1914 and 1952, with a partial index for the years 1914–1925, are also available at the archives.

Statewide indexing of marriage and divorce records began in 1952; these records are available at the state vital records office. Earlier marriage records can be found at the county clerk's office in the appropriate county, while divorce records are located in the county at the clerk of the court's office.

Cemetery and Church Records

Confederate and Federal Papers, 1858–65 (T)
Includes Civil War deaths and cemetery records.
Cumberland Presbyterian Church, African-American, 1866–94 (T)
Disciples of Christ Historical Society (T)
Collection of African-American churchmen, including biographical sketches and some materials on African-American congregations; archives of the Southern Christian Institute and Home Mission School for African Americans.

Mars Hill Presbyterian Church, Athens, McMinn County, 1823–1923 (T)

Methodist Episcopal Church, 1866–88; 1905–25 (T)

Minutes of African-American-European-American conferences; may have names and vital statistics.

Mill Creek Baptist Church, Davidson County, 1797–1814 (T)

List of African-American members.

St. Joseph Catholic Mission, Jackson, Madison County (T)

Records of mission established for African Americans.

Military Records

Confederate and Federal Papers, 1858–65 (T)

In addition to the cemetery records listed above, these papers also contain many personal materials.

Military Records, 1861–75 (T)

Ninety-nine reels of microfilm, which include an index to service records of African-American Union veterans from Tennessee.

Tennessee Confederate Pension Application, 1891 (T)

Personal and family history included for all veterans, including African Americans.

Newspapers

Colored Tennessean (Nashville). June 23?, 1865, to IW. Weekly. Continued by *Tennessean* (1866–1867?) Holdings: August 12, 1865, to July 13, 1866 (incomplete); CSdS, CSS, CU, DLC, lHi, LU-NO, MdBMC, MiKW, TNF, WHi.

Maryville Republican. October 26, 1867, to 1878. Weekly. Title varies as *Republican.* Holdings: October 7, 1876; CSS, CU, DLC, LU-NO, MdBMC, MiKW, TNF, WHi. November 2, 1867, to February 26, 1870; January 4, 1873, to October 27, 1877 (incomplete); T, USIGS.

Also see *Newspapers on Microfilm at the Tennessee State Library and Archives* at **http://www.state.tn.us/sos/statelib/pubsvs/paper-i.htm**.

Manuscript Sources: Personal Papers, Slave Records, and Diaries

African-American Chamber of Commerce; Classified directory of African Americans of Memphis and Shelby counties (T)

Berry, William Wells. Papers, 1838–96 (T)
Includes slave records relating to Berry's activities in Davidson County. MS 70–723

Buckner Papers, 1818–1923
Includes slave lists.

Buell, George P., and Brien, John S. Papers, 1805–1943 (T)
Includes Brien's slaves and Brien and Buell's joint business pursuits. MS 61–1330

Cherokee Collection. Papers, 1775–1878 (T)
Many items relate to Cherokees' ownership of slaves and their joint ownership of lands.

Dunlop, Hugh W., and John H. Papers, 1824–1905 (T)
These notes of two Henry County lawyers include over 200 documents related to slave sales, indentures, and deeds. MS 62–251

Eakin, William. Papers, 1841–46 (T)
Slave deeds included.

Fisk University Library.
The Anti-Slavery Collection has bills of sale and free papers. The African-American Collection includes estate papers, diaries, slave sales, biographies, birth records, certificates of freedom, and slave labor contracts.

Jackson, Andrew II. Account Books, 1845–77 (CCIVMi)
Includes purchase, sale, births, marriages, and deaths of slaves at Hermitage, 1845–77. MS 75–1849. Also available at (T).

Harrison, William. Papers, 1840–90 (T)
Bills of sale for slaves.

McCutchen Family Papers, 1818–1958 (T). MS 65–881
Slave records included.

Nichols-Britt Collection, 1771–1905 (T)
Extensive records of history and genealogy of Williamson and Davidson counties. Includes slave records and account books.

Owsley Charts (T)
Records of farms, slaves, and equipment in Davidson, DeKolb, Dickson, Dyer, Fayette, Fentress, Franklin, Gibson, Grainger,

Greene, Hardin, Hawkins, Haywood, Henry, Johnson, Lincoln, Maury, Montgomery, Robertson, Stewart, Sumner, and Wilson counties from the federal census schedules 1, 11, IV of 1850. Charts for all counties for 1840 and 1860.

Petitions to Tennessee State Legislature, 1796–1869 (T)
Includes manumissions.

Pryor, Jackson. Papers, 1830–97 (T)
Bills of sale for slaves in Jasper, Marion County. MS 68–495

Sanford, Henry Shelton. Papers, 1796–1901
Large group of materials related to Barnwell Island, 1868–89, and Oakley, 1869–90, sugar plantations.

Voter Registration Rolls. (T)

Westbrooks, Allie C., Collection, 1771–1935 (T)
Includes slave records of the Barton and Taylor families of Cannon and Rutherford counties. MS 73–872

Williamson Family Papers, 1833–74 (T)
Slave sales included.

Diaries

Cutchfield Family Papers, 1828–86 (T)
Includes 1852 diary, settlement of estate, and slave deeds. Records treatment of African Americans.

Perkins, Theresa Green (Ewen), date unknown (T)
Discussion about African Americans.

Porter, Nimrod, 1861–72 (T)
Sheriff of Maury County's diary referring to African Americans.

A guide to the manuscript collections of The Tennessee State Library and Archives is available at **http://www.state.tn.us/sos/statelib/ pubsvs/mguide09.htm**.

Internet Resources

In addition to the online search for births and deaths in Tennessee from 1908 to 1912 that is available through the Tennessee State Library and Archives web site, there are a number on online resources at the web site *People of Color in Old Tennessee*, **http://www.tngenweb.org/ tncolor/**.

Research Contacts

Tennessee Historical Society
War Memorial
Nashville, TN 37243
http://www.tennesseehistory.org/

University of Tennessee in Knoxville
Hoskins Library Special Collections
104 Cumberland Avenue
Knoxville, TN 37996
http://www.lib.utk.edu/spcoll/

Bibliography

Lamon, Lester C. *African Americans in Tennessee, 1791–1970.* Knoxville: University of Tennessee Press, 1981.
A treatment of the African-American experience in Tennessee, from slavery in the territory south of the river Ohio to the Civil Rights Movement in the 1960s. Includes a selected reading list.

Lovett, Bobby L. *The African-American History of Nashville, Tennessee, 1780–1930.* Fayetteville: University of Arkansas Press, 1999.

Mooney, Chase Curran. *Slavery in Tennessee.* 1957. Reprint, Westport, Conn.: Greenwood Publishing Group, 1971.
Gives a good idea of the laws affecting the hiring and selling of African Americans. Indicates what court records should be checked in each county for African-American genealogical information. Contains a list of slave owners in 1850 (p. 188), and a list of non-land-owning slave owners (pp. 203–42). Excellent bibliography gives an idea of which plantation records exist.

Taylor, Alutheus Ambus. *The Negro in Tennessee: 1865–1880.* Spartanburg, S.C.: The Reprint Company, 1941.

TEXAS

Important Dates

1530 – Spanish exploring parties included Africans.

1836 – The slave population numbered about 5,000.

1845 – Thirty thousand slaves lived in Texas when it was annexed to the U.S.

1865 – Slaves were emancipated. Juneteenth, celebrated on June 19, is the name given to emancipation day by African Americans in Texas.

State Archives

Texas State Library and Archives Division
Lorenzo de Zavala State Archives and Library Building
1201 Brazos Street   *Mailing Address:* P.O. Box 12927
Austin, TX 78711-2927   Austin, TX 78711-2927
http://www.tsl.state.tx.us/

The Genealogical Collection of the Texas State Archives has census records on microfilm for all the states through 1910 and Texas through 1930, voting records, tax rolls, and indexes to the state's vital records and a variety of Texas state and county records. The Sam Houston Regional Library and Research Center in Austin (**http://www.tsl.state.tx.us/shc/**) is part of the state archives and holds printed family, county, and local histories; maps; newspapers; and oral histories (see "Research Contacts" below).

Census Records
Federal Census Records

1850–1880; 1900–1930 (DNA, Tx, and many public libraries throughout the state)

Mortality Records

1850–1880 (DNA, Tx)

Special Census

1890: Civil War Union Veterans and Widows (DNA, Tx, TxGR, and public libraries in Dallas, Fort Worth, Longview, and Temple)

State and County Records

Birth-Marriage-Divorce-Death Records

Bureau of Vital Statistics, Texas Department of Health
P.O. Box 12040
Austin, TX 78711
http://www.tdh.state.tx.us/bvs/

Birth and death records began statewide in 1910. Statewide indexes (not the actual records) are available from the Texas State Library and Archives. Marriage records are available statewide from 1966; earlier ones can be located at the county clerk's office in the county where the marriage took place. Divorces are indexed statewide from 1968, with the actual records housed in the clerk of district court's office in the county where the divorce was granted.

Cemetery and Church Records

A growing collection of online transcriptions of African-American cemetery records in Texas can be found at **http://www.prairiebluff.com/ aacemetery/tx.htm**.

Military Records

Civil War publications and official records can be found at the Texas State Library and Archives.

Fort Davis National Historic Site, El Paso Military records, 1854–91, of "Buffalo Soldiers" and other African-American troops who served in the Indian wars.

Newspapers

Freeman's Press (Austin). July 25 to October 17, 1868. Weekly. Continues *Freedman's Press.* Holdings: July 25 to October 17, 1868 (incomplete); CSdS, CSS, CU, DLC, IHi, LU-NO, MdBMC, MiKW, TNF, WHi.

See also *Texas Newspapers on Microfilm at the Texas State Library* at **http://www.tsl.state.tx.us/ref/abouttx/news.html.**

Manuscript Sources: Personal Papers, Slave Records, and Diaries

Affleck, Thomas. Papers, 1847–66 (TxGR)
Records of the Glen Blythe Plantation near Brenham.
Billingsley, James B. Account Book, 1856–94 (TxU)
Billingsley was a planter in Marlin. MS 62–4834
Borden, Gail. Papers, 1832–82 (TxGR)
Letters and papers dealing with slaves and Texas property. MS 67–1996
Bryan, Moses Austin. Papers, 1824–95 (TxU)
Peach Point Plantation in Brazoria County; includes slave sales.
Cartwright, Matthew. Papers, 1831–71 (TxU)
Slave sales and account book. MS 62–4018
Chambers, Thomas W. Papers, 1824–95 (TxU)
A Bastrop planter's personal and business letters, with slave sales. MS 62–4044
Darragh, John L. Papers, 1839–93 (TxGR)
A Galveston lawyer's slave-trading papers. MS 67–1999
Fulmore, Zachary Taylor. Papers, 1735–1911 (TxU)
Fulmore was a lawyer, and secretary of the Colored Knights of Pythias. This is a large collection of personal material including letters on Texas history and genealogy (1880–1911). MS 64–748
Graham, Edwin S. Papers, 1825–1917 (TxU)
Contains diaries, bills of sale for slaves, indentures, and account books. MS 64–754
Green, Thomas Jefferson. Papers, 1789–1872 (TxU)
Deeds for slaves are included. MS 64–755

Kauffman, Julius. Papers, 1834–79 (TxGR)
   Includes slave sale papers, 1859.
Morgan, James. Papers, 1809–80 (TxGR)
   Bills, receipts, and slave trade papers. MS 67–2011
Rosenberg, Henry. Papers, 1845–1907 (TxGR)
   This collection includes Mrs. Mollie Rosenberg's papers on slaves.
Thompson, Ishan. Papers, 1830–75 (TxGR)
   Business letters, deeds, and bill of slave sales.

Diaries

Groce, Jared E., 1866–67 (TxU)
   Transcript on care of slaves, including bills of sale. MS 64–756

Internet Resources

A large number of resources are available on the Texas State Library and Archives' web site (**http://www.tsl.state.tx.us/arc/index.html**). Information available on the web site includes the following:

An index to Confederate pension applications
An index of county records on microfilm
An index to Republic claims
An index to Texas Adjutant General service records, 1836–1935
1867 Voters' Registration. The Reconstruction Act of March 13
Newspapers available on microfilm
Selected Texas city directories
A selection of past Texas telephone directories
Texas county tax rolls on microfilm

Addresses and telephone numbers for Texas county and district clerks are available online.

Research Contacts

Sam Houston Regional Library and Museum
P.O. Box 310
Liberty, TX 77575-0310
http://www.tsl.state.tx.us/shc/

In addition to the resources available on the Texas State Library and Archives' web site (see "Internet Resources" above), there are twenty-five Regional Historical Resource Depositories [RHRD] in the state, which all hold some of the microfilm of local and county record sources. However, the only RHRD that holds the entire collection of county records on paper and microfilm is the Sam Houston Library in Liberty. Only records on microfilm can be borrowed through interlibrary loan. See **http://www.tsl.state.tx.us/arc/local/index.html** for a listing of those records available on microfilm.

East Texas Resource Center
Ralph Steen Library, Stephen F. Austin University
P.O. Box 13055
Nacogdoches, TX 75962
http://www.lib.sfasu.edu/etrc/etrchome.htm

One of the twenty-five RHRDs in the state, the East Texas Resource Center has a variety of family records and photographs, including an exhibit of African-American lumbermen in East Texas.

Bibliography

Baker, T. Lindsay, and Julie P. Baker, ed. *Till Freedom Cried Out: Memories of Texas Slave Life.* Illustrated by Kermit Oliver. College Station: Texas A&M University Press, 1997. Thirty-two reminiscences of slaves from the Oklahoma slave narrative project.

Barr, Alwyn. *Black Texans: A History of African-American in Texas, 1528–1995.* Norman: University of Oklahoma Press, Second Edition, 1996.

Barr examines the African American experience in Texas during the periods of exploration and colonization, slavery, Reconstruction, the struggle to retain the freedoms gained, the twentieth-century urban experience, and the modern civil rights movement.

Carlson, Shawn Bonath. *African-American Lifeways in East-Central Texas: The Ned Peterson Farmstead Brazos County, Texas.* Contributions by Sue Winton Moss, Sunny Nash; technical editor, Robyn P. Lyle [submitted to the Office of Facilities Planning and Construction, Texas A & M University, by the Center for Environmental Archaeology, Texas A & M University]. College Station: The Center, 1995.

Campbell, Randolph B. *An Empire for Slavery: The Peculiar Institution in Texas, 1821–1865*. Baton Rouge: Louisiana State University Press, 1989.

Devereaux, Linda Ericson. *Nacogdoches County, Texas: The African-American Marriages, 1866–1874*. Nacogdoches, Tex.: Erickson Books, 1991.

Institute of Texan Cultures. *The Afro-American Texans*. San Antonio: University of Texas Institute of Texan Culture at San Antonio, 1992.

Kennedy, Imogene K., and Leon Kennedy. *Genealogical Records in Texas*. Baltimore: Genealogical Publishing Company, 1992.

Muir, Andrew Forest. "The Free Negro in Fort Bend County, Texas." *Journal of Negro History* 33 (1948): 79–85.

Redwine, W.A. "History of Five Counties." *Chronicles of Smith County* (Fall 1972): 13–68.
This reprint of a 1901 book was reissued by the Smith County Historical Society and contains biographies and pictures of several prominent African Americans, mainly from Smith and Rusk counties in eastern Texas. Migration routes are indicated, along with a listing of African-American property owners, including their place of birth, age, value of property, etc.

Smallwood, James. *Time of Hope, Time of Despair: African-American Texans During Reconstruction*. Port Washington, N.Y.: Kennikat Press, 1981.

Williams, David A., ed. *Bricks Without Straw: A Comprehensive History of African Americans in Texas*. Austin, Tex.: Eakin Press, 1997.

Utah

Important Dates

1847 – Permanent settlement of African Americans began with the arrival of Mormons. The James family was the first free African-American family to settle in Utah.

1850 – Approximately sixty African Americans lived in the Utah territory, the majority slaves. Laws sanctioning slavery were not enacted until 1852.

1862 – Slavery was officially ended when Congress abolished slavery in the territories.

State Archives

Utah State Archives and Records Service
Archives Building, State Capitol *Mailing Address:* P.O. Box 141021
Salt Lake City, UT 84114   Salt Lake City, UT 84114
www.archives.state.ut.us/

The Utah State Archives houses the state and local records of permanent historical interest and makes them available for public research.

Census Records

Federal Census Records

1850–1880*; 1900–1930 (DNA, USIGD, UPB, UL)

---

*The 1850 Slave Schedules for Davis and Salt Lake counties list twenty-nine slaves by name. The 1860 Slave Schedules enumerated twenty-six slaves living in Utah County, but they are not named; one slave was en-route to California.

Mortality Records

1850–1880 (DNA); 1870 (Tx)

Special Census

1890: Civil War Union Veterans and Widows (DNA, USlGD, UL)

State and County Records

Birth-Marriage-Divorce-Death Records

Utah Bureau of Vital Records
288 North 1460 West   *Mailing Address:* P.O. Box 141021
Salt Lake City, UT 84114-1012   Salt Lake City, UT 84114
http://hlunix.hl.state.ut.us/bvr/

Utah began filing birth and death records statewide in 1905. These are available from the Bureau of Vital Records. Some earlier records exist for the cities of Salt Lake and Ogden. These are available at the respective city's Board of Health. Death records between 1905 and fifty years ago are available to the public at the Utah State Archives Research Center. Marriage and divorce records began being centrally recorded at the Bureau of Vital Records in 1978. Before this, the county clerk or court in the respective county held the records. Marriage records go back to the mid-19th century.

Newspapers

Broadax (Salt Lake City). 1895 to June 6, 1899. Weekly. Holdings: August 31, 1895, to 1899; CSdS, CtY, GLC, FtaSU, ICU, MB, MdBJ, MnU, NcU, TNF, WHi.

Research Contacts

Family History Library
35 North West Temple
Salt Lake City, UT 84101
http://www.familysearch.com

The world's largest collection of family history research materials is maintained by the Family History Library and accessible at both the Salt Lake City location and through a system of local Family History Centers, from which it is possible to order material from the library in Salt Lake City on microfilm or microfiche. The Family History Library's catalog is available online at the above URL, under "Library."

Utah State Historical Society
300 Rio Grande
Salt Lake City, UT 84101
http://history.utah.org/

Manuscripts, newspapers, city directories, yearbooks, telephone directories, and photographs are included in the Historical Society's collections.

Bibliography

Bringhurst, Newell. *Saints, Slaves, and Blacks: The Changing Place of Black People within Mormonism.* Westport, Conn.: Greenwood Press, 1981.

Carter, Kate B. *The Negro Pioneer.* Salt Lake City: Utah Printing, 1965.

Coleman, Ronald C. "African-Americans in Utah History: An Unknown Legacy," in Helen Papanikolas, ed. *The Peoples of Utah.* Salt Lake City, 1976.

_____. "A History of African-Americans in Utah, 1825–1910" (Ph.D. dissertation, University of Utah, 1980).

Lythgoe, Dennis Leo. "Negro Slavery in Utah" (Master's thesis, University of Utah, 1966).

Vermont

Important Dates

1777 – Vermont was the first state to prohibit slavery when it adopted its constitution.

1790 – African Americans maintained a small presence in Vermont throughout its history. In 1790 census enumerators identified 269 people as "all other free persons."

1820 – Three members of a free African-American family with the surname of Virginia appeared in Fletcher, Vermont.

1830 – Calvin Virginia remained in Vermont, living in Burlington. Jeremiah, over 100 years old, re-appeared, living with a white family in St. Albans in 1840.

1830–1860s – Vermont played an active role in the Abolitionist movement and Underground Railroad.

State Archives

Vermont State Archives
Redstone Building
26 Terrace Street
Montpelier, VT 05602
http://www.vermont-archives.org/

Mailing Address: 109 State Street
Montpelier, VT 05609-1101

The Vermont State Archives maintains state governmental records related to the executive, legislative, and judicial branches of government in the state, but does not keep town or county records.

Census Records

Federal Census Records

1790–1880; 1900–1930 (DNA); 1790–1880, 1900–1920 (Vt, VtU)

Mortality Records

1850–80 (Vt); 1850–60 (DNDAR); 1870 (DNA, Tx)

Special Census

1890: Civil War Union Veterans and Widows (DNA)

State and County Records

Birth-Marriage-Divorce-Death Records

Vermont Department of Health, Vital Records Section
108 Cherry Street   *Mailing Address:* P.O. Box 70
Burlington, VT 05402   Burlington, VT 05402
http://www.state.vt.us/health/_hs/vitals/records/vitalrecords.htm

Although this is the state's official office for vital records, it only maintains birth, marriage, and death records for the past five years. All earlier vital records—including those recorded after mandatory record-ing began in 1857, those included in town records back to the early settlement period (1760s), and a statewide divorce index—are main-tained by the Public Records Division:

Public Records Division, Reference Research
General Services Administration Bldg.
Rt 2   *Mailing Address:* Drawer 77
Middlesex, VT   Montpelier, VT 05609

Other State and County Records

Vermont records are organized primarily by the state's 251 towns and municipalities, not by counties. All town clerks' offices have a wide variety of original source material for genealogical research. A large portion of these records are also microfilmed and available at the Public Records Division (see above) and through the Family History Library and its branches. For online addresses of town clerks, see **http://www. vitalrec.com/vt.html#State**.

Cemetery and Church Records

All extant and known cemeteries in Vermont were indexed statewide in 1919, although the index only covers graves pre-dating mandatory recording (1857). These transcriptions are included in the statewide vital records index 1760–1870.

The W.P.A. inventory of extant church records and their locations in 1941 is located at the Public Records Division in Middlesex, Vermont.

Military Records

The Vermont Civil War web site provides a list of African Americans who served in the U.S. Navy; see **http://www.vermontcivilwar.org/navy/afam.shtml**. See also James Fuller's *Men of Color, To Arms! Vermont African Americans in the Civil War* (San Jose, Calif.: University Press, 2001) and "Minority Military Service, New Hampshire and Vermont, 1775–1783." (Washington, D.C.: National Society of the Daughters of the American Revolution, 1991).

Newspapers

The Vermont State Library maintains an extensive collection of newspapers published in the state (see "Research Contacts" below).

Manuscript Sources: Personal Papers, Slave Records, and Diaries

The Vermont Historical Society has an extensively indexed manuscript collection, which has some references to topics of interest to African-American genealogical research (see "Internet Resources" below).

Internet Resources

The Vermont Historical Society has a web site devoted to the Underground Railroad's history in the state (**http://www.state.vt.us/vhs/educate/ugrr.htm**), which provides a listing of statewide newspapers, manuscript repositories, and suggestions for researching the topics of slavery, abolition, and the Underground Railroad in Vermont.

The full text of Elizabeth Merwin Wickham's document, "A Lost Family Found: An Authentic Narrative of Cyrus Branch and His Family, Alias John White," published in Manchester, Vermont in 1869, is available through the University of North Carolina-Chapel Hill Library web site at **http://docsouth.unc.edu/neh/wickham/menu.html**.

Research Contacts

Vermont Historical Society Library and Museum
60 Washington Street
Barre, VT 05641-4209
http://www.state.vt.us/vhs/

Vermont State Library
109 State Street
Montpelier, VT 05609-0601
http://dol.state.vt.us/

Bibliography

Daley, Yvonne, "Vermont's History Reveals Uneven Race Relations." *Boston Globe*, February 18, 1990, p. 75.

Virginia

Important Dates

1619 – Twenty Africans arrived in Jamestown, Virginia.

1770s–1780s – Such congregations as the Negro Baptist Church in Williamsburg, the Harrison Street Baptist Church in Petersburg, and the First African Baptist church in Richmond were all established.

1775 – Several hundred African Americans entered the Revolutionary War on the British side.

1782 – A new state law facilitated manumission.

1863 – The Emancipation Proclamation freed slaves in federally controlled area.

1910–1920s – The Great Migration north resulted in the loss of 50,000 African Americans.

State Archives

The Library of Virginia
Archives And Research Services
800 East Broad Street
Richmond, VA 23219
http://www.lva.lib.va.us

The Library of Virginia serves as the state archives for Virginia. Archival collections include local records (such as county and city land, probate, tax, court, and marriage records; bonds; oaths; etc.), maps, private papers and manuscripts, census reports and other state records, and an extensive collection of books and printed materials. Online catalogs exist for books, newspapers, manuscripts, and archives, although the entire collection is not cataloged online.

Census Records

Federal Census Records

1810–1880; 1900–1930 (DNA); 1810–1880, 1900–1920 (Vi, ViU)

Mortality Records

1860–1870; 1860 (DNA, NcD); 1870 (USIGD)

Special Census

1890: Civil War Union Veterans and Widows (DNA)

State and County Records

Birth-Marriage-Divorce-Death Records

Office of Vital Records and Health Statistics
James Madison Building
P.O. Box 1000
Richmond, VA 23218-1000
http://www.vdh.state.va.us/vitalrec/f_08.htm

Birth and death records begin for the entire state in 1912, although records are available for the cities of Hampton, Newport News, Norfolk, and Richmond between 1896 and 1912. Extant records from 1853 to 1896 are available through the Archives Division of the Library of Virginia. Extant marriage and divorce records from 1853 are available from the county in which the event took place, although some marriage records from 1853 to 1936 are also on microfilm at the Archives.

Cemetery and Church Records

There are numerous resources for church and cemetery records in Virginia, including some African-American records. See "Internet Resources" below and the Library of Virginia's web site (**http://www.lva. lib.va.us**) for online African-American church records.

Military Records

There are extensive military records, beginning with the colonial period, available for Virginia. The Library of Virginia's web site (**http://www.lva.lib.va.us**) provides searchable databases and guides.

Newspapers

People's Advocate (Alexandria). 1876–? Weekly. Moved to Washington, D.C. some time before April 19, 1879. Holdings: April 22, September 9, 1876; CSdS, CtY, CU, DLC, InNd, MB, MdBJ, MnU, NcD, NcU, NcU, NiP, TNF.

Richmond Planet. December 1883–1945? Weekly. Holdings: February 21, 1885, to July 12, 1890 (incomplete); 1895–1898; July 1899, to September 1900; CSdS, CtY, CU, DLC, FTaSU, ICU, InNd, MB, MdBJ, MnU, NcD, NcU, NIP, TNF, WHi. 1890–94; 1899–1945; McP, Vi. 1890–94; 1899 to May 1938 (incomplete); ViU, ViW.

Virginia Gazette (Williamsburg). 1736–80. Weekly. Holdings: 1736–80; A-Ar, ArU, AU, CFIS, CLS, CoU, CSdS, CSmH, CSt, CU, DeU, DLC, FTaSU, GEU, GStG, loHi, IaU, InNd, KyHi, KU, LU-No, MB, MBAt, MdAA, MdBJ, MeU, MiD, MiDW, MiMtpT, MiU, MnU, MoS, MoSHi, MoSW, MoU, MsHaU, MsSM, MU, MWA, NbOU, NcD, NcU, NdU, NhD, NHi, NIC, NiP, NiR, NmU, NN, NvU, OC, OCI, OkentU, OkS, OrU, OU, PPiD, PPiu, ScU, TU, TxF, TxU, ViU, ViW, WHi, Wv-Ar. Includes extracts related to runaway slaves and slave sales.

Virginia Star (Richmond). April 1877–1888? Weekly. Holdings-September 8, 1877; May 11, 1878, to September 27, 1879 (incomplete); April 30, 1881, to December 23, 1882 (incomplete); CSdS, CSS, CLI, DLC, FTaSU, LU-NO, McIBMC, MiKW, TNF, WHi.

The Library of Virginia has microfilm or original copies of most extant Virginia newspapers published since 1736. Several African-American newspapers published in Virginia are included in the collection. There are few newspaper indexes available, but an obituary may be found if the approximate date of death is known.

Manuscript Sources:
Personal Papers, Slave Records, and Diaries

Bill of Sale, 1737 (NN)
> Collection contains bonds for delivery after the 1783 sale of Nathan Lyttleton Savage, a Virginia planter. Also included is his account book concerning African Americans, 1768–85.

Brock, Robert Alonzo. Collection of Virginiana, 1582–1914 (CSmH)
> Extensive county records, family papers, and slave merchants' records, manumissions, etc. MS 61–1834.

Cabell Family Papers, 1719–1839 (ViW)
> Includes a list of Dr. William Cabell's slaves of Amherst, Albemarle, and Nelson counties, Virginia. MS 67–735

Cummins Family Papers, 1815–80 (ViU)
> Includes slave lists for the Cummins family of Fauquier County, Virginia. MS 69–1254

Davis Preston and Company, Lynchburg and Bedford, Virginia. (FTaSU; also available at NHi)
> This company bought and hired out slaves to farmers for commodities (cotton, tobacco, wheat, etc.). MS 69–204

Description of Slaves Being Transported. Manifests of Negroes, Mulattoes and Persons of Color taken on Board Various Vessels, 1835–55 (NHi)
> Most vessels went from Alexandria, Virginia, to New Orleans. Document gives slave's name, age, sex, height, color, and owner or shipper's name and place of residence.

Gilliam Family Papers, 1794–1920 (ViU)
> Includes indentures and slave records (1830–60) of this family from Dinwiddie County, Virginia. MS 69–1269

Glasgow Family Papers, 1795–1889 (TxU)
> Virginia planter's family letters and bills of sale for slaves and land. MS 64–751

Madden Family Papers, 1760–1874 (ViU)

Diaries

Carter, Robert Wormley, 1776 (ViW)
> "Sabine Hall" personal and business affairs.

Gray, M.R., 1822–31 (ViU)
> Includes his slave sales.

Taylor, Francis, 1786–92; 1794–99 (Vi)

Midland Plantation births, deaths, and marriages in Orange County, Virginia.

The Library of Virginia has copies of more than five thousand Bible records in its collection, which contain some references to African-American individuals, including slaves. This collection can be searched through the library's web site. For a listing of Bible records that mention slaves, search using the keywords "slave" or "slaves."

Internet Resources

Search the Library of Virginia web site (**http://www.lva.lib.va.us**) under "Archives and Manuscripts" for many materials relevant to Afri-can-American genealogy.

A web site called *Afro-American Sources in Virginia: A Guide to Manuscripts,* edited by Michael Plunkett (**http://www.upress.virginia. edu/plunkett/mfp.html**), contains the first book to be published by a university press on the web. It covers a wide range of manuscript sources.

Examples of material found on this outstanding Internet resource are as follows:

- Ethel Littlejohn Adams Collection, 3 items, 1848–51 (Thomas Balch Library)
Slave bills of sale, all for children who were sold to members of the Mott family.
- Archer Family Papers, 1771–1918 (ViHi)
Business, personal, and legal correspondence and accounts of this family of Amelia County. Included is a list of slaves belonging to Jane Segar Archer.
- Bailey Family Papers, 1802–1980 (ViHi)
Personal, business, and legal correspondence and accounts of this Halifax County family. Included is a list of slaves belonging to William Bailey.

The Institute for Advanced Technology in the Humanities at the University of Virginia provides technical support for its Fellows and other partners to make historic collections available for database-searching on the Internet. See, for example, *The Valley of the Shadow* project for Franklin and Augusta counties at **http://jefferson.village. virginia.edu/vshadow2/**.

Research Contacts

Virginia Historical Society
428 North Boulevard   *Mailing Address:* P.O. Box 7311
Richmond, VA 23220   Richmond, VA 23211-0311
http://www.vahistorical.org/

National Genealogical Society Library
4527 Seventeenth Street, N.W.
Arlington, VA 22207-2399
http://www.ngsgenealogy.org

Bibliography

Boyd-Rush, Dorothy A. *Register of Free African-Americans, Rockingham County, Virginia, 1807–1859.* Bowie, Md.: Heritage Books, 1992.

Bushman, Katherine G. *Registers of Free African-Americans, 1810–1864, Augusta County, Virginia and Staunton, Virginia.* Verona, Va.: Mid-Valley Press, 1989.

Carter, Landon. *The Diary of Colonel Landon Carter of Sabine Hall, 1752–1778.* Edited by Jack P. Greene. Virginia Historical Society Documents, vols. 4–5. Charlottesville: Virginia Historical Society, 1987.
This is an excellent example of the valuable African-American genealogical source material found in diaries. All of the names of the Carter slaves are listed under "slave." There are probably many African-American families from Virginia with the name Carter whose ancestral search will lead them to one of the Carter plantations (see "Diaries" on page 344 for location of his papers).

Dickinson, Richard B., comp. *Entitled!: Free Papers in Appalachia Concerning Antebellum Freeborn Negroes and Emancipated African Americans in Montgomery County, Virginia.* Edited by Varney R. Nell. Arlington, Va.: National Genealogical Society, 1981.

First Families of Virginia Staff. *Adventurers of Purse and Person: Order of First Families of Virginia.* Petersburg, Va.: Dietz Press, 1956.
This includes a census of African Americans in 1623, including the 19 original African Americans.

Heinegg, Paul. *Free African Americans of North Carolina, Virginia, and South Carolina.* 4th ed. Baltimore: Clearfield Company, 2001.

This book consists of detailed genealogies of about 300 free African-American families. This edition traces many families further back to their seventeenth and eighteenth century roots.

Hopkins, Margaret Lail. *Index to the Tithables of Loudoun County, Virginia, and to Slaveholders and Slaves: 1758–1786*. Baltimore: Clearfield Company, 1991.
Among the annual lists of tithes for Loudoun County are lists of slaveholders and slaves. Altogether about 6,000 slaves and slaveholders are named in this section.

Houston, William R., and Jean M. Mihalyka. *Colonial Residents of Virginia's Eastern Shore Whose Ages Were Proved Before Court Officials of Accomack and Northampton Counties*. Baltimore: Genealogical Publishing Company, 1985.

Ibrahim, Karen, Karen White and Courtney Gaskins. *Fauquier County, Virginia Register of Free Negroes, 1817–1865*. Westminster, Md.: Willow Bend Books, 1993.

Jefferson, Thomas. *Thomas Jefferson's Farm Book*. Edited by Edwin Morris Betts. Charlottesville: University Press of Virginia, 1987.
This includes extensive records of births, deaths, and other records of Thomas Jefferson's slaves. A truly outstanding example of the types of records plantation owners kept on their slaves.

Johnson, June W. *Prince William County, Virginia, Will Book G: Liber H, 1792–1803*. Westminster, Md.: Willow Bend Books, 1986.
There are over 730 slave listings in this book, and these are indexed under the subject of "slaves."

Koger, Celestine G. *The 1850 Slave Inhabitants of Accomac County, VA*. Bowie, Md.: Heritage Books, 1995.

Latimer, Frances Bibbins. *The Register of Free Negroes: Northampton County, Virginia, 1853 to 1861*. Bowie, Md.: Heritage Books, 1992.

_____. *The Register of Free Negroes, Northampton County, Virginia, 1853 to 1861*. Bowie, Md.: Heritage Books, 1992.

McLeRoy, Sherrie, and William McLeRoy. *Strangers in Their Midst: The Free Black Population of Amherst County, Virginia*. Bowie, Md.: Heritage Books, 1993.
The last section is alphabetical by name and lists individual data on all known free Negroes in Amherst County during 1761 to 1865.

Perdue, Charles L., Thomas E. Barden, and Robert K. Phillips., eds. *Weevils in the Wheat: Interview with Virginia Ex-slaves*. Reprint. Charlottesville: University Press of Virginia, 1992.

Provine, Dorothy S. *Alexandria County, Virginia Free Negro Registers 1797–1861*. Bowie, Md.: Heritage Press, 1991.

Redford, Dorothy Spruill. *Somerset Homecoming: Recovering a Lost Heritage*. Chapel Hill: University of North Carolina Press, 2000.

Sutton, Karen E. *Northumberland County Registers of Free African-Americans*. Bowie, Md.: Heritage Books, 1999.

Swem, Earl C. *Virginia Historical Index*. Baltimore: Genealogical Publishing Company, 2003.
A masterful index that includes hundreds of references to African-American slaves, plantations, and families who owned slaves.

Sobel, Mechal. *The World They Made Together: Black and White Values in Eighteenth Century Virginia*. Princeton, N. J.: Princeton University Press, 1987.

Washington

Important Dates

1844 – Wealthy African-American Missouri landowner George Washington Bush and his family arrived in Oregon Territory and settled near Olympia.

1860s – Many towns had African-American barbers, boot blacks, bathhouse operators, and restaurateurs.

1880 – African Americans arrived as coal miners.

State Archives

Washington State Archives
1120 Washington Street, S.E.
P.O. Box 40238
Olympia, WA 98504-0238
http://www.secstate.wa.gov/archives/

The Washington State Archives consists of the state government archives in Olympia and five regional offices. The state office maintains the governmental records connected with statewide functions, while the regional branches (Northeast, Southwest, Central, Eastern, and Puget Sound) maintain county, city, and local records.

Census Records

Federal Census Records

1860–1880; 1900–1930 (DNA); 1860–1880, 1900–1920 (Wa, WaSp, WaHi)

Mortality Records

1860–1880 (DNDAR, Wa)

349

Special Census

1890: Civil War Union Veterans and Widows (DNA, Wa, WaHi, WaSp)

State and County Records

Birth-Marriage-Divorce-Death Records

Washington State Center for Health Statistics
P.O. Box 9709
Olympia, WA 98507-9709
http://www.doh.wa.gov/EHSPHL/CHS/cert.htm

Mandatory recording of birth and death records began in 1907, and marriage and divorce records in 1968. These records are available at the state office. Marriage and divorce records before this date, and extant birth and death records before 1907 are located in the county where the event took place. However, the regional branches of the Washington State Archives also maintain either original or microfilm copies.

Other State and County Records

Each of the branches of the Washington State Archives holds either original or microfilm copies of a wide variety of useful resources for genealogical research. See **http://www.secstate.wa.gov/archives/archives.aspx** for information on each of the regional branch facilities.

Military Records

See the Washington State Archives for information on all military records for Washington.

Newspapers

Seattle Republican. 1894–1915? Weekly. Holdings: January 4, 1896– May 2, 1913; WSL.

The newspapers below can be found at the University of Washington Suzzalo Library in the Special Collections, Manuscripts, and University Archives Division:

Afro-American Journal (Seattle). 11/16/1967–5/27/1971 (incomplete).
Cayton's Monthly (Seattle). 1921–1922. Continuation of *Cayton's.*
Weekly 1916–1921.
Citizen (Spokane). 1908–1915.
Facts (Seattle), 1962. (Tacoma), 1970–1980.
K-ZAM Kazette (Seattle), 1962.
Medium (Seattle), 1970.
Northwest Bulletin (Seattle), 1937–1940.
Northwest Enterprise (Seattle), 1920–1962.
Pacific Dispatch (Seattle), 1946–1947; continued as *Seattle Dispatch,*
1947–1949.
Pacific Northwest Bulletin (Seattle), 1944–1948.
Pacific Northwest Review Bulletin (Takoma), 1936–1949.
Searchlight (Seattle), 1904–1925.
Seattle Observer (Seattle), 1964.
Trumpet (Seattle), 1967.
Western Journal of Black Studies (Pullman), 1977.

Research Contacts

Black Heritage Society of Washington State, Inc.
P.O. Box 22961
Seattle, WA 98122-0961
A collection of local oral history, obituaries, and photographs is included in the Society's archives, which are permanently housed at the Museum of History and Industry (2700 24th Avenue East, Seattle, Washington 98112). A current project is the oral history of African Americans who attended local (King County) high schools during the 1930s.

Black Genealogy Research Group, Seattle
5834 N.E. 75th Street, B-301
Seattle, WA 98115–6394
The Research Group was organized in 1992 to bring together those individuals interested in researching their family ancestry.

Douglass-Truth Library
2300 East Yesler Way
Seattle, WA 98122
The Douglass-Truth branch of the Seattle Public Library houses a large collection of African-American publications, many of them related to the history of African Americans in Washington State.

See *Let's Take a Walk,* self-published by Jacqueline E. A. Lawson, which contains names of prominent local African Americans from the 1920s and 1940s.

Bibliography

Davis, Lenwood G. *Blacks in the Pacific Northwest, 1788–1974: A Bibliography of Published Works and Unpublished Source Materials on the Life and Contributions of Black People in the Pacific Northwest.* Thousand Oaks, Calif.: Sage Publications, 1975.

Franklin, Joseph. *All Through the Night, The History of Spokane Black Americans, 1860–1940.* Fairfield, Wash.: Ye Galleon Press, 1989.

Hanford, Cornelius Holgate, ed. *Seattle and Environs, 1852–1924.* Salem, Mass.: Higginson Book Company, 1997.
Contains a list of African Americans from the Seattle area who served in World War I (p.664).

Henry, Mary. *Tribute: Seattle Public Places Named for Black People.* Seattle: Elton-Wolf Publishing, 1997.

Killian, Crawford. *Go Do Some Great Thing: The Black Pioneers of British Columbia.* Seattle: University of Washington Press, 1978.

Kirk, Ruth, and Carmela Alexander. *Exploring Washington's Past: A Real Guide to History.* Seattle: University of Washington Press, 1990.

Mumford, Esther Hall. *Seattle's Black Victorians, 1862–1901.* Seattle: Ananse Press, 1980.
Based on interviews conducted in the 1970s. Includes business, property, migration, etc.

_____. *Calabash: A Guide to the History, Culture, and Art of African Americans in Seattle and King County, Washington.* Seattle: Ananse Press, 1993.

_____. *Seven Stars & Orion: Reflections of the Past.* Seattle: Ananse Press, 1986.
Features interviews with seven Washington State pioneers.

Taylor, Quintard. *The Forging of a Black Community: Seattle's Central District, from 1870 Through the Civil Rights Era.* Seattle: University of Washington Press, 1994.

_____. *A History of Blacks in the Pacific Northwest, 1790–1970.* Photocopy of Transcript, Ann Arbor, Mich: University Microfilm International, 1978.

_____. *In Search of the Racial Frontier: African Americans in the*

American West, 1528–1990. New York: W.W. Norton and Company, 1998.

_____. "The Emergence of Afro-American Communities in the Pacific Northwest, 1865–1910," *Journal of Negro History* 64:4 (Fall 1979): 342–351.

_____. "The Great Migration: The Afro-American communities of Seattle and Portland during the 40's." *Arizona and the West* 23 (1981): 109–126.

_____. "Discovering the Rich History of African Americans in the Pacific Northwest." *Columbia: The Magazine of Northwest History* 7 (Fall 1993): 3–6.

Washington State Library. *The Negro in the State of Washington, 1788–1967: A Bibliography of Published Works and of Unpublished Source Materials on the Life and Achievements of the Negro in the Evergreen State.* Olympia: Washington State Library, January 1968.
One of the few bibliographies on African Americans in Washington. It covers much of the manuscript sources in the library.

West Virginia

Important Dates

1750s – African Americans first entered the western region of the Virginia colony. They settled in the Greenbrier and New River valleys, with the slaveholding family of William and Mary Ingles.

1861–63 – Virginia seceded from the Union and those living in the western part of the state formed a separate state, which was part of the Union.

1865 – In February the state ratified the Thirteenth Amendment, outlawing slavery.

1890s – Over twenty percent of West Virginia's total mining labor force from the 1890s through the early 20th century were African Americans.

State Archives

West Virginia Archives and History
The Cultural Center
1900 Kanawha Boulevard East
Charleston, WV 25305-0300
www.wvculture.org/

The West Virginia Archives is part of the Division of Culture and History—located at the Cultural Center at the State Capitol in Charleston—which also includes a museum, theater, and a genealogical research library.

Census Records

Federal Census Records

1810 (incomplete)–1860 (as Virginia counties), 1870–1880; 1900–1930 (DNA, Wv-Ar)

Mortality Records

1850–1860 (as Virginia counties), 1870–1880 (Wv-Ar)

Special Census

1890—Civil War Union Veterans and Widows (DNA, Wv-Ar, and several other public libraries)

State and County Records

Birth-Marriage-Divorce-Death Records

West Virginia Vital Registration
350 Capitol Street
Charleston, WV 25301-3701
http://www.wvdhhr.org/bph/oehp/hsc/vr/birtcert.htm

Statewide birth and death records beginning in 1917 are available from the above office, although many counties have earlier records located at the office of the county clerk. Marriage records are also housed at the county clerk's office, divorce records at the county court.

Cemetery and Church Records

Lambert, Frederick B. Collection, 1809–1959 (WvU)
Materials include cemetery records and obituaries from Guyandotte Valley and area.

Military Records

For military records before 1860, see the chapter on Virginia. For information on the availability of military service records for West Virginia, see Virgil Lewis's *The Soldiery of West Virginia* (Baltimore: Genealogical Publishing Company, 1972).

Newspapers

Pioneer Press (Martinsburg, W. Va.). 1882–1918? Weekly. Holdings: September 1886 to November 1868; Wv-Ar, WvU. September 6,

1890; January 16, 1892; August 28, 1915; CsdS, CSS, CU, DLC, LU-NO, MdBMC, MiKW, TNF, WHi.

See also the West Virginia State Archives web site (**http://www. wvculture.org/history/newspapers/newsmic.html**) for a listing of all newspapers in the state and their availability.

Manuscript Sources: Personal Papers, Slave Records, and Diaries

Campbell Family Papers, 1795–1901 (WvU)
>Microfilm of plantation and store operations near Arden in Berkeley County, West Virginia.

Fannie Cobb Carter, 1872–1972; Educator; Superintendent of First Industrial Home for Colored Girls in Huntington (1926–1936); Director of Adult Education for Negroes in Kanawba County; Dean and Acting President of National Trade and Professional School for Women and Girls in Washington, D.C.

Fox, William. Papers, 1762–1895 (WvU)
>Accounts and items related to slaves in Romney and Hampshire County, West Virginia.

Goff, David. Papers, 1826–1904 (WvU)
>Berkeley County letters and slave sales.

Johnson Papers, 1778–1848 (Wv-Ar)
>Abraham Johnson, justice of the peace and high sheriff of Hampshire County (later Mineral County area). Collection consists of correspondence, land grants, promissory notes, court orders, receipts, and bills of sale for slaves.

Lewis Family Papers, 1825–1936 (WYU)
>Kanawha County slave sales.

Lewis, Jarnes V.
>Bill of sale of slave to Guy P. Mathews, 1856 Nov. 16.

Morgan County Archives, 1772–1923 (WvU)
>The Free Negro Register and numerous county records are held in these archives.

Internet Resources

The West Virginia State Archives has a web site devoted to African-American research in the state. **http://www.wvculture.org/history/blacks.html**.

Research Contacts

West Virginia and Regional History Collection
West Virginia University Library
P.O. Box 6069
Morgantown, WV 26506-6069
http://www.libraries.wvu.edu/wvcollection/index.htm

Library of Virginia
800 East Broad St.
Richmond, VA 23219-1905
http://www.lva.lib.va.us/

See listing in this book under Virginia.

Bibliography

McGinnis, Carol. *West Virginia Genealogy: Sources & Resources*. Baltimore: Genealogical Publishing Company, 1998.
This is a guide to the sources available in West Virginia, not a "how to" book. The guide is arranged by type of materials, including vital records, Bible records, church records, cemetery records, newspapers, naturalizations, military records, county and regional records, census records, land records, maps, and city directories. Also included is a detailed bibliography of West Virginia genealogical sources. Appendices include a complete inventory of the Historical Records Survey Archives on microfilm, and a list of West Virginians who filed Civil War damage claims.

For an excellent bibliography of West Virginia publications, see the West Virginia Archives and History web site at **http://www.wvculture.org/history/biblio.html**.

Wisconsin

Important Dates

1634–1760 – The French Period took place during this time period.

1760–1783 – The British Period took place during this time period.

1783–present – The Federal Period took place during this time period.

1790s – Canadian African-American Jean Bonga and family arrived on the south shore of Lake Superior.

1793 – Marie Anne la Buche, a New Orleans born African American, was living in Prairie du Chien along the Mississippi River with her second husband, Claude Gagnier.

1820–30s – African-American slaves owned by miners and army officers arrived at Fort Crawford in Prairie du Chien and Fort Winnebago in Portage.

1848 – With the arrival of statehood, many African Americans arrived in Wisconsin and settled in cities and small towns.

1855 – African-American farmers clustered around Pleasant Ridge near Lancaster in Grant County, and in Cheyenne Valley near Hillsboro in Vernon County. Other settlements were near Delavon in Walworth County, at Fox Lake in Dodge County, and Prescott in Pierce County.

1910 – Fewer than 3,000 African Americans lived in Wisconsin.

State Archives

Wisconsin Historical Society (State Historical Society of Wisconsin)
816 State Street
Madison, WI 53706
http://www.shsw.wisc.edu

The Wisconsin Historical Society serves as the state archives and includes a museum, library, and research facility in Madison, as well as the Area Research Centers Network (ARCN). The ARCN consists of local facilities throughout the state that make state, county, and local records available outside of the main facility in Madison. See **http:// www.shsw.wisc.edu/archives/arcnet/index.html** for more information. Collections at these research centers include state and local records, books, periodicals, maps, manuscripts, and newspapers.

Census Records

Federal Census Records

1820–1880; 1900–1930 (DNA; some also available at WHi and WM)

Mortality Records

1850–1880 (WHi); 1850–70 (DNDAR); 1860–70 (WM)

Special Census

Territorial Censuses: 1836, 1842, 1846, 1847 (DNA)
1890: Civil War Union Veterans and Widows (DNA, WM, WU)

State and County Records

Birth-Marriage-Divorce-Death Records

Vital Records
1 West Wilson Street   *Mailing Address:* P.O. Box 309
Madison, WI 53701   Madison, WI 53701
http://www.dhfs.state.wi.us/vitalrecords/index.htm

Statewide recording of births, deaths, marriages, and divorces began in 1907, although earlier records may be available. It is estimated that before 1907 only about fifty percent of the events were recorded. For a chart indicating the years for which some birth, death, and marriage records are available for each county, see **http://www.dhfs.state.wi.us/ vitalrecords/genereq.htm#Earliest**.

Cemetery and Church Records

See the Wisconsin Historical Society web site at **http://www.shsw. wisc.edu** for further information about accessing church and cemetery records in the state.

Military Records

Gilson, Norman Shepard: Papers, 1860–1901 (WHi)
Muster rolls for the 58th Infantry Regiment of U.S. Colored Troops from Wisconsin. MS 62–2651

Newspapers

Northwestern Recorder (Milwaukee). 1892–93. Weekly, monthly, and irregular. Continues *Wisconsin Afro-American* (see below). Holdings: December 3, 1892; January 14, 1893; February–March 1893; CSdS, CSS, CU, DLC, LU-NO, MdBMC, MiKW, TNF, WHi.

Wisconsin Afro-American (Milwaukee). April to November, 1892. Weekly, monthly, and irregular. Continued by *Northwestern Recorder* (see above). Holdings: August 13 to November 19, 1892 (incomplete); CSdS, CSS, CU, DLC, LU-NO, MdBMC, MiKW, TNF.

Wisconsin Weekly Advocate (Milwaukee). 1898–1915. Weekly. Holdings: May 1898 to September 19, 1907; CSdS, CtY, DLC, FTaSU, InNd, MB, MdBJ, MnU, MoSW, NcU, NjP, TNF.

A study sponsored by the Wisconsin Historical Society and conducted by James P. Danky developed a comprehensive guide of African-American newspapers in the U.S. See "African American Newspapers and Periodicals: A National Bibliography and Union," a description of more than 6,500 titles and their locations, at **http://www.shsw.wisc.edu/library/newspaper/aabib.html**.

Manuscript Sources: Personal Papers, Slave Records, and Diaries

Remsen, Peter A. Papers, 1817–52 (WHi)
>Letters in 1820s concerning the rescue of Henry Hicks, an indentured African-American apprentice. MS 62–2876

Holzhueter, Jack. Afro-Americans in Early Wisconsin. 1969 (WHi)
>Miscellaneous items located at the Wisconsin Historical Society connected with research on the African-American population in early Wisconsin, including clippings, notes, bibliographical citations, a card file on "African Americans" in the U.S. censuses of 1850, 1860, and 1870, and articles summarizing some of the results; with explanatory notes on the project by Jack Holzhueter.

Shepard, Charles. Papers, 1850–1958 (WHi)
>Shepard was a freed slave and farmer of Beetown Township in Grant County. The collection includes family letters and manuscripts containing Grant County history. MS 61–1057

Wisconsin. Circuit Court (Iowa County) Title: Clerk of Court papers, 1809–1868. Summary: Files including records of territorial courts of the area of southern Wisconsin formerly in Saint Clair County, Territory of Illinois; Crawford County, Territory of Michigan; and Iowa County, Territory of Wisconsin (WHi) Papers include manumissions of slaves.

Internet Resources

See the Wisconsin Historical Society web site (**http://www.shsw.wisc. edu/website/search.html**) to access its electronic catalogs and search for documents related to African Americans, slavery, slaves, etc. One example of the resources available is the Pleasant Ridge Negro Community collection of materials (1848–1959), which pertains to the Greene (Green), Shepard, and Richmond families in Beetown township, Grant County.

Research Contacts

In addition to the thirteen Area Research Centers in the network of the Wisconsin Historical Society (**http://www.shsw.wisc.edu/archives/arcnet/index.html**), the following societies may provide helpful information:

Wisconsin State Genealogical Society
2109 20th Avenue
Monroe, WI 53566

Rock County Historical Society
P.O. Box 8096
Janesville, WI 53547-8096
    The Rock County Historical Society has a fine collection of materials
on African Americans in Rock County, covering the years 1895–1950.

Bibliography

Cooper, Zachary. *Black Settlers in Rural Wisconsin*. Second Edition.
    Madison: Wisconsin Historical Society, 1994.

Strache, Neil E. *Black Periodicals and Newspapers: A Union List of
    Holdings in Libraries of the University of Wisconsin and the
    Library of the State Historical Society of Wisconsin*. Second
    Edition, revised. Madison: State Historical Society of Wiscon-
    sin, 1979.

The Wisconsin Magazine of History, published quarterly by the State
    Historical Society of Wisconsin in Madison and available at
    most research libraries, has several articles dealing with Afri-
    can Americans. See **http://www.shsw.wisc.edu/website/
    search.html**.

Wyoming

Important Dates

1800s – African Americans in Wyoming played many important roles throughout the territorial era.

1890 – Wyoming became a state.

1900 – The African-American population exceeded 1,000.

1950 – The African-American population was 3,000.

State Archives

Wyoming State Archives
2301 Central Area
Cheyenne, WY 82002
http://wyoarchives.state.wy.us/

In addition to being the central repository for state and local governmental records, many of value to genealogical research, the Wyoming State Archives also houses a collection of books, periodicals, and manuscripts pertaining to Western history. A listing of useful genealogical records available at the archives can be found at **http://wyoarchives. state.wy.us/geneal1.htm**.

Census Records

Federal Census Records

1860–1880; 1900–1930 (DNA, WSA)

Mortality Records

1870–1880 (DNDAR)

Special Census

    1869: Wyoming Territorial Census (WSA)
    1890: Civil War Union Veterans and Widows (DNA)

State and County Records

Birth-Marriage-Divorce-Death Records

Vital Records Services
Hathaway Building
Cheyenne, WY 82002
http://wdhfs.state.wy.us/vital_records/certificate.htm

    Birth and death records from 1909 are available from the state office, as are marriage and divorce records from 1941. Earlier ones are located at the county in which the event occurred. However, all death, marriage, and divorce records more that fifty years old are located at the Wyoming State Archives.

Cemetery and Church Records

    See the list of genealogical sources at the Wyoming State Archives at http://wyoarchives.state.wy.us/geneal1.htm.

Military Records

    These are available at the Wyoming State Archives.

Newspapers

    These are available at the Wyoming State Archives.

Manuscript Sources: Personal Papers, Slave Records, and Diaries

    See the Wyoming State Archives.

Internet Resources

A 1924 petition, filed with the Sheridan County clerk and signed by ministers and other individuals regarding the employment of Church Woods as janitor at the county jail, is an example of the kind of information that is available on the Wyoming State Archives' web site (**http://wyoarchives. state.wy.us/articles/blacksii.htm**).

Research Contacts

Wyoming Genealogical & Historical Society
Laramie County Library
2800 Central Avenue
Cheyenne, WY 82001

Bibliography

Steuart, Christensen Raeone, ed. *Wyoming 1870 Census Index.* Bountiful, Utah: Heritage Quest, 2000.

Canada

Important Dates

1629 – Olivier Le Jeune, an African from Madagascar, was sold as a slave and arrived in New France (Canada). He later died as a freeman.

1759 – Slaves in New France numbered 3,604; 1,132 were African Americans, the rest largely Indians.

1783 – About 3,500 African Americans who fought on the British side in the American Revolution ("Black Loyalists") were granted land in the maritime provinces of Nova Scotia and New Brunswick.

1791 – Eleven hundred "Black Loyalists" immigrated to Sierra Leone.

1813 – African-American "Refugees" arrived in Halifax during the War of 1812.

1820 – Ninety-five African-American families moved to Trinidad.

1829 – The community of Wilberforce located on Lake Huron was established with African Americans from Cincinnati, and was disbanded in 1836.

1865 – After the passage of the Thirteenth Amendment, many African Americans returned to the United States.

1907 – Thirteen hundred African-American farmers from Oklahoma immigrated to the provinces of Alberta and Saskatchewan, where most settled near Edmonton.

National Archives

National Archives of Canada
395 Wellington Street
Ottawa, Ontario K1A 0N3
http://www.archives.ca

The National Archives of Canada web site provides extensive information in both English and French on genealogical resources throughout the provinces. Included are census, vital, land, probate, military, immigration, citizenship, Loyalist, and school records and newspapers.

Census Records

The National Archives of Canada web site (**http://www. archives.ca**) details the extent and availability of census records for all of the provinces.

Canadian Provincial Records

Civil registration of vital events began in the provinces in the late nineteenth century. Previous records were kept extensively by local churches. For civil registration information, see the National Archives of Canada web site.

Cemetery and Church Records

Halifax, Nova Scotia, Catholic Church, Parish Registers for Colored People, 1827–35 (USIGD)

A microfilm copy of baptism, marriage, and burial records; includes an index.

Internet Resources

Among the outstanding web links for African-American genealogy in Canada are the following:

Canadian GenWeb: **http://www.rootsweb.com/~canwgw/**

Canadian Genealogy and History Links: **http://www.islandnet.com/ ~jveinot/cghl/cghl.html**

Black Loyalists—The Online Institute for Black Loyalists: **http:// www.royalprovincial.com/military/black/black.htm**

A History of the Black Cultural Centre for Nova Scotia: **http:// www.bccns.com/bcc_history.html**.

Bibliography

Baxter, Angus. *In Search of Your Canadian Roots: Tracing Your Family Tree in Canada*. 3rd ed. Baltimore: Genealogical Publishing Company, 2000.
This book covers the National Archives in Ottawa, with its holdings of censuses, parish registers, naturalization records, land and homestead records, and military records; and even summarizes the holdings of the LDS Church relating to Canada. Several chapters are devoted to each province's available records, archives, genealogical societies, and libraries. Good bibliography.

Drew, Benjamin. *A North-Side View of Slavery the Refugee: Or the Narratives of Fugitive Slaves in Canada*. New York: Johnson Reprint Corp., 1969.

Gregorovitch, Andrew. *Canadian Ethnic Groups Bibliography*. Toronto: Department of the Provincial Secretary and Citizenship, 1972.
Lists forty-two items relating to African-American history in Ontario, some with applicability to genealogical research.

Jain, Sushil Kumar. *The Negro in Canada: A Select List of Primary and Secondary Sources for the Study of the Negro Community in Canada from the Earliest Times to the Present*. Unexplored Fields of Canadiana, vol. 3. Regina: University of Saskatchewan, 1967.

Newman, Debra L., and Marcia Eisenberg. "An Inspection Roll of Negroes Taken on Board Sundry Vessels at Staten Island Bound for Nova Scotia, 1783." *Journal of the Afro-American Historical and Genealogical Society*. 1#2 (1980).

Rawlyk, George A. "The Guysborough Negroes: A Study in Isolation." *Dalhousie Review*. 40 (1961): 103–20.
A study of the Loyalist Negroes who settled in Nova Scotia after the American Revolution.

Spray, W. *The Blacks in New Brunswick*. Fredericton: Brunswick Press, 1972.
A short history, with some bibliographical references.

Walker, James W., St. G. *The Black Loyalists: The Search for a Promised Land in Nova Scotia and Sierra Leone 1783–1870*. Toronto: University of Toronto Press, 1992.
Includes a bibliography.

West Indies

Important Dates

1700s – Many West Indians arrive in the American colonies as part of the slave trade and as domestic servants belonging to white settlers from the West Indies.

1972–1992 – Jamaica accounted for 373,972 legal entrants into this country, followed by 249,953 from Haiti; 161,530 from Guyana; and 109,594 from Trinidad. For more information on immigration to the West Indies, read pages 1344–1355 in Jack Salzman, David Lionel Smith, and Cornel West's *Encyclopedia of African-American Culture and History* (see Bibliography on page 380).

Island Archives

When searching through ship manifest records, one fact becomes clear: most African Americans brought to the United States were not brought directly from Africa, but rather had been previously enslaved in the West Indies. Consequently, tracing African-American roots to Africa, in many cases, requires a detour to the West Indies. In addition, many members of the African-American community are recent immigrants from the West Indies. Therefore, it is important to know where to go on each island for genealogical research. Listed below are the important locations for that essential information. See also **http://www.rootsweb.com/~caribgw/**.

Antigua

Museum of Antigua & Barbuda
(Antigua Historical & Archaeological Society)
P.O. Box 103, Long Street
St. Johns, Antigua

Antigua National Archives
Factory Road
St. Johns, Antigua

Available records include vital records from 1856; slave registers, 1817-1831; and newspapers. Some records may be at the Court House, a few blocks away.

Registrar General
High Street
St. John's, Antigua

Birth, marriage, and death records are available from August 1856 to the present.

Bahamas

Archives Section
Ministry of Education and Culture
P.O. Box N3913
Nassau, New Providence, Bahamas

Bahamas Historical Society
P.O. Box SS-6833
Nassau, Bahamas
http://www.bahamas.net.bs/history/

Barbados

Barbados Department of Archives
Lazaretto Building
Black Rock
St. James, Barbados

Available records include baptism, marriage, and burial records; wills; land records; newspapers; and other resources.

Bermuda

Bermuda Historical Society
c/o Bermuda Library
Par-la-ville Park
Hamilton, Bermuda
St. George's Historical Society Museum
St. George's, Bermuda

National Archives
Government Administration Building
30 Parliament Street
Hamilton 12, Bermuda

Bahamas

Archives Section
Ministry of Education and Culture
P.O. Box N3913
Nassau, Bahamas

Bahamas Historical Society
P.O. Box SS-6833
Nassau, Bahamas
http://www.bahamas.net.bs/history/bhs/index.html

Bahamas Public Library
Rawson Square
Nassau, Bahamas

Nassau Public Library
P.O. Box N3210
Nassau, Bahamas

Bahamas Department of Archives
P.O. Box SS-6341
Nassau, Bahamas

Cayman Islands

National Archives
Government Administrative Building
Georgetown, Grand Cayman

Grenada

Registrar General
Church Street
St. George's, Grenada

Birth, marriage, and death records are available from 1 January 1866
to the present.

Guyana

Ministry of Education and Cultural Development
20 Main Street
Cummingsburg
Georgetown, Guyana

Haiti

Bibliotheque Nationale d'Haiti
Rue Hammerton Killick
Port au Prince, Haiti

Centre de Documentation
Port au Prince, Haiti

Institut d'Ethnologie d'Haiti
Rue Capois
Port au Prince, Haiti

Jamaica

African-Caribbean Institute of Jamaica
12 Ocean Boulevard
Kingston 6, Jamaica

The Jamaica Archives
Spanish Town, Jamaica

Available records include baptism, marriage, and burial records, 1664–1871; registers of return of slaves, 1817–1832; books of gifts, deeds, and manumissions, 1732–1832; wills and deeds; land grants; and other important records.

Trinidad

National Archives
105 St. Vincent Street
P.O. Box 763
Port-of-Spain, Trinidad and Tobago

The Registrar General
Registrar General's Office
Ministry of Legal Affairs
Red House, St. Vincent Street
Port-of-Spain, Trinidad and Tobago

National Heritage Library
8 Knox Street
Port-of-Spain, Trinidad and Tobago

Virgin Islands

Department of Health
Bureau of Vital Records
Charlotte Amalie
St. Thomas, VI 00810

Director of Libraries and Museums
Department of Conservation and Cultural Affairs
Government of the Virgin Islands
P.O. Box 599
St. Thomas, VI 00802

Island Records

For examples of the range of materials that are housed in the above island archives, see **http://www.rootsweb.com/~caribgw/islands.html**. Listed below are examples of the types of slave records that can be found on many of the islands:

List of Negroes Imported 1707–26
Accounts of Negroes Imported October 14, 1746, to April 14, 1747
Returns of Slaves Imported, 1747–51

Barbados

Accounts of Burials and Christenings and Slaves Imported, 1751–56
    and 1756–59
Accounts of Burials and Christenings and Slaves Imported, 1773
Accounts of Negroes Imported, October 14, 1746, to April 14,1747
Census of Barbados by Parishes, 1783
Christenings and Burials of Negroes, December 1, 1802, to December
    1, 1803
List of Negroes Imported, 1707–26
Plantation Bonds and Certificates, January 6, 1777, to January 5,
    1778
Returns of Christenings and Burials of Negroes and Negroes Im-
    ported, August 11, 1772, to August 11, 1773

Returns of Christenings and Burials of Negroes by Parishes, 1766
Returns of Negroes, May 27, 1766, to May 27, 1767 (shows number
    in each cargo received and number of consignees)
Returns of Slaves Imported, 1747–51
Revenue Accounts, May 1803 to May 1804
Shipping Returns from 1680 to 1806 with Inward and Outward
    Records

Jamaica

Assembly Journals, 1770–has a list of slaves
Jamaica Board of Trade Entry Books Shipping Returns, 1683–1784

    The Institute of Jamaica (IJ) on King Street in Kingston and the Island Records Office (IRO) have the following records:

Births, Marriages, and Deaths before 1815 (IRO)
Kingston Register of Slaves (manumitted) 1744–95 (IJ)
Manumission Records, 1747–1832 (66 vols. IRO)
Memorandum of Slaves Sold at Kingston, 1738–43 (IJ)
Parochial Tax Rolls before 1815 (N)
Port Royal Sale of Slaves, 1783–94; 1800–1806 (IJ)
Slave Returns, 1817–32 (141 vols. IRO)
Slaves Sold in Kingston Toll Book, 1738–43 (IJ)
Wills and Inventories (IRO)

Internet Resources

    A growing, island-by-island online archive continues to develop at **http://www.rootsweb.com/~caribgw/cgw_archive/index.html**. Some examples of the information currently available are as follows:

Antigua

Extracts from Antiguan Baptismal Records

Bahamas

Loyalists who went to the Bahama Islands
Early Settlers of the Bahamas
Early Burial Records and Inscriptions

Barbados

Names found on Richard Ligon's map of Barbados, 1657
Extracts from Barbados Christ Church Baptisms

Bermuda (see http://www.BermudaGenWeb.com)

Emigration Lists
Association Oath Rolls: British Plantations, Bermuda
Devonshire Parish Church Records
A Survey of the Inhabitants of Bermuda
The Names of ye Govern' & Councill of ye Assembly

British Virgin Islands

Wesleyan Methodist Church 1815–1933
Society of Friends (Quakers) 1740–1760
St. George's Episcopal 1862–1934, Marriages 1862–1866

Caribbean (General)

Emigration Lists
Slave Movement in the 18th and 19th Centuries

Jamaica

Newcomers, White Settlers to Jamaica
Index of Jamaican Probate Records
Extracts from Some Wills, Spanish Town, Jamaica
List of microfilms available from the LDS Family History Center

Trinidad

Selections from Trinidad Colonial Handbooks
Selected Cemetery Inscriptions
Governors of Trinidad
Trinidad Civil Service Offices, 1899

U.S. Virgin Islands

List of Landowners of the 1841 St. John Census
List of Colonists of Danish W.I. 1678
List of Lutheran Clergy

Land Lister (tax records) 1672–1680
Land Lister (tax records) 1686–1693
St. Croix 1841 Census, Part 1
List of Shareholders of the Danish West India Company, Part 1
List of Shareholders of the Danish West India Company, Part 2
List of Shareholders of the Danish West India Company, Part 3
List of Shareholders of the Danish West India Company, Part 4

Bibliography

Bush, Barbara. *Slave Women in Caribbean Society—1650-1838*. London: James Currey, 1990.

Craton, Michael. *A Jamaican Plantation: A History of Worthy Park, 1670-1970*. London, 1970.

Dunn, Richard C. *Sugar and Slaves (The Rise of the Planter Class in the English West Indies, 1624–1713)*. Chapel Hill: University of North Carolina Press, 2000.
A excellent background source for information on slavery in the English West Indies.

Grannum, Guy. *Tracing Your West Indian Ancestors/Sources at the Public Record Office*. London: Public Record Office, 1995.

Green, William A. *British Slave Emancipation—The Sugar Colonies and the Great Experiment 1830–1865*. Oxford: Oxford University Press, 1991.

Higman, B. W. "The Slave Family and Household in the British West Indies, 1800–1834." *Journal of the Interdisciplinary History* (6), 1975.

Ingram, K. E. *Sources of Jamaican History 1655–1838*. 2 vols. Inter Documentation Co. Ag Zug Switzerland, 1976.
Comprehensive list of documents around the world.

Kapp, Kit S. *The Printed Maps of Jamaica up to 1825*. Kingston, Jamaica: Bolivar Press, 1968.

Rice, C. Duncan. *The Rise and Fall of Black Slavery*. New York: Macmillan, 1975.

Salzman, Jack, David Lionel Smith, and Cornel West. *Encyclopedia of African-American Culture and History*. 5 vols. New York: Simon and Schuster, 1996).
Includes an excellent bibliography on West Indian immigration.

Walvin, James. *Black Ivory—A History of British Slavery*. New York: Harper Collins, 1992.

Appendix A
General References

Bentley, Elizabeth P. *The Genealogist's Address Book,* 4th ed. Baltimore: Genealogical Publishing Company, 1998. Contains an excellent list of African-American research contacts.

Carmack, Sharon D. *A Genealogist's Guide to Discovering Your Female Ancestors: Special Strategies for Uncovering Hard-to-Find Information About Your Female Lineage.* Cincinnati: Betterway Books, 1998. Includes sources created by and about women. Appendixes include an overview of women's legal rights in America, matrilineal research and genetics, and a checklist for researching female ancestors.

Carothers, Diane F., ed. "Genealogy and Libraries." *Library Trends.* 32 (Summer 1983). This entire issue is on genealogy. Chapters, written in a scholarly manner, cover such topics as National Archives and Library of Congress sources, African-American family research, and genealogical research in LDS Church facilities.

Croom, Emily, Anne. *Unpuzzling Your Past: A Basic Guide to Genealogy,* 3rd ed. White Hall, Va.: Betterway Publications, 1995. A good general "how-to" book.

Doane, Gilbert and James Bell. *Searching for Your Ancestors: The How and Why of Genealogy.* Minneapolis: University of Minnesota Press, 1980.

Eichholz, Alice, ed. *Ancestry's Red Book: American State, County and Town Sources,* rev. ed. Salt Lake City: Ancestry, Inc., 1992. An extensive guide to local sources for family history research, with information on sources for African-American family research included for each state.

Everton, George. *The Handy Book for Genealogists,* rev. ed. Logan, Utah: The Everton Publishers, 1991.

Gilmer, Lois C. *Genealogical Research and Resources: A Guide for Library Use.* Chicago: American Library Association, 1988. A general guide and discussion of the genealogical process. A brief look at key primary and secondary sources is included.

Greenwood, Val D. *The Researcher's Guide to American Genealogy*, 3rd ed. Baltimore: Genealogical Publishing Company, 2002.

Hefner, Loretta L. *The WPA Historical Records Survey: A Guide to the Unpublished Inventories, Indexes, and Transcripts.* Chicago: Society of American Archivists, 1980.

Makower, Joel, ed. *The American History Sourcebook.* New York: Prentice Hall, 1988.

Meyer, Mary K., ed. *Meyer's Directory of Genealogical Societies in the U.S.A. and Canada.* Mt. Airy, Md.: Author, 1990.

Mills, Elizabeth S. "Ethnicity and the Southern Genealogist: Myths and Misconceptions, Resources and Opportunities." In *Going to Salt Lake City to Do Family History Research*, edited by Ralph J. Crandall and Parker, J. Carlyle. 3rd ed. rev. & exp. Turlock, Calif.: Marietta Publishing Co., 1996. The Family History Library in Salt Lake City contains the world's largest collection of genealogical research materials. This guide begins with a long discussion on how to prepare for a trip to the Library.

Schaefer, Christina K. *The Center: A Guide to Genealogical Research in the National Capital Area.* Baltimore: Genealogical Publishing Company, 1996. Contains information on hundreds of libraries and other repositories in the Washington, D.C. area, including The National Archives and Library of Congress. Some sections are arranged by type of research material.

The Sourcebook of State Public Records: the Definitive Guide to Searching for Public Record Information at the State Level. Tempe, Ariz.: BRB Publications, 1994. Information given for each type of record includes the name of the contacting agency, what specific records are available, and how to access the records.

Szucs, Loretto Dennis, and Sandra Hargreaves Luebking, eds. *The Source: A Guidebook of American Genealogy*, rev. ed. Salt Lake City: Ancestry Publishing, 1996. An essential guide to the large variety of research materials available for genealogical research. In particular, see David Thackery's section, "Tracking African-American Family History."

Taylor, Robert M., ed. *Generations and Change: Genealogical Perspectives in Social History.* Macon, Ga.: Mercer, 1986.

Wheeler, Mary B., ed. *Directory of Historical Organizations in the United States*, 14th ed. Nashville: American Association for the Study of State and Local History, 1993.

Wright, Raymond S., III. *The Genealogist's Handbook: Modern Methods for Researching Family History.* Chicago: American Library Association, 1995. An excellent guide that provides an overview of the full family history research process. Information covered includes how to get started, computers and genealogy family records, local and national records, and how to write a family history.

U.S. Department of Health and Human Services. *Where to Write for Vital Records*, updated ed. Washington, D.C.: U.S. Government Printing Office, 2002.

Internet Resources

Crowe, Powell Elizabeth. *Genealogy Online*, 6th ed. Berkeley, Calif.: McGraw-Hill, 2001. Covers the resources available to online genealogists, including descriptions of more than 100 web sites.

Howells, Cyndi. *Cyndi's List: A Comprehensive List of 70,000 Genealogy Sites on the Internet.* Second edition. Baltimore: Genealogical Publishing Company, 2001. A printed version of Cyndi's popular web site **(www.cyndislist.com)**.

Howells, Cyndi. *Netting Your Ancestors: Genealogical Research on the Internet.* Baltimore: Genealogical Publishing Company, 1997. An essential guide written by the creator of *Cyndi's List* (**www.cyndislist.com**), a comprehensive list of sources on the Internet.

Kemp, Thomas Jay. *Virtual Roots: A Guide to Genealogy and Local History on the World Wide Web.* Wilmington, Del.: Scholarly Resources, 1997. A road map to genealogy and local history sites on the Internet.

Appendix B
African-American Family History Research Bibliography

Books

Beasley, Donna. *Family Pride: The Complete Guide to Tracing African-American Genealogy.* New York: Macmillan, 1997.

Blockson, Charles L., and Ron Fry. *Black Genealogy.* Englewood Cliffs, N.J.: Prentice-Hall, 1977.

Burroughs, Tony. *Black Roots: A Beginner's Guide to Tracing the African American Family Tree.* New York: Simon & Schuster, 2001.

Byers, Paula, K., ed. *African-American Genealogical Sourcebook,* 1st ed. New York: Gale Research, 1995.

Catterall, Helen H., ed.. *Judicial Cases Concerning American Slavery and the Negro.* 5 vols. Washington, D.C.: Carnegie Publications, 1926-1937.

Cross, Lee Elzey. *The Thomas W. Cross Family Records: From 1826–1986.* Lansing, Mich.: L.E. Cross, 1987.

Curtis, Annette, ed. *African-American Genealogy Sources at MCPL—Histories & Resources.* St. Louis, Mo.: Mid-Continent Public Library, 2001. An outstanding bibliography of African-American genealogical resources.

Fears, Mary L. Jackson. *Slave Ancestral Research: It's Something Else.* Bowie, Md.: Heritage Books, 1995.

Free Negro Heads of Families in the United States in 1830. Washington, D.C.: Association for the Study of Negro Life and History, 1925.

Glover, Denise, M. *Voices of the Spirit: Sources for Interpreting the African-American Experience.* Chicago: American Library Association, 1996.

Guttman, Herbert. *The Black Family in Slavery and Freedom, 1750–1925.* New York: Pantheon, 1976.

Lawson, Sandra M., comp. *Generations Past. A Selected List of Sources for Afro-American Genealogical Research.* Washington, D.C.: Library of Congress, 1988.

Linder, Bill R. *African-American Genealogy. Basic Steps to Research.* Technical Leaflet #135. Nashville: American Association for State and Local History, 1981.

Merritt, Carole. *Historical Black Resources: A Handbook.* Atlanta: Georgia Department of Natural Resources, 1994.

Miller, Joseph C. *Slavery: A Worldwide Bibliography, 1900–1982.* White Plains, N.Y.: Kraus International, 1985.

Miller, Randall, and John D. Smith. *Dictionary of Afro-American Slavery.* Detroit: Greenwood Publishing Group, 1988.

Morton-Young, Tommie. *Afro-American Genealogy Sourcebook.* New York: Garland Publishing, 1987 (Garland Reference Library of Social Science; vol. 321).

Oakes, James. *The Ruling Race: A History of American Slaveholders.* New York: Knopf, 1982.

Olson, James Stuart. *Slave Life in America: A Historiography and Selected Bibliography.* Langham: University Press of America, 1983.

Peters, Joan W. *Local Sources for African-American Family Historians: Using County Court Records and Census Returns.* Broad Run, Va.: J.W. Peters, 1993. Demonstrates use of county-level resources and state archives, including nineteenth-century personal property tax records, county registers of free Negroes, overseers of the poor indentures in court minute books.

Rawick, George P., ed. *The American Slave: A Composite Autobiography.* 42 vols. Westport, Conn.: Greenwood Press, 1979. Includes a name and subject index.

Smith, Allen. *Directory of Oral History Collections.* Phoenix, Ariz.: Oryx Press, 1988.

Smith Carney, Jessie, ed. *Ethnic Genealogy: A Research Guide.* Foreword by Alex Haley. Westport, Conn.: Greenwood Press, 1983. Basic background reading for African-American genealogy. Overview of African history, slave trade, Underground Railroad, and records of African-American communities. More than 200 libraries and historical organizations were surveyed for their holdings, including manuscript collections.

Smith, John D. *Black Slavery in the Americas: An Interdisciplinary Bibliography, 1865–1985.* Westport, Conn.: Greenwood Press, 1983.

Streets, David, H. *Slave Genealogy: A Research Guide with Case Studies*, Bowie, Md., Heritage Books, 1986. Provides a clear discussion of slave genealogy, with emphasis on the non-plantation slaves; vividly demonstrates the research methods and types of analysis that must be employed, and the importance of researching both owners and slaves.

Sutton, Karen E. *The Nickens Family: How to Trace a Non-slave African-American Lineage from Virginia to Maryland and Back.* Baltimore, Md.: Author, 1993.

Thackery, David. *A Bibliography of African-American Family History at the Newberry Library.* Chicago: The Newberry Library, 1988.

Thackery, David, and Dee Woodtor. *Case Studies in Afro-American Genealogy.* Chicago: The Newberry Library, 1988.

Thompson, Edgar T. *The Plantation: An International Bibliography.* Boston: G.K. Hall, 1983.

Tucker, Veronica. *An Annotated Bibliography of the Fisk University Library's Black Oral History Collection.* Nashville, Tenn.: Fisk University, 1974.

Vlach, John M. *Back of the Big House: The Architecture of Plantation Slavery.* Chapel Hill, N.C.: University of North Carolina Press, 1993.

Walker, James D. *Black Genealogy, How to Begin.* Athens, Ga.: University of Georgia Center for Continuing Education, 1977.

Walton, Angela Y. *Black Indian Genealogy Research.* Bowie, Md.: Heritage Books, 1993.

Wilson, Emily. *Hope and Dignity: Older Black Women of the South.* Philadelphia: Temple University Press, 1983.

Witcher, Curt Bryan. *A Bibliography of Sources for Black Family History in the Allen County Public Library Genealogy Department.* Fort Wayne, Ind.: Allen County Public Library, 1989.

————. *African American Genealogy: A Bibliography and Guide to Sources.* Fort Wayne, Ind.: Round Tower Books, 2000.

Woodson, Carter C. *Free Negro Owners of Slaves in the United States in 1830: Together with Absentee Ownership of Slaves in the United States in 1830.* Reprint. New York: Negro Universities Press, 1968.

Articles on the Research Process

Alger, Alexandra. "Bringing an Ancestor to Life." *Forbes,* 158(6) Sept. 9, 1996: 232–236.

Alger, Alexandra. *"Where to Find Civil War Records."* *Forbes,* 158(6) Sept. 9, 1996: 233.

Blockson, Charles. "Black American Research and Records." In *Ethnic Genealogy: A Researcher's Guide*, edited by Jessie Carni Smith. Westport, Conn.: Greenwood Press, 1983.

Elkin, Lisa. "Unearthing of Freed-Slave Cemetery. May Put Dallas Road Project on Hold.*" New York Times (National),* August 13, 1990.

Lucas, Ernestine. "Good Queries Bring Excellent Results." *American Visions,* 10(5) Oct. 1995: 44.

Mannis, Margaret. "Plugging into Your Roots." *U.S. News & World Report,* 121(25) Dec. 23,1996: 73–76.

Merritt, Carole. "Slave Family History Records: An Abundance of Materials." *Georgia Archives* 6 (Spring 1978): 16–21.

Mintz, Steven and Susan. "The Shaping of the Afro-American Family." In *Domestic Revolutions: A Social History of American Family Life*. New York: Free Press, 1988.

Nordmann, Chris. "Basic Genealogical Research Methods and Their Application to African-Americans." In *African-American Genealogical Sourcebook*, edited by Paula K. Byers. Detroit: Gale Research, 1995.

Redford, Dorothy Spruill, with Michael D'Orso. *Somerset Homecoming: Recovering a Lost Heritage.* New York: Doubleday, 1988. This family research project turned into the history and genealogy of an entire plantation. It is a remarkable example of a family research project, very readable, and highly recommended for everyone attempting African-American genealogical research.

Reese, Shelly. "Shrouded by Slavery." *American Demographics*, 17(12) Dec. 1995: 51.

Thomas, Kenneth. "A Note on the Pitfalls of Black Genealogy: The Origins of Black Surnames." *Georgia Archives,* 6 (Spring 1978).

"Tracing Free People of Color in the Antebellum South: Methods, Sources, and Perspectives." *National Genealogical Society Quarterly* 78 (December 1990).

Woodtor, Dee Parmer. "African-American Genealogy: A Personal Search for the Past." *American Visions* 8(6) Dec./Jan. 1994: 20–25.

Journals

Journal of the Afro-American Historical and Genealogical Society. The Afro-American History and Genealogical Society, 1980–present.

Newspapers

Beryl, Susan, and Erwin K. Welch. *Black Periodicals and Newspapers: A Union List of Holdings in Libraries of the University of Wisconsin and the Library of the State Historical Society of Wisconsin,* 1975.

Jacobs, Donald M. *Antebellum Black Newspapers.* Westport, Conn.: Greenwood Press, 1976.

Henritze, Barbara K. *Bibliographic Checklist of African American Newspapers.* Baltimore Md.: Genealogical Publishing Company, 1995.

Hutton, Frankie. *The Early Black Press in America, 1827 to 1860.* Westport, Conn.: Greenwood Press, 1993.

Spradling, Mary Mace. *In Black and White: A Guide to Magazine Articles, Newspaper Articles, and Books Concerning More Than 15,000 Black Individuals and Groups.* 3rd ed. Detroit, Mich.: Gale Research Company, 1980.

Spradling, Mary Mace. *In Black and White. Supplement: A Guide to Magazine Articles, Newspaper Articles, and Books Concerning More Than 6,700 Black Individuals and Groups.* 3rd ed. Detroit, Mich.: Gale Research Company, 1985.

Appendix C
National Archives and Records Administration Facilities

National Archives Building, Washington, D.C.

National Archives and Records Administration, 700 Pennsylvania Avenue, N.W., Washington, DC 20408; Telephone: 866-325-7208 (customer service); Web: www.nara.gov.

Regional Records Services Facilities

Alaska

NARA's Pacific Alaska Region (Anchorage), 654 West Third Avenue, Anchorage, Alaska 99501-2145; Telephone: 907-271-2443; E-mail: alaska.archives@nara.gov; Web: www.nara.gov/regional/anchorag.html; Fax: 907-271-2442. Holdings: Archival holdings from federal agencies and courts in Alaska, and extensive microfilm holdings of value for genealogy research.

California

NARA's Pacific Region (Laguna Niguel), 24000 Avila Road, First Floor-East Entrance, Laguna Niguel, California 92677-3497; Telephone: 949-360-2641; E-mail: laguna.archives@nara.gov; Web: www.nara.gov/regional/laguna.html; Fax: 949-360-2624. Holdings: Archival holdings from federal agencies and courts in Arizona, southern California, and Clark County, Nevada.

NARA's Pacific Region (San Francisco), 1000 Commodore Drive, San Bruno, California 94066-2350; Telephone: 650-876-9009; E-mail: sanbruno.archives@nara.gov; Fax: 650-876-9233; Web: www.nara.gov/

regional/sanfranc.html. Holdings: Archival holdings from federal agencies and courts in northern California, Hawaii, Nevada (except Clark County), the Pacific Trust Territories, and American Samoa.

Colorado

NARA's Rocky Mountain Region, Building 48, Denver Federal Center, West 6th Avenue and Kipling Street, Denver, Colorado 80225 (mailing address: P. O. Box 25307, Denver, Colorado 80225-0307); Telephone: 303-236-0804; E-mail: denver.archives@nara.gov; Web: www.nara.gov/regional/denver.html; Fax: 303-236-9297. Holdings: Archival holdings from federal agencies and courts in Colorado, Montana, New Mexico, North Dakota, South Dakota, Utah, and Wyoming.

Georgia

NARA's Southeast Region (Atlanta), 1557 St. Joseph Avenue, East Point, Georgia 30344-2593; Telephone: 404-763-7474; E-mail: atlanta.center@nara.gov; Web: www.nara.gov/regional/atlanta.html; Fax: 404-763-7059. Holdings: Archival holdings from federal agencies and courts in Alabama, Florida, Georgia, Kentucky, Mississippi, North Carolina, South Carolina, and Tennessee.

Illinois

NARA's Great Lakes Region (Chicago), 7358 South Pulaski Road, Chicago, Illinois 60629-5898; Telephone: 773-581-7816; E-mail: chicago.archives@nara.gov; Web: www.nara.gov/regional/chicago.html; Fax: 312-353-1294. Holdings: Archival holdings from federal agencies and courts in Illinois, Indiana, Michigan, Minnesota, Ohio, and Wisconsin. Records center holdings from federal agencies in Illinois, Minnesota, and Wisconsin, and from federal courts in Illinois, Indiana, Michigan, Minnesota, Ohio, and Wisconsin. Microfilm holdings of value for genealogy research.

Maryland

Office of Regional Records Services (College Park), National Archives and Records Administration, 8601 Adelphi Road, College Park, Maryland 20740-6001; Telephone: 301-713-7200; Fax: 301-713-7205.

Washington National Records Center (Suitland), 4205 Suitland Road, Suitland, Maryland 20746-8001; Telephone: 301-457-7000; E-mail: suitland.center@nara.gov; Web: www.nara.gov/records/wnrc.html; Fax: 301-457-7117. Holdings: Records center holdings for federal agency headquarters offices in the District of Columbia, Maryland, and Virginia; federal agency field offices in Maryland, Virginia, and West Virginia; federal courts in the District of Columbia; and U.S. Armed Forces worldwide.

Massachusetts

NARA's Northeast Region (Boston), 380 Trapelo Road, Waltham, Massachusetts 02452-6399; Telephone: 781-647-8104; E-mail: waltham.archives@nara.gov; Web: www.nara.gov/regional/boston.html; Fax: 781-647-8088. Holdings: Archival holdings from federal agencies and courts in Connecticut, Maine, Massachusetts, New Hampshire, Rhode Island, and Vermont.

NARA's Northeast Region (Pittsfield), 10 Conte Drive, Pittsfield, Massachusetts 01201-8230; Telephone: 413-445-6885; E-mail: pittsfield.archives@nara.gov; Web: www.nara.gov/regional/pittsfie.html; Fax: 413-445-7599. Holdings: Records center holdings from selected federal agencies nationwide.

Missouri

NARA's Central Plains Region (Kansas City), 2312 East Bannister Road, Kansas City, Missouri 64131-3011; Telephone: 816-926-6272; E-mail: kansascity.archives@nara.gov; Web: www.nara.gov/regional/kansas.html; Fax: 816-926-6982. Holdings: Archival holdings from federal agencies and courts in Iowa, Kansas, Missouri and Nebraska.

NARA's Central Plains Region (Lee's Summit), 200 Space Center Drive, Lee's Summit, Missouri, 64064-1182; Telephone: 816-478-7079; E-mail: kansascitycave.center@nara.gov; Web: www.nara.gov/regional/leesumit.html; Fax: 816-478-7625. Holdings: Records center holdings from federal agencies and courts in New Jersey, New York, Puerto Rico, and the U.S. Virgin Islands, and from most Department of Veterans Affairs and Immigration and Naturalization Service offices nationwide.

NARA's National Personnel Records Center (St. Louis), Civilian Personnel Records, 111 Winnebago Street, St. Louis, Missouri 63118-4199; E-mail: cpr.center@nara.gov; Web: www.nara.gov/regional/

cpr.html; Fax: 314-538-5719. Holdings: Civilian personnel records from federal agencies nationwide; selected military dependent medical records.

NARA's National Personnel Records Center (St. Louis), Military Personnel Records, 9700 Page Avenue St. Louis, Missouri 63132-5100; E-mail: mpr.center@nara.gov; Web: www.nara.gov/regional/mpr.html; Fax: 314-538-4175. Holdings: Military personnel records, and military and retired military medical records from all services; selected dependent medical records, morning reports, rosters, and Philippine army and guerilla records.

New York

NARA's Northeast Region (New York City), 201 Varick Street, New York, New York 10014-4811; Telephone: 212-337-1300; E-mail: newyork.archives@nara.gov; Web: www.nara.gov/regional/newyork.html; Fax: 212-337-1306. Holdings: Archival holdings from federal agencies and courts in New Jersey, New York, Puerto Rico, and the U.S. Virgin Islands. Microfilm holdings of value for genealogy research.

Ohio

NARA's Great Lakes Region (Dayton), 3150 Springboro Road, Dayton, Ohio 45439-1883;Telephone: 937-225-2852; E-mail: dayton. center@nara.gov; Web: www.nara.gov/regional/dayton.html; Fax: 937-225-7236. Holdings: Records center holdings from federal agencies in Indiana, Michigan, and Ohio; federal bankruptcy court records from Ohio since 1991/92; Defense Finance Accounting System records nationwide and from Germany and Korea; and Internal Revenue Service records from selected sites nationwide.

Pennsylvania

NARA's Mid Atlantic Region (Center City Philadelphia), 900 Market Street, Philadelphia, Pennsylvania 19107-4292; Telephone: 215-597-3000; E-mail: philadelphia.archives@nara.gov; Web: www.nara.gov/regional/philacc.html; Fax: 215-597-2303; Holdings: Archival holdings from federal agencies and courts in Delaware, Maryland, Pennsylvania, Virginia, and West Virginia. Microfilm holdings and original records of value for genealogy research.

NARA's Mid Atlantic Region (Northeast Philadelphia),14700 Townsend Road, Philadelphia, Pennsylvania 19154-1096; Telephone: 215-671-9027; E-mail: philadelphia.center@nara.gov; Web: www.nara.gov/regional/philane.html. Fax: 215-671-8001. Holdings: Records center holdings from federal agencies in Delaware and Pennsylvania and federal courts in Delaware, Maryland, Pennsylvania, Virginia, and West Virginia.

Texas

NARA's Southwest Region (Fort Worth), 501 West Felix Street, Building 1, Fort Worth, Texas 76115-3405, P. O. Box 6216, Fort Worth, Texas 76115-0216; Telephone: 817-334-5525; E-mail: ftworth.archives@nara.gov; Web: www.nara.gov/regional/ftworth.html; Fax: 817-334-5621. Holdings: Archival holdings from federal agencies and courts in Arkansas, Louisiana, Oklahoma, and Texas. Records center holdings from federal agencies and courts in the same states. Microfilm holdings of value for genealogy research.

Washington (State)

NARA's Pacific Alaska Region (Seattle), 6125 Sand Point Way NE, Seattle, Washington 98115-7999; Telephone: 206-526-6501; E-mail: seattle.archives@nara.gov; Web: www.nara.gov/regional/seattle.html; Fax: 206-526-6575. Holdings: Archival holdings from federal agencies and courts in Idaho, Oregon, and Washington (State). Records center holdings for federal agencies and courts in the same states and Alaska. Microfilm holdings of value for genealogy research.

Appendix D
Library Symbols

A-Ar	Alabama Department of Archives and History, Montgomery
Ar-Hi	Arkansas History Commission, Department of Archives and History, Little Rock
A-Sr	Alaska State Archives, Juneau
ArU	University of Arkansas, Fayetteville
ATT	Tuskegee Institute, Tuskegee, Ala.
AU	University of Alabama, University, Ala.
Az	Arizona State Department of Library and Archives, Phoenix
AzML	Mesa Branch Genealogical Library, Mesa, Ariz.
AzTP	Arizona Pioneers' Historical Society, Tucson
C	California State Library, Sacramento
C-Ar	California State Archives, Sacramento
CChiS	California State University, Chico
CFls	California State University, Fullerton
CFS	California State University, Fresno
CLCM	Los Angeles County Museum, Los Angeles
CLS	California State University, Los Angeles
CNoS	California State University, Northridge
CoD	Denver Public Library
CoFS	Colorado State University, Fort Collins
COG	Oakland Branch Genealogical Library, Oakland, Calif.
CoHi	Colorado State Historical Society, Denver
CoU	University of Colorado, Boulder
CSdS	San Diego State University
CSf	San Francisco Public Library
CSfGS	California Genealogical Society, San Francisco

CSfSt	San Francisco State University
CshS	Stephen H. Hart Library, Colorado Historical Society
CSmarP	Palomar College, San Marcos, Calif.
CSmH	Henry E. Huntington Library, San Marino, Calif.
CSS	California State University, Sacramento
CSt	Stanford University, Stanford, Calif.
Ct	Connecticut State Library, Hartford
CtD	West Connecticut State College, Danbury
CtU	University of Connecticut, Storrs
CtY	Yale University, New Haven
CU	University of California, Berkeley
CU-B	University of California, Bancroft Library, Berkeley
CU-Riv	University of California, Riverside
De-Ar	Delaware Public Archives, Dover
DeH	History Society of Delaware, Wilmington
DeU	University of Delaware, Newark
DeWl	Wilmington Institute Free Library, Wilmington, Del.
DeWint	Henry Francis Dupont Winterthur Museum, Winterthur, Del.
DHU	Howard University, Washington, D.C.
DLC	U.S. Library of Congress, Washington, D.C.
DNA	U.S. National Archives, Washington, D.C.
DNDAR	Daughters of The American Revolution, Washington, D.C.
F-Ar	Florida State Archives
FM	Miami Public Library, Miami, Fla.
FTaSU	Florida State University, Tallahassee
FU	Florida State University, Gainesville
G-Ar	Georgia State Department of Archives and History, Atlanta
GAU	Atlanta University, Atlanta
GEU	Emory University, Atlanta
GHi	Georgia Historical Society, Savannah
GSSC	Savannah State College, Savannah
GStG	Georgia Southern College, Statesboro
GU	University of Georgia, Athens
HU	University of Hawaii, Honolulu

IaCft	University of Northern Iowa, Cedar Rapids
IaDH	Historical, Memorial and Art Department of Iowa, Des Moines
IaDM	Des Moines Public Library, Iowa
IaHi	State Historical Society of Iowa, Iowa City
IaMpl	Iowa Wesleyan College, Mount Pleasant
I-Ar	Illinois State Archives, Springfield
IaU	University of Iowa, Iowa City
IC-Hi	Chicago Public Library, George Cleveland Hall Branch
ICHi	Chicago Historical Society
ICIU	University of Illinois at Chicago Circle, Chicago
ICN	Newberry Library, Chicago
ICU	University of Chicago
IdHi	Idaho State Historical Society, Boise
IHi	Illinois State Historical Library, Springfield
In	Indiana State Library, Indianapolis
InFw	Public Library of Fort Wayne and Allen County
InIB	Butler University, Indianapolis
InMuB	Ball State University, Muncie, Ind.
InNd	University of Notre Dame, Notre Dame, Ind.
InU	Indiana University, Bloomington
IU	University of Illinois, Urbana
Kcpl	Kansas City Public Library
KH	Kansas State Historical Society, Topeka
KU	University of Kansas, Lawrence
KXSM	Saint Mary College, Xavier, Kans.
KyBgW	Western Kentucky State University, Bowling Green
KyHi	Kentucky Historical Society, Frankfort
KyLoF	Filson Club, Louisville, Ky.
KyLxT	Transylvania College, Lexington, Ky.
KyMoreU	Morehead State University, Morehead, Ky.
KyU	University of Kentucky, Lexington
LN	New Orleans Public Library
LNT	Tulane University, New Orleans
LU	Louisiana State University, Baton Rouge
LU-Ar	Louisiana State University, Department of Archives and Manuscripts, Baton Rouge

LU-NO	Louisiana State University in New Orleans
M-Ar	Archives Division, Secretary of State, Boston
MB	Boston Public Library
MBAt	Boston Athenaeum
MBU	Boston University
McA	Microfilming Corporation of America, 21 Harristown Road, Glen Rock, N.J. 07452
MdAA	Hall of Records Commission, Annapolis, Md.
MdBj	Johns Hopkins University, Baltimore
MdBMC	Morgan State College, Baltimore
MdHi	Maryland Historical Society, Baltimore
MdPM	University of Maryland Eastern Shore
MeB	Bowdoin College, Brunswick, Maine
MeHi	Maine Historical Society, Portland
MeU	University of Maine, Orono
Me-Vs	Maine Office of Vital Statistics, Augusta
MH	Harvard University, Cambridge, Mass.
MH-B	Harvard University, Baker Library, Cambridge, Mass.
MHi	Massachusetts Historical Society, Boston
Mi	Michigan State Library, Lansing
MiD	Detroit Public Library
MiD-B	Detroit Public Library, Burton Historical Collection
MiDW	Wayne State University, Detroit
Mi-HC	Michigan Historical Commission, State Archives Library, Lansing
Mi-Hi	Michigan Historical Commission, Lansing
MiKW	Western Michigan University, Kalamazoo
MiMtpT	Central Michigan University, Mount Pleasant
MiU	University of Michigan, Ann Arbor
MiU-C	University of Michigan, William L. Clements Library, Ann Arbor
MiYEM	Eastern Michigan University, Ypsilanti
MMeHi	Medford Historical Society, Medford, Mass.
Mn-Ar	Minnesota State Archives, St. Paul
MnHi	Minnesota Historical Society, St. Paul
MnU	University of Minnesota, Minneapolis
MoIG	Genealogical Services, Independence, Mo.
MoJcL	Lincoln University, Jefferson City, Mo.

MoS	St. Louis Public Library
MoHistSoc	Missouri Historical Society, St. Louis
MoMcpl	Mid-Continent Public Library Genealogy Branch, Independence
MoSW	Washington University, St. Louis
MoU	University of Missouri, Ellis Library, Columbia
MSaE	Essex Institute, Salem, Mass.
MSoP	Peabody Museum of Salem, Mass.
Ms-Ar	Mississippi Department of Archives And History, Jackson
MsHaU	University of Southern Mississippi, Hattiesburg
MsSM	Mississippi State University, State College
MsU	University of Mississippi, University, Miss.
MsVHi	Vicksburg and Warren County Historical Society, Vicksburg, Miss.
MtHi	Montana Historical Society, Helena
MU	University of Massachusetts, Amherst
MWA	American Antiquarian Society, Worcester, Mass.
MWalAj	American Jewish Historical Society, Waltham, Mass.
MWiW	Williams College, Williamstown, Mass.
N	New York State Library, Albany
NAll	Albany Institute of History and Art
NbHi	Nebraska State Historical Society, Lincoln
NbO	Omaha Public Library
NbOU	University of Nebraska at Omaha
Nc-Ar	North Carolina State Department of Archives and History, Raleigh
NcD	Duke University, Durham, N.C.
NcGrE	East Carolina University, Greenville, N.C.
NcHiC	North Carolina Historical Commission, Raleigh
NcU	University of North Carolina, Chapel Hill
NcWsM	Moravian Archives, Winston-Salem, N.C.
NdHi	State Historical Society of North Dakota, Bismarck
NdU	University of North Dakota, Grand Forks
NGcA	Adelphi College—Nassau County Historical and Genealogical Society, Garden City, N.Y.
Nh	New Hampshire State Library, Concord
NhD	Dartmouth College, Hanover, N.H.
NhHi	New Hampshire Historical Society, Concord

NHi	New York Historical Society, New York
NIC	Cornell University, Ithaca, N.Y.
Nj	New Jersey State Library, Trenton
Nj-Ar	New Jersey Bureau of Archives and History, Trenton
Nj-Hs	New Jersey Historical Society, Newark
NjGbS	Glassboro State College, Glassboro, N.J.
NjP	Princeton University, Princeton, N.J.
NjR	Rutgers, The State University, New Brunswick, N.J.
NjRuF	Fairleigh Dickinson University, Rutherford, N.J.
NjT	Trenton Free Public Library, Trenton, N.J.
NmU	University of New Mexico, Albuquerque
NN	New York Public Library
NNC	Columbia University, New York
NNGB	New York Genealogical and Biographical Society, New York
NN-Sc	Schomburg Collection for Black Culture, New York
NRU	University of Rochester, N.Y.
NSyU	Syracuse University, Syracuse, N.Y.
NvHi	Nevada State Historical Society, Reno
NvL	Las Vegas Public Library, Las Vegas, Nev.
NvU	University of Nevada, Reno
OC	Public Library of Cincinnati and Hamilton County
OCHP	Cincinnati Historical Society
OCI	Cleveland Public Library
OCIWHi	Western Reserve Historical Society, Cleveland
OCX	Xavier University, Cincinnati
OFH	Rutherford B. Hayes Library, Fremont, Ohio
OHi	Ohio State Historical Society, Columbus
OKentU	Kent State University, Kent, Ohio
OkHi	Oklahoma Historical Society, Oklahoma City
OkOkU	Oklahoma City University
OkS	Oklahoma State University, Stillwater
OkTG	Thomas Gilcrease Foundation, Tulsa
OkU	University of Oklahoma, Norman
OOxM	Miami University, Oxford, Ohio
Or-Ar	Oregon State Archives, Salem
OrHi	Oregon Historical Society, Portland
OrU	University of Oregon, Eugene
OU	Ohio State University, Columbus

OWibfU	Wilberforce University, Wilberforce, Ohio
P	State Library of Pennsylvania, Harrisburg
P-Ar	Pennsylvania State Archives, Harrisburg
PBL	Lehigh University, Bethlehem, Pa.
PCC	Crozer Theological Seminary, Chester, Pa.
PDoBHi	Bucks County Historical Society, Doylestown, Pa.
PEsS	East Stroudsburg State College, East Stroudsburg, Pa.
PHarH	Pennsylvania Historical and Museum Commission, Harrisburg
PHC	Haverford College, Haverford, Pa.
PHi	Historical Society of Pennsylvania, Philadelphia
PluL	Lincoln University, Lincoln University, Pa.
PP	Free Library of Philadelphia
PPAmP	American Philosophical Society, Philadelphia
PPiD	Duquesne University, Pittsburgh
PPiU	University of Pittsburgh
PPT	Temple University, Philadelphia
PSC-Hi	Swarthmore College, Friends Historical Library, Swarthmore, Pa.
PSt	Pennsylvania State University, University Park
PU	University of Pennsylvania, Philadelphia
PV	Villanova University, Villanova, Pa.
R	Rhode Island State Library, Providence
Readex	Readex Microprint Corporation, 5 Union Square, New York, N.Y. 10003
RHi	Rhode Island Historical Society, Providence
RP	Providence Public Library
RPB	Brown University, Providence
RPPC	Providence College, Providence
Sc-Ar	South Carolina Department of Archives and History, Columbia
ScCC	College of Charleston, Charleston, S.C.
ScHi	South Carolina Historical Society, Charleston
ScRhW	Winthrop College, Rock Hill, S.C.
ScU	University of South Carolina, Columbia
SdHi	South Dakota State Historical Society, Pierre

SHSM	State Historical Society of Missouri, Columbia
T	Tennessee State Library, Nashville
TC	Chattanooga Public Library
TJoS	East Tennessee State University, Johnson City
TKL	Public Library of Knoxville and Knox County
TNF	Fisk University, Nashville
TNJ	Joint University Libraries, Nashville
TrC	Tayloreel Corporation, 155 Murray Street, Rochester, N.Y. 14606
TU	University of Tennessee, Knoxville
Tx	Texas State Library and Historical Commission, Austin
TxF	Fort Worth Public Library
TxFS	Southwestern Baptist Theological Seminary, Fort Worth
TxGR	Rosenberg Library, Galveston, Tex.
TxH	Houston Public Library
TxHR	Rice University, Houston
TxHTSU	Texas Southern University, Houston
TxU	University of Texas, Austin
UL	Cache County Public Library, Logan, Utah
UNC	University of North Carolina, Wilson Library
UMC	University of Missouri, Columbia, Ellis Library
UPB	Brigham Young University, Provo, Utah
USIGD	Genealogical Department of the Church of Jesus Christ of Latter-day Saints, Salt Lake City
Vi	Virginia State Library, Richmond
ViHai	Hampton Institute, Hampton, Va.
ViHi	Virginia Historical Society, Richmond
ViU	University of Virginia, Charlottesville
ViW	College of William and Mary, Williamsburg, Va.
ViWl	Institute of Early American History and Culture, Williamsburg, Va.
Vt	Vermont State Library, Montpelier
VtU	University of Vermont and State Agricultural College, Burlington

Wa	Washington State Library, Olympia
WabeW	Western Washington State College, Bellingham
WaHi	Washington State Historical Society, Tacoma
WaOE	The Evergreen College, Olympia, Wash.
WaSp	Spokane Public Library
WaSpG	Gonzaga University, Spokane
WaU	University of Washington, Seattle
WHi	State Historical Society of Wisconsin, Madison
WHMC	University of Missouri-Columbia, Joint Collection— Western Historical Manuscript Collection.
WM	Milwaukee Public Library
WU	University of Wisconsin, Madison
Wv-Ar	West Virginia Department of Archives and History, Charleston
WvU	West Virginia University, Morgantown
WvU-J	West Virginia University, School of Journalism, Morgantown
Wy-Ar	Wyoming State Archives and History Department, Cheyenne

INDEX

Abolitionist Movement, 337. *See also* names of antislavery organizations
Adams, Eliphalet, 89
Advent Episcopal Parish Register, 267
advertisements, slave, 32, 38, 196
Affleck, Thomas, 329
African American Archives of Maine Reading Room, 177
African American Genealogical Society of Northern California, 76
African American Resource Center, 241
African Association of New Brunswick, 246
African Benevolent Society, 304
African Colonization Society, 296
African Humane Society, 304
African Methodist Episcopal Church Records, 279
African Republic of Liberia, 14
African School Society Papers, 97
African Union Church Cemetery, 96
African Union Society, 304
Afro-American Genealogical Society, 102, 141, 190
agricultural revolution, 31, 33
Alabama Department of Archives & History, 53, 54
Alabama, records concerning African Americans, 53–60
Alaska Historical Society, 62
Alaska, records concerning African Americans, 61–62

Alaska State Archives, 61, 62
Alcorn, Governor James L., 211
Alexander Collection, 75
Allen County Indiana Public Library, 147, 148–49
Allen, Eliza A., 119
Allen, Eliza Harriet, 119
Allen, Wade Hampton, 56
American Colonization Movement, 299
America Freedmen's Inquiry Commission, 196
American Home Missionary Society Records, 200
American Negro Historical Society, 296
Anderson, Edward Clifford, 119, 120
Antigua, 373–74, 378. *See also* West Indies
Applegate, Lisbon, 220
apprenticeships, 97, 99, 116, 196, 215, 266. *See also* indentures; bonds
Archer Family, 345
Archer, Jane Segar, 345
Archives, National. *See* National Archives, Washington, D.C.
archives, state, 48. *See also* individual states
Ardrey, William E., 269
Arizona, records concerning African Americans, 63–65
Arizona Pioneers Historical Society, 64

Arizona State Library, Archives and Public Records, 63, 64
Arkansas History Commission, 67, 69
Arkansas Humanities Resource Center, 70
Arkansas, records concerning African Americans, 67–71
army records. *See* military records
Arnett, Benjamin William, 279
Arnold and Screvan Family, 120
Arrington, Archibald Hunter, 267
Ashtabula County Female Anti-Slavery Society Records, 281
Atkins, James A., 81
Atlanta University, 15

Bacot Family, 311
Bahamas, 374, 375, 378. *See also* West Indies
Bailey, Everett Hoskins, 207
Bailey Family, 345
Bailey, John Lancaster, 267
Bailey, William, 345
Ball, John, Sr., 311
Ball, William J., 311
Bank of the United States, mortgages on slaves, 213
Banneker, Benjamin, 99
baptism records, 38–39. *See also* church records
Barbados, 374, 377, 379. *See also* West Indies
Barnett, William J., 281
Barrow, Clara Elizabeth, 121
Barrow, Col. David Crenshaw, 121
Bartholomew's Episcopal Church, 117
Bass Family, 56
Batchelor, Albert A., 171
Bateman, (Mary), 171, 269
Beale, Edward, 269
Beech Creek Baptist Church, 163
Bell, George, 99

Bellinger, Carnot, 56
Bennett, Reuben, 56
Bermuda, 374–75, 379. *See also* West Indies
Berrien, John McPherson, 119
Berry, William Wells, 324
Bethel African-American Methodist Episcopal Church, 235
Bethel Methodist Church, 118
Bethlehem Baptist Church, 117
Bibles, as genealogical records, 7–8
Billingsley, James B., 329
birth records, 38–39. *See also* vital records; diaries
Black American West Museum and Heritage Center, 82
"Blackdom," in New Mexico, 249, 250
Black Genealogy Research Group, Seattle, Washington, 351
Black Genealogy Search Group, Denver, Colorado, 82
Black Heritage Council of the Alabama Historical Commission, 69
Black Heritage Society of Washington State, 351
Black Loyalists. *See* Loyalists
Black Renaissance Project, 102
Blacks in Alaska History Project, 62
Blackspear, Alexander, 56
Blessed Sacrament Catholic Church, 107
Blockson Afro-American Collection, Philadelphia, Pennsylvania, 297
Blount, Richard A., 56
Boise County [Idaho], 129
Bolton and Dickens Company Slave Trade Records, 169
bonds
  Barbados, 377
  Georgia, 116
  Louisiana, 170
  Maryland, 181–88

Missouri, 222
New Jersey, 244, 247
North Carolina, 264, 266
Virginia, 341, 344
See also indentures
books, for genealogical research, 4, 6,
43, 381–83. *See also* individual
states
Borden, Gail, 329
Botts-Lewis Family, 220
Bowen, George Washington, 281
Bradley, T.T., 220
Branscomb Family, 56
Bratton Family, 311
Breckenridge Family, 220
Bridgeport Public Library, 90
Brigham Young University, 7
Brinckerhoff, Isaac W., 311
Brock, Robert Alonzo Collection, 344
Brotherhood of Sleeping Car Porters,
140
Broughton Family, 311
Brown, James, 220
Brown, Thomas, 56
Bryan, Moses Austin, 329
Buche, la Anne Marie, 359
Buckner, James, 220
Buckner Papers, 324
Buell, George P., 324
Buffalo Lick Baptist Church, 163
Buffalo Soldiers, 157, 231, 328. *See
also* Indians of North America
Bureau of Refugees, Freedmen and
Abandoned Lands. *See*
Freedmen's Bureau
Burgwyn, Capt. William Hyslop
Sumner, 269
Burlington Iowa Public Library, 152
Burr Oak Cemetery, 137
Burt, Franklin, 220
Burton Historical Collection, 202
Burwell Family, 268
Bush, George Washington, 349

Cabell Family, 344
California Department of Health
Services, 74
California, records concerning
African Americans, 73–77
California State Archives, 73, 74
California Supreme Court, 75
Cameron Family, 119
Campbell Family, 357
Canada, records concerning African
Americans, 369–71
Capell, Eli J., 171, 211
Cape Verdean Islands, 175
Caples, J. A., 89
Carter, Fannie Cobb, 357
Carter, Robert Wormley, 344
Carter Temple C.M.B. Church, 138
Cartwright, Matthew, 329
Catholic Church, St. Augustine, 108
Cayman Islands, 375. *See also* West
Indies
Cedar Park Cemetery, 137
cemetery records, 8, 49, 55, 74, 85,
87, 96, 99, 107, 117, 130, 131,
137, 147, 162, 163, 190, 195, 202,
210, 259, 267, 278, 279, 286, 290,
310, 318, 322, 328, 339, 356, 361,
366. *See also* names of individual
cemeteries
census records, 4–6, 7, 22–24, 25, 35,
39, 48, 54, 61, 63, 68, 70, 74, 79–
80, 82, 85–86, 95–96, 100, 106,
111, 130, 131, 146, 151–52, 155–
56, 161–62, 167–68, 175–76, 180,
193, 199, 202, 206, 209, 218, 227–
28, 230, 235–36, 240, 243–44,
249–50, 253–54, 259, 263, 274,
277–78, 285, 290, 293–94, 300,
307–08, 317–18, 321–22, 327–28,
333–34, 337–38, 342, 349–50,
355–56, 360, 365–66, 370
Central State Hospital Cemetery
Records, 117

Chambers, Thomas W., 329
Chapron, Jean Marie, 56
Chelette, Atala, Family, 170
Cherokee Collection, 324. *See also*
Indians of North America
Chestnut-Miller-Manning, 311
Cheves Family, 326
Chew, Benjamin, 296
Chicago Historical Society Library,
141
Chicago Public Library, 137, 138,
139, 141
Chickasaw Nation Records, 287
Chicote, Samuel, 287
Christenburg Baptist Church, 163
Christine's Genealogy Website, 213
Church of Jesus Christ of Latter-day
Saints, Family History Library, 5,
8, 25, 37, 48, 74, 259, 334–35
church records, 6, 49, 55, 74, 87, 96,
99, 105, 107, 117–18, 137–38,
146, 152, 163, 168, 173, 188, 190,
195, 200, 202, 207, 210–11, 219,
231, 259, 267, 279, 310, 322–23,
339, 342, 361, 366, 370. *See also*
names of individual churches
Circuit Court Clerk of Cook County
Archives, 136
city directories, 131, 142, 259, 330,
335
Civil War records. *See* military
records
Civil War Regimental Papers, 280
Clark, Charles, 211
Clements Family, 56
Cocke Family, 56
Coffee, John, 56
Coker, William, 312
Colleges, African-American, 15, 99,
176
Colonization, records of, 102
Colorado Historical Society, 81
Colorado Newspaper Project, 80

Colorado, records concerning African
Americans, 79–83
Colorado State Archives, 79
Confederate Pension Application
Files, 108, 118
Confederate States of America,
African Americans in, 55, 69, 163,
310, 322, 323. *See also* military
records
Connecticut General Assembly
records, 86–87
Connecticut, records concerning
African Americans, 85–93
Connecticut State Library, 85, 86, 87,
88
Convention of Colored Men, 199
Conway, Joseph, 220
Cook County Cemetery, 137
Cooper, Mark Anthony, 119
Cooper, James Hamilton, 121
Cooper, William, 211
Coppin, Levi Jenkins, 279
Corby Family, 221
county records, 6, 49. *See also* deeds,
wills, court records, military
records
court records, 39, 41, 79, 96, 116,
135, 136, 147, 162–63, 181–88,
194–95, 219, 230, 236, 341, 362
Cowan, Mrs. F. B., 119
Cowboys, 63
Cox Family, 312
Crenshaw, Edward, 56
Crickmore, H.G., 280
Cross, Paul, 312
Crowell, John, 56
Crudup, E.A., 269
Culin, Beppie, 64
Cumberland Presbyterian Church,
322
Cummins Family, 344
Cunningham, Valerie, 241
Cutchfield Family, 325

Darden Family, 212
Darragh, John L. 329
Daughters of the American Revolution Library, 103
Davis Preston and Company, 344
death records, 38–39, 41. *See also* vital records
deeds, 6, 37, 68, 162–63, 221, 222, 245. *See also* land records
DeClouet, Paul L., 171
Delaware Public Archives, 95
Delaware, records concerning African Americans, 95–98
Denver Public Library, 82
De Rosset Family, 268
Detroit Public Library, 202
DeWolf, James, 303
Diamant, Henry A., 221
diaries, 10, 50, 56–57, 75, 102, 121, 164, 171–72, 173, 201, 202, 211–13, 249, 269–70, 311–14, 325, 330, 344–45. *See also* papers, personal
Diary of Joshua Hempstead of New London, 10
Dickey, William J., 121
Disciples of Christ Historical Society, 322
District of Columbia Public Library, 2
District of Columbia, records concerning African Americans, 99–103
divorce records. *See* vital records
DNA testing, 7
Donnon, Elizabeth, 88
Douglass-Truth Library, 351
Dred Scott, 205
Duke University Special Collections, 270
Dunbar School, 65
Dunderhook slave community, 247

Dunlop, Hugh W., 324
Dupree, H.T.T., 212
Dutilh and Wachsmuth, 296

Eakin, William, 324
Eastern Illinois University, 134
Eggleston, Dick Hardeway, 212
Elliott, Newton G., 221
Emancipation Proclamation, 15, 41
emancipations, 86, 164, 221
emigration and immigration
    freedmen to Liberia, 14
    in Canada, 369
    year of, in census, 23
    West Indians, 373
Emmons Family, 221
Employment
    in military records, 118, 138
    in state constitutions, 289
Enoch Pratt Free Library, African American Collection, 190
Erwin, William, 269
Ethelbert, William Ervin Journals, 212
Everard, Green Baker, 212

family history, 85, 79, 120–21, 146, 159, 167, 202, 259, 314, 327, 335, 385–89. *See also* papers, personal; diaries
Family History Library. *See* Church of Jesus Christ of Latter-day Saints
federal censuses. *See* census records
federal records, 21–25
Federal Writers Project, 101. *See also* Works Progress Administration
Female African Benevolent Society, 304
First Bethel Baptist Church, 105
First Baptist Church for the Colored, 117
First Christian Church, 267

Fisk University Library, 324
Five Civilized Tribes, 287. *See also*
Indians of North America
Fleetwood, Christian Abraham, 102
Florida, records concerning African
Americans, 105–09
Florida State Archives, 105–06
Floyd, Charles, 56
Folsom Prison records, 73
Foster, Robert Watson, 171
Fox, William, 357
Foy, Robert Lee Collection, 268
Franklin, Nicholas, 99
Fred J. Reynolds Historical Geneal-
ogy Department, 147
Free Will Baptist Church Records,
279
Freedmen's Aid Society, 196
Freedmen's Bank, CD-ROM, 8, 22
Freedmen's Bureau, 15, 53, 99
Freedmen's records, 25, 116
Freedmen's Relief Association, 158
Freedmen's Savings and Trust
Company, 25, 58
French and Indian War. *See* military
records
Fulmore, Zachary Taylor, 329
funeral records, 70, 107
Futrell, Elliott, will of, 40–41

Galloway, James Clarence, 268
Gaudet, James Amedee, 170
genealogical research, basic prin-
ciples, 3–6
Georgia Department of Archives and
History, 39, 111
Georgia Department of Human
Resources, 112
Georgia Historical Society, 122
Georgia Normal and Industrial
Institute, 111
Georgia, records concerning African
Americans, 111–123
Gholson, William Yates, 281

Gilliam Family, 344
Gilman, Robbins, 207
Gittings Family, 189
Glasgow Family, 344
Goff, David, 357
Gold Rush, blacks in, 61, 62, 73
Grabill, Levi, 75
Grace Presbyterian Church, 138
Graham, Edwin S., 329
Gray, M.R., 344
Greater Metropolitan Missionary
Baptist Church, 138
Green, Thomas Jefferson, 329
Greene, Richard Appling, 119
Greenwood Cemetery, Jackson, 210
Grenada, 365. *See also* West Indies
Griffin, John A., 138
Griffith, Dr. David J., 138
Grimball, John Berkely, 312
Groce, Jared E., 330
Groom, William B., 221
Guyana, 376. *See also* West Indies
Gwyn, James, 269

Hairston and Wilson Family, 212
Haiti, 376. *See also* West Indies
Hale Collection of Newspaper
Marriage and Death Notices, 88
Halifax, Nova Scotia, 369, 370
Hall Family, 57
Hall, William, 56
Hamilton, Frederick A., 221
Hamilton Library, University of
Hawaii, 126
Hammond, Eli Shelby, 196
Harden, Edward, 269
Harrison Family, 57
Harrison, William, 324
Haverford College Library, 296
Hawaii, records concerning African
Americans, 125–27
Hawaii State Archives, 125
Hawaii State Library, 126
Haynes, Richard, 241

Hebron Presbyterian Church, 118
Hector Davis and Company Account
    Books, 140
Hempstead, Joshua. *See* Diary of
    Joshua Hempstead
Hempstead, Stephen, 89, 221
Heritage Quest, 5
Herndon, Archelaus, 221
Hickman-Bryan, 164, 171, 221
Hill, Col. John, 269
Hill Memorial Library, Special
    Collections, 173
Hilliard, Isaac H. (Mrs), 172
Hinson, Joseph Benjamin, 312
Historical Society of Pennsylvania, 296
history, and genealogy, 9
history, important dates in, 13–16, 48
Hollis, Deborah R., 81
Holy Angels Church, 138
Home Mission School for African
    Americans, 322
homesteaders, 232
Homewood Memorial Gardens, 137
Hooker, Joseph, 75
Hooper, William, 241
Hopeton Plantation, 121
Hord, William, 164
Houmas Plantation, 170
Howard, Oliver Otis, 176
Howard University, 99, 176
Hubard Family, 268
Hunter, David, 221
Hunter, Nancy, 221

Idaho, records concerning African
    Americans, 129–31
Idaho State Historical Society Library
    and Archives, 129, 130
Illinois, records concerning African
    Americans, 133–34
Illinois Regional Archives Deposito-
    ries [IRAD], 134
Illinois State Archives, 134, 136, 139,
    140

Illinois State Historical Library, 141
Illinois State University, 134
Immaculate Conception Parish, 139
immigration. *See* emigration and
    immigration
indentures, 69, 97, 99, 113, 116, 133,
    141, 158, 181–88, 247, 255, 310,
    311
Independent Presbyterian Church,
    118
Indiana Commission on Public
    Records, 146
Indiana Historical Society Library,
    148
Indiana, records concerning African
    Americans, 145–150
Indiana State Library and Historical
    Building, 147, 148
Indians of North America, 53, 195,
    274, 287, 324, 369, 287
Indies. *See* West Indies
Internet resources, 5, 11, 19, 43, 50,
    57–59, 62, 64–65, 70, 76, 81, 90,
    97, 102, 108, 121, 159, 164, 172,
    190, 197, 202, 207, 213, 223, 237,
    241, 259–60, 270, 274, 282, 287,
    291, 297, 303–04, 319, 325, 330,
    339–40, 345, 358, 362, 366, 370,
    378–79
interviewing, 4, 18–19. *See also* oral
    history
intestate records, 40. *See also* wills,
    intestate records, and inventories
inventories, 40, 69, 173, 181, 182.
    See also wills, intestate records,
    and inventories
Iowa Conference Historical Society
    of the United Methodist Church,
    152
Iowa, records concerning African
    Americans, 151–53
Iowa, State Historical Society, 151
Iowa Wesleyan College Archives,
    153

Jacobs, George R., 221
Jacobs, Phillip, 196
Jackson, Andrew II, 324
Jamaica, 376, 378, 379. *See also* West
    Indies
James Brown African Room, Newark
    Public Library, 247
Jean Byers Sampson Center for
    Diversity in Maine, 177
Jefferies Family, 312
Jenkins, Dr. John Carmichael, 172
Jenks, Michael Hutchinson, 296
Johnson, Abraham, 357
Johnson, Rev. Floyd D., 138
Jones, Benjamin Rush, 57
Jones, John J., 119
Jones, Robert, 89
Jones, William B., 119, 175
Jordan Grove Baptist Church, 117
Juneteenth, in Texas, 343
Justis, Horace Howard, 269

Kansas, records concerning African
    Americans, 155–160
Kansas State Historical Society, 155,
    157
Kauffman, Julius, 330
Kendrick, John F., 139
Kentucky Colonization Society
    Reports, 164
Kentucky Department for Library and
    Archives, 161
Kentucky Historical Society, 162,
    163, 164, 165
Kentucky, records concerning African
    Americans, 161–66
King, Martin Luther, Jr., Collection,
    76
King, Parrington, 119
King, Richard Hugg, 269
King, William R., 57

Ladies Aid Society, 281
Lahainaluna School, 125

land records, 37, 41
    Alabama, 55
    Arkansas, 70
    Barbados, 374
    Colorado, 79
    Connecticut, 86
    Delaware, 96
    District of Columbia, 99
    Indiana, 147
    Jamaica, 376
    Maryland, 181–88
    Michigan, 202
    Rhode Island, 300
    South Carolina, 310
    West Virginia, 358
Laurel Grove Cemetery Records, 117
Laurens, Henry, 312
Law, African-Americans and the, 15,
    29, 73
Law, Lyman, 89
Law, Thomas Cassels, 312
Lawton, Alexander James, 269
Lee, Huston, 312
Le Jeune, Olivier, 369
Lewis Family, 357
Lewis, Jarnes V., 357
Lewis, Junius R., 81
Liberia College, 196
Library of Congress, 51, 101
Liddell, St. John R., 172
Lincoln, William, 196
Lincoln Cemetery, 137
Linville, Richard, 10–11
Liverpool, Moses, 99
Lopez, Aaron, 303
Louisiana, records concerning
    African Americans, 167–74
Louisiana State Archives, 167, 168
Lovell, William S., 269
Lowery, William, 57
Loyalists, 369, 370
lumbermen, in Texas, 331
Lumpkin, Wilson, 121
Lyman, Carlos Parsons, 279

McCall, Duncan G., 212
McCanse, William A., 222
McCollan, Ellen E., 172
McCollum, Andrew, 170
McCutchen Family, 324
McGovern, Patrick Francis, 212
McIver, Sarah Witherspoon Ervin, 312
McKeag Family, 247
Madden Family, 344
Magruder, Eliza L., 172
Maine, records concerning African Americans, 175–77
Maine State Archives, 175, 176, 177
Manigault Family, 312
manumissions, 8, 41–42, 86, 97, 141, 147, 181–88, 189, 190, 202, 213, 245, 246, 254, 255, 256, 281, 297, 325, 376
manuscript sources, 50
marriage records, 38. *See also* vital records
Marshall Family, 222
Marshall, Henry Grimes, letters, 87
Mars Hill Presbyterian Church, 323
Marstella Family, 158
Marston, Henry W., 172
Martin, Charles, 170
Maryland Hall of Records, 179, 180–90
Maryland Museum of African-American Historical & Cultural Commission, 189
Maryland, records concerning African Americans, 179–92
Maryland State Archives, 179, 180–90
Maryland State Colonization Society, 189
Massachusetts Anti-Slavery Society, 196
Massachusetts Colonization Society, 196
Massachusetts Historical Society, 197

Massachusetts, records concerning African Americans, 193–97
Massachusetts State Archives, 193, 194, 195
Mather, Joseph, 172
Maxwell Family, 57
Mckee, Robert, 57
medical records, 40
Methodist Episcopal Church, 323
Michigan, records concerning African Americans, 199–203
Michigan State Archives and Library, 199, 202
Middleton, Nathaniel Russell, 312
Midland Plantation, KY, 164
Migration, Great, 253, 293, 307, 341
migration patterns, 7, 31–33, 37
military records, 7, 25, 27–30, 36, 49, 55, 69, 75, 79, 87, 96, 118, 138–39, 147, 152, 157, 163, 169, 177, 188, 193, 200–01, 202, 207, 219, 231, 240, 246, 259, 267, 279, 286, 290, 295–96, 303, 308, 310, 318, 321, 322, 328, 339, 343, 350, 356
Mill Creek Baptist Church, 323
Miller, Howard, 164
Minnesota Historical Society, 205, 207
Minnesota, records concerning African Americans, 205–08
Mississippi Baptist Church, 210
Mississippi Church of Christ Records, 210
Mississippi Department of Archives and History, 209, 214
Mississippi Historical Society, 213–14
Mississippi Methodist Church, 210
Mississippi Presbyterian Church, 210
Mississippi Primitive Baptist Church, 211
Mississippi, records concerning African Americans, 209–16
Missouri Compromise, 14

Missouri, records concerning African Americans, 217–25
Missouri, University of, 223
Monette, James, 172
Montana Historical Society, 227
Montana, records concerning African Americans, 227–28
Montgomery, Thomas, 207
Montgomery, William Thornton, 273
Moore, Samuel Preston, 196
Morgan County Archives, 357
Morgan, James, 330
mortality records, 24, 54, 63, 68, 74, 80, 86, 95, 99, 106, 111, 130, 135, 146, 151, 156, 162, 168, 176, 180, 194, 200, 206, 209, 218, 227, 230, 235, 240, 244, 250, 254, 263, 274, 278, 290, 294, 300, 308, 318, 322, 323, 328, 334, 338, 342, 356, 360. *See also* census records
Moreland, William F., 172
mortality records, 24
Moseley, Lewis B., 57
Mount Glenwood Memory Gardens South, 137
Mt. Vernon Plantation, Fla., 108
mulattoes, 168, 170, 194, 294, 295, 344
Mulberry Plantation, S.C., 312
Murrell Family, 170
Museum of Antigua & Barbuda, 373

Nacosa Plantation, Fla., 108
Nailer Plantation, Claiborne County, Miss., 212
Nanechehaw Plantation, Miss., 213
Nashoba Colony, Ohio, 281
National Afro-American Museum, 282
National Archives of Canada, 369, 370
National Archives, Washington, D.C., 5, 21–22, 28–30

Regional Records Services Facilities, 391–95
National Association for the Advancement of Colored People [NAACP], 102, 177
National Funeral Directors and Morticians Association, 8
National Genealogical Society Library, 346
National Guard records, 73
National Negro Convention, 175
National Urban League, 102
naturalizations, 69, 106, 134, 181–88, 193, 229. *See also* emigration and immigration
Nebraska, records concerning African Americans, 229–33
Nebraska State Farmers Alliance Records, 232
Nebraska State Historical Society, 229–32
Nephew, James, 119
Nevada Historical Society, 236, 237
Nevada, records concerning African Americans, 235–37
Nevada State Library and Archives, 235
Newark Public Library, 247
Newberry Library, Chicago, Ill., 141
New Brunswick Colonization Society Records, 247
Newburg Christian Church, 163
New England Freedman's Aid Society, 196
New England Historic Genealogical Society, 197
New England, records concerning African Americans. *See* Connecticut, New Hampshire, Maine, Massachusetts, Rhode Island, Vermont
New Hampshire Historical Society, 241

New Hampshire, records concerning
  African Americans, 239–42
New Hampshire State Archives,
  239
New Hope Presbyterian Church, 118
New Jersey, records concerning
  African Americans, 243–48
New Jersey State Archives, 243, 244
New London, Connecticut, 10, 85
New Mexico Commission of Public
  Records, 249
New Mexico, records concerning
  African Americans, 249–52
New Mexico State Archives, 249
New Orleans Public Library, 173
New Orleans Slave Trade, 170
Newport Congregational Church, 303
Newport Historical Society, 301, 302,
  304
Newspapers, 49–50, 56, 69, 75, 80,
  85, 88, 90, 97, 99, 118, 130, 139,
  141, 148, 153, 157, 163, 188–89,
  195, 201, 211, 220, 228, 231–32,
  240, 246, 256–57, 267, 280, 287,
  291, 296–97, 310, 319, 323, 329,
  330, 334, 335, 341, 343, 350–51,
  356–57, 360, 361, 366, 374
New York City vital records, 254
New-York Historical Society, 259
New York National Freedmen's
  Relief Association, 281
New York, records concerning
  African Americans, 253–61
New York State Archives, 253
New York State Library, 259
Nichols-Britt Collection, 324
Nicodemus [Kansas] Historical
  Society, 159
Niles [Mich.] Public Library, 201
North Carolina, records concerning
  African Americans, 263–71
North Carolina State Archives, 263,
  264

North Carolina, University of, Wilson
  Library, 270
North Dakota, black towns of, 274
North Dakota, records concerning
  African Americans, 273–75
North Dakota State Archives and
  Historical Research Library, 273
North Dakota State University
  Archives, 275
Northeastern Illinois University, 134
Northern Illinois University, 134
Norton Family, 170
Nova Scotia, records concerning
  African Americans, 370–71

Oak Grove Cemetery, 117
Oak Hill Cemetery, 137
Oakland Memory Lanes, 137
Oakley Plantation, Tenn., 325
Oak Woods Cemetery, 137
Obituaries, 8, 49
  Arkansas, 70
  Michigan, 202
  Mississippi, 216
  South Dakota, 319
  Washington, 351
  West Virginia, 356
Ohio Historical Society, 277, 278,
  279
Ohio, records concerning African
  Americans, 277–83
Oklahoma cemeteries, 286
Oklahoma Federal Land Tract Books,
  286
Oklahoma Historical Society, 285,
  286
Oklahoma, records concerning
  African Americans, 285–88
Old Negro Cemetery, 117
Oliver, William K., 57
oral history, 17–19, 351
Oregon Archives Division, 289, 290,
  291

Oregon Genealogical Society Library, 291
Oregon Historical Society, 291
Oregon, records concerning African Americans, 289–92
Oregon, University of, Library, Oregon Collection, 292
Orr, James M., 119
Owsley Charts, 108, 324

Palfrey, William T., 172
Palmer, William Pendleton, 280
papers, personal, 50, 56–57, 64, 69, 75–76, 81, 88–89, 97, 101–02, 108, 119–20, 140, 148, 158, 164, 169–71, 189, 196, 201, 207, 211, 220–23, 232, 246–47, 249, 267–69, 281, 287, 291, 296–97, 303, 311–14, 324–25, 344, 345, 357, 362. *See also* diaries
Paris Archives, 202
Parker, William Foster, 121
Pascal, Paul, 172
passenger lists, 82, 170, 193, 259
Payne, Daniel Alexander, Collection, 279
Peabody, George Foster, 102, 189, 196
Peach Point Plantation, Brazoria County, Tex., 329
Pennsylvania clubs and societies, records of, 297
Pennsylvania Colonization Society, 296
Pennsylvania, records concerning African Americans, 293–98
Pennsylvania Society for Promoting the Abolition of Slavery, 296
Pennsylvania State Archives, 293, 294, 295
Pennsylvania, University of, Library, 297
pension records, 30, 330. *See also* military records

Perkins, Theresa Green (Ewen), 325
Perot, Joseph, 170
Perrin Family, 312
Perry, Mr., 202
Perry, Sally, 57
Peyton, Polly, 281
Phelps Family, 213
Pickens, Isreal, 57
Pilgrim Baptist Church, St. Paul, Minn., 207
Pitkin, Perley Peabody, 281
Poine, J.W., 280
Porcher-Ford Family, 313
Porcher, Isaac DuBose, 313
Porcher, Thomas, 313
Porter, Nimrod, 325
Powell, L. H., 89
Princeton University Library, 50
Prince Whipple, 239
Pringle, Elizabeth W., 269
prison records, 76
probate records, 69, 73, 79, 96, 99, 126, 136, 176, 202, 236, 300, 301, 302, 341. *See also* wills, intestate records, and inventories
Providence Shelter for Colored Children, 303
Prudhomme, J. Alphonse, 170
Prudhomme, Phanor, 170
Pullman Company archives, 141

Quakers. *See* Society of Friends
Quinn Chapel A.M.E., 138

Ramsey, Richard C., 57
Rankin, John, 281
Ransom, Reverend Cassius, 279
Ravenel, Dr. Henry, 121
Ravenel Family, 313
Ravenel, Thomas Porcher, 121
Reese, Ann, 97
Remsen, Peter A., 362
Restvale Cemetery, 137

Revolutionary War records. *See* military records

Rhode Island Genealogical Society, 304

Rhode Island Historical Society, 301, 303, 304

Rhode Island, records concerning African Americans, 299–305

Rhode Island State Archives, 299, 300

Rhode Island State Historical Society Library, 302, 303, 304

Rice, Nannie Herndon, 212

Richardson Family Bible, 107

Richardson, Gilbert M., 121

Richardson, Levin, 189

Richardson-Nelson Families, 313

Rock County Historical Society, 363

Root Cellar—Sacramento Genealogical Society, 73

Rosenberg, Henry, 330

Ross, Isaac, 213

Rowell, James, 268

Ruby, Reuben, 175

Sacramento Genealogical Society, 73

Sam Houston Regional Library and Museum, 330

Sams Family, 313

Sandy Creek Baptist Church, 117

Sanford, Henry Shelton, 325

Sauters, Charles, 212

Schoharie County (N.Y.) Historical Society, 256

Schomburg Center for Research in Black Culture, 256, 259, 260

school records
Canada, 370
Colorado, 81
Delaware, 97
Georgia, 114, 115
Massachusetts, 196
Missouri, 222

New York, 256

North Carolina, 268

schools, black, 53, 111. *See also* colleges, black

Seale, H. M., 172

seamen, 195

Seattle Public Library, Douglass-Truth Branch, 351

Shaffer, J.J., 269

Shaffer, William Rufus, 75

Shannon, Wesley, 291

Sheftall, Mordecai, 196

Shepard, Charles, 362

Sherman, Adelbert C., 246

Siebert, Wilbur Henry, 281, 196

Silver City [Idaho], 129

Simpson, Samuel, 269

Singleton Family, 313

Sizer, Henry E., 213

Skinner, Tristin Lowther, 269

Slack Family, 171

slave advertisements. *See* advertisements, slave

Slave Narrative Collection, Library of Congress, 101

slave records, 31–32, 35–43, 50, 56–57, 64, 89–90, 96, 102, 105, 119–20, 140, 141, 148, 158, 164, 169–71, 181–88, 189, 196, 211–13, 220–23, 241, 245–46, 247, 254–56, 264–66, 267–69, 281–82, 287, 291, 294–95, 296–97, 303, 308–10, 311–14, 324–25, 329–330, 344, 357, 362, 377–78

slave schedules, 36, 54, 68, 82, 99, 106, 112, 162, 168, 180, 210

Smith, A.F. Records, 213

Smith, Blanche, 61

Smith, Daniel Elliot Huger, 313

Smith, Ephram H., 268

Smith, Miles C., 247

Smith, Peter Evans, 268

Smith, Thomas Adams, 222

Smyth, Thomas, 313
Snoddy, Daniel F., 222
Society of Friends, 95, 145, 243, 279, 296, 302, 346, 379
South Carolina Department of Archives and History, 307
South Carolina Episcopal Church Records, 310
South Carolina, records concerning African Americans, 307–15
South Carolina State Library, 314
South Dakota, records concerning African Americans, 317–19
South Dakota State Archives, 317, 318, 319
South Dakota State Library, 319
Southern Christian Institute, 322
Southern Illinois University, 134
Spanish-American War records. See military records
special census schedules. See census records
Spradlin, William, 222
Spratlin, James A., 121
St. Anne's Parish, St. Charles, 138
St. Anthanasius Episcopal Church, 117
Stapleton, John, 313
Stark, Armistead, 268
state records, 49. See also individual states
St. Croix, 380. See also West Indies
Steinmetz, Mary Owen, 297
St. Elizabeth Catholic Church records, 138
Stephen F. Austin University, Ralph Steen Library, 331
Stephen H. Hart Library, 81
Stephens, Alexander H., 57
St. Francis Xavier Parish Records, 147
St. George Plantation, Dorchester County, S.C., 311

Still, Peter, 247
St. Joseph Catholic Mission, 323
St. Joseph's Parish, 138
St. Louis Cathedral Archives, New Orleans, 168
St. Mark's African Methodist Episcopal Church, 207
St. Michael's Catholic Church (Pensacola) Parish Records, 107
Stoney, Peter Gaillard, 313
St. Philips Episcopal Church, Kirkwood, 211
Strange, Agatha Jane (Rochester), 164
Strong, George W., 152
Sublette Family, 222
surnames, 37, 291
Swilley's Funeral Home Records, 107

Talbot Family, 177
Tallcott, Joseph, 297
Taylor, Francis, 164, 344
Taylor, William, 172
tax records, 39, 69, 96, 116, 162, 220, 256, 330, 341, 378
Telfair Family Plantation, 120
Temple University's web site, 297
Tennessee Historical Society, 326
Tennessee, records concerning African Americans, 321–26
Tennessee State Library and Archives, 321, 322, 325
Tennessee, University of, Hoskins Library, 326
Thompson Family, 213
Thompson Ishan, 330
Thurston, Charles Brown, 177
Tiffany, P. Dexter, 222
Tinley Park Mental Health Cemetery, 137
Torbet, James, 57
Trapier, Paul, 313

Traylor, John G., 57
Trinidad, 376, 379. *See also* West
    Indies
Trinity United Methodist Church
    (Tallahassee) Records, 107
Trumbull papers, 89
Tucker, D.M., 223
Tucker, J.H., 223
Turner, Daniel, 120

Underground Railroad, 31, 32, 33,
    98, 196, 259, 337
Union Congregational Church, 304
United States Customs Service
    records, 171
university and college records. *See*
    school records
Utah State Archives and Records
    Service, 333, 334
Utah State Historical Society, 335
Utah, records concerning African
    Americans, 333–35

Van Liew-Voorhees, 247
Vass, Elise Virginia Jones, 57
Vermont Historical Society, 339, 340
Vermont, records concerning African
    Americans, 337–40
Vermont State Archives, 337
Vermont State Library, 339, 340
Vick Family, 213
Virginia, records concerning African
    Americans, 341–48
Virginia Historical Society, 346
Virginia, State Library of, 341, 345,
    358
Virginia, University of, 345
Virgin Islands, 377, 379. *See also*
    West Indies
vital records, 38–39, 54–55, 61–62,
    64, 68, 74, 80, 85, 86, 96, 99, 105,
    106, 112, 113–16, 126, 130, 135–
    36, 146, 152, 156, 162, 168, 176,
    180, 193, 194, 200, 202, 206, 210,
    218, 219, 221, 228, 230, 235, 240,
    243, 244, 250, 254, 259, 264, 265,
    266, 274, 278, 286, 290, 291, 294,
    330, 308, 318, 321, 322, 328, 334,
    338, 342, 350, 356, 366, 374, 375,
    376
voting records, 112, 142, 330
voter registration, 49
    Florida, 106
    Illinois, 134
    Texas, 327

Wade, Walter, 213
Walker Family, 57
Walker, James Dent, 102
Walker, Timothy, 281
War of 1812 records. *See* military
    records
Washington, D.C. *See* District of
    Columbia
Washington Memory Gardens, 137
Washington, records concerning
    African Americans, 349–53
Washington State Archives, 349, 350
Washington, University of, Suzzalo
    Library, 350
Webb, Daniel Cannon, 313
Weedon Family, 108
West Indies, records concerning
    African Americans, 373–80
Westbrooks, Allie C., 325
Westerly Public Library, 301
Western Illinois University, 134
Weston Family, 313
West Virginia and Regional History
    Collection, 358
West Virginia Archives and History,
    355, 357
West Virginia, records concerning
    African Americans, 355–58
West Virginia University Library, 358
White, John R., 223
Whitehurst Family, 108
Wilberforce Colony, Canada, 369

Williams, Fred Hart, 201
Williams, Samuel Wesley, 279
Williamson Family, 57, 325
wills, intestate records, and invento-
ries, 10–11, 40–41, 99, 126, 136,
162, 176, 182, 245, 249, 310, 374,
376
Wisconsin Historical Society (State
Historical Society of Wisconsin),
359–60, 361, 362
Wisconsin, records concerning
African Americans, 359–63
Wisconsin State Genealogical
Society, 363
Withers, Francis, 314

Wood, Anna Wharton, 297
Works Progress Administration, 81,
140, 282, 318. *See also* Federal
Writers Project
Wormoth, Henry Clay, 270
Wyoming Genealogical & Historical
Society, 367
Wyoming, records concerning
African Americans, 365–67
Wyoming State Archives, 365, 366,
367

Yancy, D.C., 120
Yancy, William, 57
Young, Allen, 268

11/04 φ